British Friends of **The Hebrew University** BFHU

1926 – 2006

Presented in celebration of the
British Friends of the Hebrew University
80th Anniversary Celebratory Dinner

The Banqueting House
7th June 2006

Support the University – Benefit the World
www.bfhu.org

With grateful thanks to our anonymous donor
for sponsoring this gift

MAN IN THE SHADOWS

MAN
IN THE
SHADOWS

INSIDE THE MIDDLE EAST CRISIS WITH
A MAN WHO LED THE MOSSAD

EFRAIM HALEVY

Weidenfeld & Nicolson
LONDON

First published in the USA in 2006
by St. Martins Press

First published in Great Britain in 2006
by Weidenfeld & Nicolson

1 3 5 7 9 10 8 6 4 2

A CIP catalogue record for this book
is available from the British Library.

ISBN-13   978 0 297 84831 8
ISBN-10   0 297 84831 3

Printed in Great Britain by
Butler & Tanner Ltd, Frome and London

Weidenfeld & Nicolson

The Orion Publishing Group Ltd
Orion House
5 Upper Saint Martin's Lane
London, WC2H 9EA
www.orionbooks.co.uk

The Orion Publishing Group's policy is to use papers that are natural,
renewable and recyclable products and made from wood grown in s
ustainable forests. The logging and manufacturing processes are expected
to conform to the environmental regulations of the country of origin.

To the unsung and unnamed men and women of the Mossad
whose courage, devotion, and professional excellence
have made an indescribable and unique contribution to the
security of the State of Israel and the defense of the free world.

CONTENTS

ACKNOWLEDGMENTS

The writing of this book and much of what it relates would not have been at all possible were it not for the unstinted support and devotion that I have experienced for the last fifty years from Hadassa—my wife, partner, and watchful and constructive critic. I owe her an unpayable debt of gratitude for making it possible for me to lead such a life.

The constant support from my two children, Michal and Gilead, and their spouses, Alexander and Arielle, has been a source of strength and pride that has sustained me for many long years.

I wish to thank those friends who were generous in their help and encouragement whenever these were in need. And I cannot forget colleagues and counterparts throughout my career who cooperated in many an endeavor and so often turned the sensitive scales in midair and pulled success from the threatening jaws of failure.

I owe so much to successive heads of the Mossad and prime ministers of Israel, who expressed confidence in me for a period of forty years and placed me time and time again in positions that permitted me to make my contribution to our people and country.

My thanks to my literary agent, Lynne Rabinoff, who saw me safe and sound through the minefield of book production, which was uncharted waters for me.

My deep appreciation of the outstanding professionalism of my experienced and sensitive editor, Michael Flamini, whose deft strokes tweaked and shaped the prose of this book and who treated me with an original blend of firmness, flexibility, and grace.

My thanks to Katherine Tiernan, who shepherded the manuscript through all its stages and treated the writer with infinite patience. And to St. Martin's Press and to Orion/Weidenfeld and Nicolson, who gave me the confidence to try my hand at an art and craft that was entirely new to me.

And one final note: This is not an autobiography, nor is it a blow-by-blow recital of the feats of the Mossad; but there are, I hope in proportion, elements of both of these as well, enough, I hope, to encourage persons of good faith, vision, and ambition to go out and serve their country with all their heart, brain, and might in the never-never world of intelligence. The very future of the free world depends on them.

MAN IN THE SHADOWS

EMERGING FROM THE SHADOWS

My name is Efraim Halevy. I was born in London in 1934. I grew up during World War II and toward its end vividly remember the V-1 and V-2 rocket missiles that fell on London, causing, very often, hundreds of deaths among the civilian population.

With my parents I moved to what was then known as Palestine in April 1948. A month later the State of Israel came into being, and I lived through the War of Independence as a teenager. In my early twenties, I served as president of the National Union of Israeli Students and traveled extensively to Eastern Europe, Asia, and Africa on its behalf. I was in Moscow and Prague in 1956, a tumultuous period in the history of the Communist bloc. I joined the Mossad in 1961 and served as a combination analyst, case officer, and executive department head until 1967, when I became a deputy division chief. In that capacity I was a member of the governing body of the Mossad for the next twenty-eight and a half years. I served in Washington, D.C., for four years, mostly under the ambassadorship of Yitzhak Rabin, who later served twice as Israel's prime minister. I also served in Paris for three years in a senior posting, and commanded two operational divisions, each for a period of five years.

My last five years before retirement were spent as deputy chief of the

Mossad. I left at the end of October 1995, a week before Yitzhak Rabin was assassinated, for Brussels to serve as Israel's ambassador to the European Union. Two and a quarter years later, I was hastily recalled by Prime Minister Benjamin Netanyahu to become head of the Mossad at a time of crisis. I became director of one of the most powerful and prestigious undercover governmental agencies in the world and served as chief for four and a half years. All in all I served at the senior executive level for thirty-three years.

During all my years in the Mossad, I have seen the Middle East crisis from the inside. There have been times when certain events totally took my by surprise, along with the public at large. There have been occasions when I knew what was about to happen shortly, or long, before events unfolded. It has also been my great privilege to participate in a few instances that made history, serving as an instrument to change the landscape of the region. I have seen leaders in times of acute stress and have learned much from their conduct about human frailties and human strengths. I have seen heads of state cringe as the destiny of their nations and their own careers hung in the balance, and I have observed and witnessed acts of courage and loyalty. I have seen and lived through moments of great hope and enthusiasm and I have also been around in times of despair and despondency.

In Israel, on the afternoon of September 11, 2001, I was attending a meeting chaired by Prime Minister Ariel Sharon in the cabinet room in Jerusalem devoted to an issue concerning the Palestinian territories. I well recall that the discussion was calm and orderly when suddenly a young female soldier entered the room and handed a piece of paper to the military secretary and to the prime minister. He read it himself and then told us all in the room that there had been an attack from the air against the Twin Towers in New York. I immediately left the room to call my office and find out if there had been any further reporting, of any kind. I was told that we knew nothing at all beyond what was in the public domain. We did not linger. Each of us rushed to his office to take up as best we could. Within a very short time it was clear to each and every one of us at the top of the intelligence community that the events of 9/11 would become turning points in the history of the world.

As the hours went by, my concern rose for my son, then living in London, who had left that very morning for New York on a British Airways aircraft. John F. Kennedy International Airport had been closed and I was anxious to learn where he had landed. It was many hours before I located him at one of the more distant airports used for planes flying to the United States. He was stranded in the States for many days until he could get back to the U.K.

Of all the events that took place during my tenure as head of the Mossad, this was the one that caught me in a feeling of almost total helplessness. The information level was at zero. The exact nature and scope of the threat were initially impossible to evaluate and their immediate derivatives for the Middle East were too vast and too serious to contemplate. I remember saying to a close colleague, after a day or two, that the Middle East war had penetrated the shores of the American continent and that the United States was now at war in the Middle East. It could not win that war on its own soil and therefore sooner rather than later, the United States would have to come to the Middle East and engage the enemy in order to win that war. I had no idea how this would come about, but I was convinced, then and there, that this would happen—one way or another. As happens during such times, one's mind casts back to earlier times of crisis.

IT WAS MEMORIAL DAY IN ISRAEL, THE EVE OF INDEPENDENCE DAY 1994, and I was about to cross Allenby Bridge on the river Jordan and make my way back to Israel. I had spent four days in Jordan with my wife as guests of His Majesty King Hussein and had held extensive talks with him and his brother, Crown Prince Hassan. Prime Minister Rabin, who had approved my mission, had not attached much importance to this round of meetings. He viewed it as a "maintenance operation," and the truth of the matter was that he had little patience for the king of Jordan at that particular time. He was bent on pursuing peace with Syria and all his efforts were focused in that direction. Jordan would have to wait. In the meantime, contact with the Hashemite kingdom would be maintained on a low profile.

But the talks in Jordan had taken a dramatic turn. As I reached the Israeli side of the river, I was convinced that we had worked out the parameters of a strategic agreement between Israel and Jordan that would also serve as a platform for the rehabilitation of the traditional U.S.-Jordanian alliance. This traditional link had been almost fatally damaged when Jordan appeared to side with Saddam Hussein during the 1991 Desert Storm campaign of the American-led coalition.

I was truly buoyed with a spirit of historic achievement, but my colleagues who met me greeted me with somber news. That very morning, two major terrorist acts had been committed in two Israeli central bus stations in Afula and Hadera; there was a heavy toll of dead and wounded. On the next day, Israel was destined to mark Independence Day with a large number of funerals. The mood would be bitter and there would be strong calls for retribution. I decided that this was not the time to report to the prime minister on a peace initiative. This could wait.

The following day, public opinion in Israel erupted in fury. Conventional wisdom had it that these two terrorist attacks had been perpetrated by the Khammas movement headquartered in Amman, Jordan. If the Jordanians were incapable of controlling hostile elements in their own country, Israel would have to do the job on her own. Newspaper headlines even raised the possibility that Israel would go to war against Jordan. Tensions, obviously, were running high.

The mood in Israel was becoming uglier as the day wore on. I went to visit a friend and left his telephone number with the duty officer. No sooner had I arrived than I received a phone call. The prime minister wished to talk to me. A minute later Yitzhak Rabin was on the line. He told me that Foreign Minister Shimon Peres had just left his residence and the two had resolved to take a very tough stand against Jordan. The situation was intolerable, he said, and immediately after the traditional Independence Day reception in the Rose Garden of the Ministry of Defense, the two would denounce Jordan, publicly, at a midnight press conference. Given the awkward relationship between the two Israeli leaders, their joint appearance was going to be a rather unusual event in Israel. I was to make contact with my Jordanian liaison and tell him to alert the king that he should expect a stern public denouncement. I told the prime minister that I thought this move was wrong. I told him that I had returned only the day before and had dramatic news for him. Rabin retorted in anger that this was not a time for bickering. For once, he said, I should do what I was told. The prime minister dictated to me the exact text of what I was to say and for the first—and last—time told me that the acting military secretary would call me a couple of minutes later to make sure I had the wording right!

I contacted my Jordanian friend Colonel Ali Shukri and told him what was about to happen. He was astounded. There was no evidence that the bus station attacks had been committed by the Khammas, so he said. He told me that, as of my departure from Jordan the day before, the king had been virtually incommunicado due to a health problem and that he would not understand why the Israeli leadership was suddenly targeting him. "You must stop Rabin from holding the press conference!" my friend said. "It could end in catastrophe." "I simply cannot do this," I replied. "You will have to explain things to His Majesty the best you can."

The following morning was a Friday, a relatively calm day. The Israeli weekend press gave the joint press conference banner headlines. Leading commentators competed among themselves in explaining the volatility of the situation. Israeli-Jordanian relations appeared to be plunging into an almost all-time low and I wondered whether or not another surprise war was at hand.

In the late morning I met with the prime minister and reported to him on my visit in great detail. He appeared elated, surprised, and concerned. As I ended my report, he looked me straight in the face and said very seriously, "Why did you not tell me all this before?" I looked at him and said nothing. A moment later his face broke into a broad smile. Rabin issued clear instructions that nobody except those in the room at the time should be informed of the discussions and moves without his express approval. He also instructed me to begin putting together a list of subjects and issues that had to be addressed in order to make sure that all aspects of the future relationship be covered. He specifically made it clear that no other member of the cabinet, including Foreign Minister Peres, be kept abreast of developments without his specific approval. In the months to come he often briefed me in the greatest detail on what I should or should not impart to anybody. These were to be the ground rules and they were meticulously kept as of that moment and until the final ceremony that took place in the Arava Valley on October 26, 1994.

The peace treaty with Jordan was launched that morning in the office of Prime Minister and Defense Minister Rabin in Tel Aviv. Shortly after it transpired that the murderous attacks on the twin bus stations had nothing to do with the Khammas and certainly nothing to do with Jordan. This was a classic example of the damage that could be done when hasty conclusions were drawn based on surmise and prior to the collection of good intelligence. There was no doubt in my mind that none other than Mr. Peres had prevailed upon the prime minister during the course of that Independence Day. In my estimate, we could have easily gone to war with Jordan on false premises had my visit not taken place just at that point in time. History is so often determined by coincidence and the history of the Middle East provides ample proof of this.

ON THAT SEPTEMBER DAY IN 2001, MY MIND WAS ALSO ON AMERICAN colleagues, past and present, who shared my own concerns about the Middle East and worked with the government of Israel toward peace in the region. James Angleton was one of those people.

I last saw Jim Angleton on April 30, 1987. The legendary former counterintelligence chief was gravely ill and had passed me a message that he wished to see me one more time before he was to die. I had enjoyed a long personal relationship with this "dreaded" figure of the CIA that included four years of service in the Israeli embassy in Washington. We had spent, literally, hundreds of hours together in one-on-one meetings and had done many things together. I must have cut a very sad and humble figure as I entered his home in Arlington, Virginia, to see him lying quietly on the sofa in his living room. Within minutes we were immersed in earnest conversation and Jim gave me his views on a large variety of issues. As always, there was one condition for these talks: Reporting had to go—exclusively—directly to the top when I returned to my country.

The last point he made related to the future of Israel, a country that he dearly loved. "Never go for an international conference solution," he said. "This is courting disaster. It would lead to imposed solutions and you would be in a straitjacket. I fear Shimon [Peres] is too sure of himself. In this he is different from Moshe [Dayan], who although outwardly more dashing is extremely cautious. Shimon thinks he can convince everybody and this presents a grave danger to you all. Stay on as long as you can! Keep the faith!"

Tears welled in his eyes. Jim turned away and gradually fell asleep. I left his house, never to see him again. The following day he was taken to hospital and he died a few days later.

Jim had cast his shadow over the Agency for almost a quarter of a century. There were those who revered him and others who feared and hated him. His influence covered areas near and far. It was he who had arranged the first refresher course in physical protection for the then young and extremely vulnerable King Hussein of Jordan in the early 1950s. He was active in Europe and in other regions, but his penchant was always Soviet intelligence and, most specifically, the workings of the KGB. He left no stone unturned in his pursuit of the "forces of evil," and he always sought to reveal the hidden connection between terrorism and clandestine hostile intelligence.

Three years after he had retired from the Agency, an enforced departure engineered by the then director Bill Colby, I received one of many personal letters he regularly sent me. I was then stationed in Paris. In a few lines, he painted a panorama of the interconnections among players on the international scene, the likes of which only he was capable of doing. The letter carried the date of October 3, 1977, and focused on an incident with what Jim called "poignant implications" that was not resolved during his CIA tenure. He described a visit to Moscow by Arafat that was much discussed in the Soviet media. The coverage included a photograph showing Arafat "adorning the grave of Soviet leader Khrushchev with flowers." The photograph had three individuals pictured: Arafat, Zamyatin of the Soviet Foreign Office, and an unidentified agent with a "bald head." Angleton went on to reveal that "one of my old KGB men came running to me when we received the publication." He was excited to explain that he had worked closely with the bald man depicted. His agent described the man as a professional KGB agent who served in Karlshorst, Germany. Significantly, however, the KGB agent could only speak German and Russian. Angleton went on to note that "I instituted a crash background research and investigation of Arafat to determine whether he knew German." Nothing was revealed at first to answer this question and Arafat himself, it seemed, chose to be oblique about his youth and education when interviewed about it on television, noting that "revolutionaries lived for the moment and the future, not for the past." Yet, before leaving the service, Angleton wrote that he did have one report that, in his youth Arafat had studied engineering in Munich, Germany, and knew German. He continued, "I could never acquire confirmation nor additional information on this matter and my mind is not at rest as to the implications. What I wish is that the question of language be established beyond certainty whether it favors my views or not. I have only discussed the broadest parameter of this line of inquiry but, needless to say, if my KGB friend's information is wedded to the Arafat dossier, then we have a most significant political fact regarding the Palestine Liberation Organization [the PLO] and the Soviets. . . ."

Jim Angleton, King Hussein, Yassir Arafat, the KGB, the CIA, the Israeli body politic, the leaders of the United States and the countries of Europe, the leaders of the states of the Middle East: These are just a few strands that have crossed each other over the last few decades and, very much, entwined themselves together on that nefarious day. Of course there are so many more and on that day, I wondered about the role of policy, of individuals, of organs of state, in shaping the destiny of this twenty-first century of ours.

As I said, I served in the Mossad for close to forty years. I met heads of state, intelligence agents, persons of influence, and at the same time I was involved in countless operations, large and small, over close to fifty years. During all these years I have been bent on trying to keep the faith as Jim Angleton asked me to do, as far as possible. Concerning the complex and virtually impossible world we live in, I shall try to provide you with the insight of an intelligence officer and a one-time diplomat. I have moved and functioned in the shadows for close to forty years. Everything looks different from there, but, in truth, which is the world of shadow and which is that of light? Which is the world of fantasy and which is the world of reality, or are they a mix of the two? In truth, I am not entirely sure.

IN THIS BOOK, I HAVE CHOSEN TO DWELL ON THIRTEEN INTEGRAL YEARS, the years 1990–2003, which have changed the face of the world and have catapulted us into a new and frightening era. I will also look at the aftermath of 9/11 and consider the current international situation, including the 2005 bombings in London and what they suggest for our time.

The years 1988 and 1989 were laden with dramatic events in both the Middle East and the rest of the world. The Iranian-Iraqi war had come to an end leaving hundreds of thousands of dead on the battlefields. The original Iranian attempt to defeat the Iraqi regime of Saddam Hussein had been repulsed by Baghdad with the massive financial aid of the Arab world and critical intelligence support rendered by the United States. Saddam emerged as a true hero; he had withstood the extreme Shiite leadership of Tehran and thus had served as a bulwark, which had successfully saved not only the Arab states but also Western society from the threat of the spread of the Iranian revolution. Saddam enjoyed unsurpassed popularity in the entire region. He personified the prowess and pride of the entire Arab world. He inspired awe in others and leaders like King Hussein and President Hosni Mubarak both revered and feared him, physically and militarily.

Israel surveyed the scene with growing concern tempered by a large dose of wishful thinking. As of the time that Ayatollah Khomeini unseated the shah of Iran in 1979 and set up a radical religious regime in Tehran, Israel had been following events in that country with deepening consternation. Iran had been a strategic ally of Israel for close to two decades and the two, together with Turkey, had been able to create an effective counterbalance to the Arab world. From 1978, this strategic and secret alliance had been destroyed; however, as long as the Iraqi-Iranian war lasted, Israel was the obvious beneficiary of this continuous bloodletting between two of its potential enemies. Thus, for about ten years, the loss of Iran as an ally had been offset by the war, but now the war was over, and a debate arose in Israel as to whether Israel should seek an alliance with Iraq or prefer to team up again with Iran. In truth, neither of these options really existed. Iraq was seething with desire to take revenge against Israel for having destroyed its nuclear reactor, Osirak, provided by France in the seventies by the government of Jacques Chirac, a friend and admirer of Saddam Hussein. Iran, under Khomeini, had solemnly declared that Israel had no right to exist and had already shown its evil intent by creating a clandestine terrorist capability, which had operated with deadly effectiveness in the eighties in Lebanon and was destined to act globally from the early nineties. Looking eastward from Jerusalem, ominous threats were clear on the horizon and Jordan, under King Hussein, who had maintained discreet contacts with successive Israeli leaders from the early seventies, was more than hard-pressed to maintain a balance between his traditional ties with Israel and his growing affinity to, and trepidation of, Saddam Hussein.

Looking elsewhere round the Middle East, Israel had cause to be cautiously optimistic. Syria, under the wily Hafiz al-Assad, had despaired of reaching strategic parity with Israel. The Soviet Union was on the verge of collapse. It was unable and unwilling to supply and fund its long-standing satellite with new-generation military hardware. Arafat and his Palestinian Liberation Organization (PLO) were beginning to show signs of a strategic or tactical change in policy toward Israel. Was it a sea-change transformation or a temporary nuance in approach? In 1988, it was much too early to form a true estimate of the nature of the move. Egypt, the only Arab state that had signed a peace treaty with Israel, was about to be accepted back into the fold after having been ostracized by the Arab world. It was no longer a pariah state in the region. All in all, the prospects for a breakthrough in the conflict appeared to be better than ever before.

Ten years were to pass from 1988 till 1998 before an event was to take place that would signal the emergence of a new threat to the United States and to the free world. Two American embassies were to be blown up simultaneously in Nairobi, Kenya, and in Dar es Salaam, Tanzania, by the bin Laden terrorists. In the meantime, 1988–1989 was to be the year when it was becoming apparent that Iraq was again on the path to developing and producing nuclear weaponry.

Thus, at the same time that peace prospects in the Middle East seemed to be more promising than ever before, the clouds were gathering and the world in its entirety was destined to witness and participate in a thirteen-year cycle that would end in the outbreak of World War III.

Within this time span, the region was to experience two major U.S. campaigns targeting Iraq. The second was to mark the entry of the U.S. into the region as a power with forces stationed in a major Arab state as an occupying-liberating force. Farther to the east, the United States, with other countries rallying around it, was to invade Afghanistan in order to try to eliminate or at least contain the Al Qaeda threat and to free that backward country from the rule of Mullah Omar and the Taliban. What were, at the outset, regional threats fast became international threats en-dangering the very existence and well-being of the free world. The future of modern-day civilization was to become contingent on victory against the two threats born and nurtured in the Middle East.

Of the many aspects of this rapidly developing train of events, the role of intelligence and intelligence leaders assumed unprecedented propor-tions. Successes and failures in this vital field were to have far-reaching effects on the destiny of peoples and political leaders. The traditional games of espionage were to undergo revolutionary changes. The rules of the game practiced by Washington, London, and Moscow suddenly proved inapplicable when it came to bin Laden, the Hizbollah, Baghdad, Kabul, or Riyadh. It was to become essential to discard, quickly, traditional mind-sets and to face an entirely different list of new realities and values. Intelligence chiefs and leaders were to assume prominence not only as close and powerful counsels to their political masters but also as preferred emissaries to heads of state and leaders of national movements. Knowledge, as the ultimate difference between life and death, was never more in demand and its exchange between allies was to become a vital aspect of common destiny. The absence of it, or a false interpretation of it, could result in national disaster in the literal sense of the term. This was to become a different world within a very few years.

I shall try to map the route we have taken in order to show how we got where we are today. My hope is that by doing so, we might be able to determine a path, from here, that will lead us to a safer world.

1

THE END OF THE EIGHT-YEAR WAR
(1988–1989)

The Iran-Iraq war was nearing its end. Iraq was employing nonconventional means both to stem the tide of the Iranian-Shiite onslaught and to cow Kurdish resistance from within. For close to eight years Israel had been sitting on the fence and observing the Sunni-Shiite confrontation with considerable satisfaction. The mutual weakening of Iraq and Iran, both sworn enemies of Israel, had been serving Israel's strategic interests for quite some time and had contributed to the decline of the eastern front threat that had been a central feature of Israeli planning for decades.

Syria in the north, under the dictatorial rule of Hafiz al-Assad, had at that stage begun to realize that it had no real chance of obtaining strategic parity with Israel. Egypt, which had signed a peace treaty with Israel a decade before and had subsequently been ostracized by the Arab world, was to be shortly taken back into the fold of Arab states through readmittance to the Arab League. It had endured the Israeli incursion into Lebanon in 1982 without severing its diplomatic relations with Israel. Egypt was able to restore its status in the Arab world and to maintain its strategic peace with Israel at one and the same time. On the Israeli-Palestinian dispute, the Palestinian uprising, known as the first *in-*

tifada, had gone through its first year with little effect on Israel's power-ful status. There had been some ugly incidents, but these had not affected its basic capabilities. Surveying the scene at the time, Israel could have rightly concluded that its position in the region had rarely been stronger.

There had been one significant change in the otherwise encouraging picture. King Hussein had renounced his country's interest in the West Bank and had declared that it was now time for the Palestinians them-selves to care for their future. He had done so in 1988 after a failed attempt in 1987 to launch a joint Israel-Jordan initiative, the purpose of which was to produce a solution commonly known as the London Agreement. The agreement was concluded by the then Israeli foreign min-ister Shimon Peres and King Hussein at a secret meeting that took place in London at the residence of Lord Mishcon, a personal friend of the two. There were a variety of reasons why this understanding did not material-ize. The two authors of the document had agreed that it would be given to the American administration and that subsequently the U.S. government would present it to the parties as an American initiative. Since that was the so-called gentleman's agreement Mr. Peres refused to give his prime minister, Yitzhak Shamir, a copy of the document and told him that he would receive it later on from the American ambassador. Mr. Shamir sensed a "conspiracy" and immediately assumed a hostile approach to the whole scheme. A last-ditch effort to sway Mr. Shamir's mind by ar-ranging for him to have his own secret meeting with King Hussein in the summer of 1987 was to no avail. He did not accept the London Agree-ment because it was destined to be implemented under a joint American-Soviet patronage, and Israel had traditionally shied away from Great Power tutelage, which bore the ingredients of an imposed solution.

King Hussein assumed in the summer of 1987 that Mr. Peres would re-sign from the Israeli cabinet and would dismantle the Labor-Likud na-tional coalition following his failure to get approval for the London Agreement. Since Mr. Peres did not go through with this commitment, King Hussein felt not only that he had been let down but that he had be-come exposed to the accusation of treachery in the Arab world. He felt that Mr. Peres had undermined his position. Given the fast-diminishing support he was receiving from the Palestinian population in the West Bank, he decided to cut his losses. So, the king severed his ties with the West Bank, leaving the Palestinians to their own fate, and the Labor party—which, for many years, had championed a policy that renewed Jordanian involvement in the West Bank was the preferred solution to the Palesstinian conflict—went on to lose the 1988 general election in Israel.

The London Agreement episode was evaluated at the time as a relatively minor event in the overall scene. It so happened that, simultaneously, Israel was sensing a rapid decline in Jordanian influence on the West Bank after it had fallen into Israeli hands in 1967. During the eighties, Israel had made repeated efforts to bolster Jordanian-supported groups and individuals but to no apparent avail. In essence, both King Hussein and Mr. Shamir had similar interests; neither really wanted a rapid solution to the Palestinian issue. Neither trusted Yassir Arafat. The king always remembered that it was Arafat who had tried to overthrow the Hashemite regime in the summer of 1970 and to assassinate him. Thus neither of the two leaders was in a hurry to change the status quo. Indeed, the king was to develop a sincere admiration for Mr. Shamir, who, on the face of it, was his most implacable adversary given the latter's "extreme" positions on the Palestinian issue.

Surveying the international scene, Israel had reason to feel relatively safe and confident. The Soviet Union under Mikhail Gorbachev was rapidly losing its economic capacity to fund and equip its veteran clients in the Middle East with new-generation weaponry. There were already indications that Soviet attitudes toward Israel were to change. At the time, the Soviet Union had not resumed diplomatic relations with Jerusalem, which had been severed in 1967, but through a series of contacts it had become apparent that Moscow now had a deep interest in normalizing its relations with Israel. Mr. Shamir, the then Israeli prime minister, had a profound understanding of the Russian scene and was hoping that a thaw on this front would open the gates for renewed immigration from the Soviet Union to Israel. However, in his wildest dreams he did not believe that within a time span of three to four years, a million people would immigrate to Israel, thus enlarging the Jewish population by 25 percent. This dramatic rise in size of the population had an enormous effect on the economy and on the security of the state. Overnight, Israel had become a state comparable in population size to several key European countries, such as Denmark, Norway, and Ireland. The populations of Norway and Ireland were considerably less than that of Israel. Denmark and Israel numbered almost the same number of inhabitants.

The first *intifada* was in its second year with no visible signs of any tangible success. The Palestinians appeared to be losing rapidly in their struggle against Israel and as more and more Jews were taking up residence in Judea and Samaria, the "occupied" or "disputed" territories, a real fear of total loss and collapse was beginning to take hold of large segments of the population in the Palestinian world. In 1988, Arafat first hinted that he might change course and contemplate a reconciliation with Israel. The main question in everyone's mind was whether or not this was a tactical move designed to overcome temporary weakness or the beginning of a genuine strategic change. The issue was destined to become the touchstone of bitter debate in Israel, spanning the entire period covered by this book.

As background to these major developments, there began to lurk a sinister threat in the form of possible proliferation of nuclear know-how into the Middle East. Preliminary indications suggested that Iraq was bent on reactivating its efforts to develop its nuclear capacities, which had suffered a severe setback when Israel, in 1981, bombed and destroyed the Iraqi Osirak nuclear reactor, a reactor donated and constructed by the French government under the premiership of Jacques Chirac. We also asked ourselves if there was a real danger that Pakistan would be instrumental in creating the "Islamic bomb," or was this just a figment of the imagination of a few deranged intelligence officers who were readily willing to think the unthinkable, time and time again? And finally, we wondered whether or not other Muslim states in the Middle East were contemplating entry into the fields of weapons of mass destruction.

Consequently, just as the Middle East appeared to be emerging from a dark ten-year period of war, and on the verge of the first glimmer of hope in the Israeli-Palestinian conflict, far greater potentials for violence and regional destabilization were beginning to cloud the horizon. There was not much enthusiasm in the intelligence community to give these new threats priority over the more conventional and traditional ones. The bitter experience of the intelligence failure leading up to the Yom Kippur War of 1973 motivated those who chose to continue monitoring the threats of war as they had been perceived day in, day out over the years. Rather than cast the net wider away in order to search for new, unknown, and uncharted threats, the conventional intelligence officers preferred to concentrate on what was always closer to home and to fret over questions such as whether or not Syria was about to launch a surprise incursion into Israel and to seize territory in order to shuffle the cards and initiate a move to ward off a new political reality. This was just one example of a daily question at the very top of the Essential Elements of Information— the sacred E.E.I. The nonconventional threats were deemed to be serious but much more remote. They were taken seriously but not given their real weight and value. Thus the years 1988–1989 were to become those in which a major intelligence failure could well have occurred.

Israel was looking westward at the time and was contemplating the Libyan conundrum with all its complexity. Libya was not only a traditional host to Arab terrorist movements and murder squads. Its development and/or purchase of surface-to-air missiles placed Israel's civilian Mediterranean air corridors within range of Libyan capabilities. Israel had no adequate answer to this threat; it could not patrol the airspace because of the distance from its shores and it could not rely entirely on the capacities and goodwill of Southern European countries on the northern shores of the Mediterranean Sea.

Apart from its anxiety over the possible threat from Mu'ammar Gadhafi, Israel's involvement, in general, in Africa was reaching its climax. For several years it had succeeded in maintaining traditionally strategic relations with veteran leaders, like Felix Houphouet Boigny of the Ivory Coast. In each of these strategic relationships, Israel had invested primarily in the defense field, training and advising the troops loyal to regimes generally considered dictatorial and, in some cases, oppressive. Farther south of the Ivory Coast, Israel was allied with the white regime of South Africa and had long range agreements with Pretoria, again basically in the defense area. Israel's policies were based in the main on its reading of its strategic interests, with minimal regard to human rights and related aspects relevant to those it supported.

Israel's African policies were a subject for constant review; it established and nurtured relationships with progressive and internationally respected regimes like those of Kenya's Kenyatta and Tanzania's Nyerere; however, it also maintained strategic contacts with the likes of Mobutu Sese Seko, a man perceived as a ruthless dictator. These relationships had been cultivated in the sixties, at the height of the scramble by the West, led by the United States, and the Communist bloc, led by the Soviet Union and Communist China. Mobutu, for one, was the "darling" of the

West because he had succeeded in staving off a Soviet-led offensive to gain control of central Africa and its vitally strategic minerals. Israel had played a very effective role in furthering its own objectives of narrowing Egypt's zones of influence in Africa. The African policies allowed us to puncture the efforts of the Arab world, led at the time by Egypt's charismatic and pro-Soviet leader, Gamal Abdel Nasser, who was, at the time, working to isolate the newly born state of the Jews, internationally, and to exercise a vigorous boycott on it. At one and the same time, Israel's prominent role in Africa was clearly serving Western interests and primarily those of the United States and the latter was quick to recognize this contribution and to applaud it.

Simultaneously, hidden far from the diplomatic human eye, Israel was pursuing activities and policies during the years 1988–1989 that were of considerable consequence both to itself and to many other players on the international scene. On the African continent it had been carrying out a massive rescue operation designed to bring to its shores the Jews of Ethiopia. In the face of the refusal of the Addis Ababa regime to allow these Jews out of the country, Israel launched a rescue operation in the Sudan. The Jews of Ethiopia were encouraged to cross the border from Ethiopia into the Sudan and to find their way to refugee camps situated around five hundred kilometers away from Khartoum, the capital of this impoverished country. This heroic operation, masterminded by the Israeli Mossad, succeeded in saving the lives of close to twenty thousand over a period of about ten years. As 1989 was nearing its close, the operation was entering its final stage and was being carried out in a country that was a sworn enemy of Israel and, at the time, under the direct influence of the then extremist Libyan leader, Gadhafi. Mossad operatives gauged their success not only in terms of the number of lives saved but also by the number of losses incurred by the forces on the ground. This number was zero.

In many respects, this operation was outside the ordinary area of responsibility of an intelligence service. Whereas normally an intelligence officer strives to limit his exposure and contact with his surroundings to a bare minimum and to narrow the revelation of his true identity to a chosen few, in this case operatives had to rub shoulders with literally thousands of people whom they had never seen before and among whom a hostile individual could well have been planted, without the knowledge of the rest. Thus, in principle, the modus operandi of such an endeavor was diametrically contrary to that of a conventional intelligence service. On the other hand, the success of the operation depended, in no small measure, on the practice of many of the tools of the trade of an intelligence officer—his and her ability to assume identities and aliases, his capacity to recruit local support for seemingly innocuous tasks, and his steely courage in maintaining cover in what were often acute circumstances. The operation entailed action on the ground across distances of fifteen hundred kilometers, close overcoming roadblocks manned by local security forces who controlled all the main arteries of this vast country and functioning for a period of more than ten years without, as mentioned, the loss of even one person. All this was accomplished by the Mossad diverting less than 5 percent of its total capacity to this unique assignment.

The year 1989 was also characterized by a continued Israeli presence on Moroccan soil and the unique relationship that had been nurtured between King Hassan II of Morocco and successive Israeli governments. The liaison between the monarch and the Mossad had come into being in the early sixties of the twentieth century. At the time newly born Algeria had gone to war against its neighboring country, Morocco, and Egyptian units were fighting alongside the Algerians. The relationship between Israel and the Arab League member Morocco fast became a strategic one and ultimately enabled the king to bring together Israeli and Egyptian senior envoys at meetings which were destined, in the seventies, to produce the first peace treaty between Israel and an Arab state. Egypt was to endure close to ten years of virtual isolation in the Arab world. The year 1989 saw it beginning to emerge from this difficult phase in its history. As Cairo was again accepted into the Arab community of nations, King Hassan turned his efforts toward convincing Israel to accept the Palestinian Liberation Organization and its leader, Yassir Arafat, as a valid negotiating partner. King Hassan engaged in an intensive dialogue with the Israeli prime minister Yitzhak Shamir on this issue, but to no avail. Shamir adamantly refused to countenance a dialogue with Arafat, who was in exile in Tunisia, and rejected every overture to permit anybody to deal with the Palestinian leader. Mr. Shamir was very anxious to meet with the Moroccan monarch; he believed such a meeting was in the interests of both countries. But this was never to come about. Instead, the ongoing exchange of views was destined to be conducted between an emissary of the Israeli prime minister and the king.

The year 1989 was also the year that the Berlin wall came down and the Soviet Union began its march toward the final dissolution of the Union of Soviet Socialist Republics—the U.S.S.R. The deteriorating economic conditions in the Soviet Union were becoming extremely difficult and Mikhail Gorbachev was encountering one obstacle after another in his efforts to stem the tide that was ultimately to engulf his empire and precipitate its dramatic collapse. In his hour of great need, Gorbachev approached Israel in 1989 and secretly appealed to it to convince the United States to prop up his regime and to prevent its downfall. He seemed to believe that Israeli influence in Washington, D.C., could be instrumental in swaying the administration and Congress to advance massive financial and economic aid to the Soviet Union. After considering the Russian request, Mr. Shamir decided not to take any action on it. I doubt if he had decided otherwise, he would have been able to prevail on the powers that be in the American capital to act and save the Russian empire.

Israel, a state with a population of around four million in 1989, had become a focal player on the regional scene and was a deft and effective factor on issues well beyond the confines of the Middle East. Its most powerful adversary in the region, Egypt, had despaired of defeating the Jewish state over a decade before and had decided to sign a peace treaty with its erstwhile enemy. All issues had been settled except one—the precise delineation of the border between the two countries in the area of Taba, just south of Eilat, Israel's most southerly port city. On January 30, 1989, the Egyptian flag was raised over the 91st border stone marking the boundary between Israel and Egypt. The two states had settled the dispute by arbitration and Israel had lost the case.

The year 1989 was to be remembered as the year when Soviet forces finally withdrew from Afghanistan. At the time this was considered one of the greatest triumphs of the "free world" against the Communist empire. It was also a remarkable success of the CIA, which had led the intricate battle against the Soviets and had run one of the most successful intelligence operations on a global scale in modern times. Little did the highly competent and professional officers of the Agency realize that the recruits they had supported in the battle against the Russians were des-

tined to turn the battlegrounds of Afghanistan into bases for indoctrina-
tion and training of extreme Muslim fundamentalist terrorists, who
would shortly turn around and not only bite the hands of their benefac-
tors, but also launch a deadly world war against them within a space of
ten years. In 1998, the U.S. embassies in Nairobi, Kenya, and Dar es
Salaam, Tanzania, were bombed and destroyed within minutes of each
other, thus heralding a new era in world history. The seeds of 1989 had
not taken long to bud and to produce their lethal results. It had taken
less than ten years. Osama bin Laden, if asked, would probably say that
his countdown began during the last week of January 1989, as the Soviet
forces completed their withdrawal from Kabul, the capital of Afghanistan.

Israel was not involved in the Afghan campaign, but its presence was
felt even when, in actual fact, it was not there at all. There were no full
diplomatic relations between Israel and either India or Pakistan, but
there were constant press rumors that Israel was aiding one side against
the other. Israel did have a consulate in what was then Bombay (now
Mumbai), but there was not much more than that. However, the reporting about Israeli involvement illuminated one more facet of Israel's
global reach. Its involvement in the affairs of the world had taken on a
life of its own. It had become a regional power and was destined to act as
one and to reap the fruits of its unique "status" for better or for worse.
Its reputation had blossomed to such an extent as to permit it to reap
benefits based purely on its growing legend.

Thus was the stage set, both internationally and at a regional level, for
the impending war of the Gulf. Within two years the hero of the deadly
Iraq-Iran confrontation was to become the most reviled villain of all
time.

2

COUNTDOWN TO WAR

As the year 1990 dawned, an atmosphere of great expectations initially spread throughout the globe. The international background was more than promising. With the reunification of Germany and the impending collapse of the Soviet-led Eastern European Communist bloc, the traditional balances throughout the world were due to undergo dramatic changes. The Middle East states like Syria and Iraq, which had been for years clients of the Soviet Union, lost their superpower support and backing almost overnight and new alignments and alliances were about to appear on the scene.

In Israel, the first Palestinian *intifada* was entering its third year, but the Palestinians were simultaneously engaged in promoting an apparently new policy designed to engage Israel in political negotiations. Notwithstanding efforts, including those made by the administration of President George H. W. Bush and his secretary of state, James Baker, to prevail upon Israel on the issue of starting some kind of contact or negotiations with the Palestinian Liberation Organization—the PLO—Mr. Shamir did not budge. He felt fairly secure as he looked at the international scene and saw the Soviet empire beginning to crumble and the beginnings of a tremendous wave of Jewish immigration to Israel. The prospect of this massive influx of Jews into Israel galvanized the Arab states into making a supreme effort to convince their erstwhile benefactor and Great Power patron to desist and to close the gates again; it was to no avail. Public statements by Arab leaders denouncing the flow of immigration fell on deaf ears. Among those was King Hussein of Jordan, whose critical comments were particularly ill-received by the government of Israel in Jerusalem.

The relationship between King Hussein and the powers that be in Jerusalem had seen much better days. Ever since the late sixties, there had been a strategic relationship between Israel and Jordan. In 1970, Israeli troop movements had dissuaded Syria from intervening in the confrontation that erupted in the month of September between the monarchy and the Arafat-led PLO. In later years both King Hussein and his brother, Crown Prince Hassan, were to show me the holes in their residences that had been made by artillery shells lobbed by the Palestinian forces that converged on Amman, the Jordanian capital. As long as the Israeli Labor party was in power, very close relations had been maintained. When Menachem Begin came to power in May 1977, the Jordanian monarch had hoped that this special link would continue. Alas, this did not come about. Mr. Begin himself showed no inclination to establish personal contact and his foreign minister, General Moshe Dayan, met only once with the king, a meeting that left him with very troubled memories.

In the eighties, a national coalition between the Likud and Labor parties was formed and the Labor wing of the government maintained close contact with the king and even tried to reach a historic agreement with him on the future of the Palestinian conflict. As we saw, these efforts ended in failure.

It was against this background, in 1990, that an attempt to establish a meaningful and trustworthy relationship between the Likud-led cabinet of Prime Minister Shamir and the reigning monarch in Jordan had to be made.

The predicament of King Hussein was compounded by a series of factors which caused him mounting concern. There had been a steady and worrisome flow of West Bank Palestinians into Jordan as the Palestinian *intifada* took its toll on everyday life in the West Bank. Jordan was much concerned with the growing imbalance between the indigenous population and the Palestinian refugees whose numbers were swelling once again. As the possibility of tension in the Gulf states loomed larger, King Hussein feared a further influx of Palestinians from those countries in the East. In the months of March and April of that year he was already acutely anxious that the whole, delicate equilibrium might be upset to the point of putting the very existence of the kingdom in jeopardy.

Seen through the eyes of the Jordanian monarch in the spring of 1990, the situation was pregnant with both dangers and unique opportunities. Iraq had won the war with Iran but had suffered tremendously both in loss of life—the toll of close to a million dead was mentioned—and in stark economic terms: Iraq had been constrained to borrow tens of billions of dollars from its Arab colleague-states and was on the verge of bankruptcy. In the eyes of the king, Saddam had waged a fierce and extended battle with the hated Shiite enemy in Tehran and had saved the Arab Sunni world from virtual destruction. However, the Sunni leadership had not responded with the gratitude and debt relief that could have been expected. Especially ungrateful were the Kuwaitis, whose country would have been one of the first to succumb had the Shiites of Tehran won the day. King Hussein was aware of the vital assistance that the United States had given intelligence-wise to Saddam Hussein to ensure his ability to survive and to inflict exceedingly heavy losses on his enemy. The king told me more than once that he was particularly taken aback when United States policy changed direction virtually overnight. He felt that the invasion of Kuwait, however wrong, erased all that Saddam had done in the service of the Middle East moderates by withstanding the pressure from the Shiite East to storm the walls of the Sunni, relatively moderate West. At the same time, he was at a loss to fathom the new and, what was in his view, unjustifiable policy of estrangement that Washington had only recently embarked on, in its attitude to Saddam Hussein's aspirations. One must keep in mind that King Hussein was not entirely unsympathetic to Iraq and its aspirations. In July 1958, the then prime minister of Iraq, Nouri Sa'id, had met with the king in Amman and had told him that Iraqi claims to Kuwait were under consideration in London and that a response was awaited by the end of the month. Within a week of their meeting a bloody revolution swept through the streets of Baghdad and the body of Sa'id alongside that of King Hussein's cousin, King Faisal, was dragged through the thoroughfares of the city to the cheers of the populace.

One must also consider the history of the Middle East at this point.

The fate of the territories that had been part of the Ottoman Empire was decided after the First World War by the victorious powers of the day, namely Britain and France, with the United States hovering in the background. Some areas were accorded independence; others, like Palestine, Syria, and Lebanon, were given mandate status and were to be administered by colonial powers for close to a quarter of a century. Countries like Iraq and Transjordan were granted monarchs and rulers. The exact frontiers and boundaries were determined by the colonial powers and in conjunction with their specific interests. Special attention was accorded to the necessity of ensuring effective influence or control of the vital oil resources in the Middle East, to the advantage of the free Western world. Under these circumstances it was not surprising that King Faisal of Iraq or his prime minister, Nouri Sa'id, would turn to Britain, the country that still reigned supreme in the Gulf during the 1950s, and expect a serious consideration of their claim to Kuwait.

Thirty years later, Kuwait had become a fully fledged independent state with aspirations of its own directed at potentially oil-rich areas close to the Iraqi border. It was not only rich and ambitious, but also singularly ungrateful. As he surveyed the scene, the experienced king was turning his attention inward to a domestic situation that carried the seeds of grave instability. There had been a steady flow of Palestinians from the West Bank into Jordan during the past year as the Palestinian *intifada* went on and caused hardship and suffering to the population as a whole in the "occupied" territories. Jordan had endured a severe bout of riots the previous year and the wounds, caused by ugly confrontation between hungry mobs and the security units, had not yet been healed. Privately, the king expressed his fear, that if conditions deteriorated in the Gulf states due to rising tension with Iraq, there could be an exodus of tens or even hundreds of thousands of Palestinians from the Gulf. Most would probably move to Jordan and further aggravate the already precarious balance inside the kingdom.

A question then arose for Israel: Should it take logical steps to help Jordan and, subsequently, improve the solidity of its own position? Speaking in the spring of 1990, Hussein suggested that Israel engage the Palestinians in a political dialogue and that it put out feelers to Iraq. It was true that Saddam Hussein had threatened that he could, and would, "burn half of Israel," but the king viewed this statement as pure bravado, uttered for local consumption. When told that there was a strong group of people in Israel who preferred an attempt to open a dialogue with Iraq rather than with Iran, but that every kite flown in that direction had been shot down, Hussein simply retorted that it was only a question of choosing the right channel.

But this was not the end of the story. The Jordanian monarch had developed a great respect for the ruler of Baghdad. He was conscious of wide sympathy for Iraq in the kingdom and had begun training his fighter pilots jointly with the Iraqi air force, on Iraqi soil. When confronted with this information, the king did not deny it but simply chose to play it down. In his words, this was just a means of cutting the high cost of pilot training and did not indicate a change of policy vis-à-vis Israel. The particular item at hand highlighted the predicaments of the two leaders on each bank of the Jordan River. For years, King Hussein had enjoyed a very special and discreet relationship with his westerly neighbor. At least on one occasion, during September 1970, Israeli troop movements had dissuaded Syria from entering Jordan to support the Palestinian forces, who were battling the Jordanian Armed Forces in an effort to topple the king and his dynasty. Regardless of government changes in Israel, Jordan had steadfastly maintained security along its long border with the Jewish state and had discreetly acted to further joint strategic interests of the two countries. Was it possible that this climate of cooperation was going to change in light of Jordan's belief that it should tilt toward Iraq in the impending showdown?

In the spring of 1990, there was still room for maneuver. At that point in time the king was busy trying to achieve a compromise between Iraq and the rest of the Arab world. He linked this wider dispute with the more defined and seemingly narrow issue of the Palestinian conflict. He believed that the Palestinians had genuinely changed their policy of nonrecognition of Israel and that they were prepared for real compromise. Moreover, the king was very conscious of a growing trend of extremism in the Arab world, including Jordan. He claimed to be aware of ties established between Muslim extremists in Jordan and groups within the community of the Arab citizens of Israel. As early as 1990, he thought that Israel must reach out to the Palestinians, before the extremists gain strength even to the extent of causing the Palestinian National Movement to implode. Such an eventuality could wreak havoc throughout the Middle East. Today, in retrospect, this thought sounds truly prophetic.

Israel did not take the king up on his suggestion of reaching out to the Palestinians, considering it an unrealistic idea. Instead, Israel decided to focus on the stark realities at hand and closely monitor a situation that was becoming more volatile as the days progressed. These were not long in coming. Iraq surprised the world by overtaking Kuwait in August of that year. Only the day before, the U.S. ambassador April Gillespie had been received by Saddam Hussein and had not gone away with any sense that such a dramatic step was at hand.

Soon after this, Israel realized that Iraqi aircraft, bearing the insignia of the Royal Jordanian Air Force, had begun patrolling the Jordanian-Israeli border south of the Dead Sea, virtually in striking distance of Israel's atomic reactor in the area of Dimona. It was inconceivable that these flights could take place without the knowledge and approval of the king of Jordan. Voices, strident voices, were heard in Jerusalem advocating an end to the long and secret honeymoon between Jordan and Israel. Those who had long advocated solving the Palestinian problem on the east bank of the river saw the approaching war as a golden opportunity to kill two birds with one stone: to retaliate against a possible Iraqi missile attack against Israel by taking the war simultaneously into Iraqi territory while at the same time running roughshod over Jordan's airspace and engaging the Jordanian Armed Forces in combat. Such a scenario, if taken to its ultimate conclusion, could bring down the monarchy.

Before countenancing such a chain of events and activities, it was decided to confront the Jordanian leader and to warn him of the possible consequences of this latest development. Sometime in September he traveled to London, where he encountered a very angry and caustic Prime Minister Margaret Thatcher. The very same day he was delivered a stiff and uncompromising warning that the Iraqi flights must stop forthwith. In later conversations the king said that whereas the tone and manner of Mrs. Thatcher had been most bitter and unpleasant in form, the Israeli message was all the more polite in form, but so much more serious and threatening in content. The opportunity afforded by the necessity to pass the message was further used in order to explain and amplify the way the king saw aspects of fundamental consequence.

The king took pains to explain that in the eyes of the Arab in the street, Saddam Hussein was a true hero. He had saved the Sunni world from the onslaught of the Iranian Shiites and he had shown courage, leadership, and power. In the words of the king, every Arab wanted to see a leader in the role of a Nebuchadnezzar. At times, the leader was a military hero. On occasion, he might be a prophet. These qualities of leadership were such as to appeal to the man of the desert, to the sheikh of a tribe; he had to command not only respect but awe and fear. He had to represent the fulfillment of a dream, the dream of glory, of sacrifice, and of success. Saddam, in the eyes of the multitude, was all of this and more. What the man of a Western city considered ruthlessness and cruelty was no less than courage and strength and pride. The element of pride must never be forgotten, was what he repeated time and time again.

The king was especially bitter concerning the way he was being treated by President George H. W. Bush. He had known and dealt with every American president since President Dwight Eisenhower and had worked with Bush when the latter was director of the CIA for a short period in the mid-seventies. He maintained contact with him after he had left office and even when he had been counseled to keep his distance from the man because he was considered a pariah in Washington. Now, Bush was pushing him into a corner and he simply could not bend to such naked pressure on the Iraqi issue. Years of patient and successful cultivation of his ties with the United States were now proving futile. The relations between himself and his long-standing ally were beginning to unravel. For Jordan and for himself personally, this spelled disaster of the worst kind, but he was powerless to stop the downward slide on the eve of the war. During those months, whenever I met him, he said to me that he was convinced that he had behaved in an honorable and respectful way, that he was prepared to meet his fate just as he had been prepared in the past when faced with grave threats to his life and to the survival of the kingdom. As the coalition of countries led by President Bush was taking shape, I was seeing a leader in a somber and fatalistic mood, at peace with himself, mentally and emotionally resigned to meeting whatever Allah had ordained for him.

At a very early stage it had become clear that the United States was striving to include as many Arab states as possible in the effort to confront Iraq. In addition to its traditional allies, like Saudi Arabia and some strategically positioned states like Oman, situated at the southern tip of the Persian Gulf, there was a distinct desire to bring in Egypt and even Syria. Of all the countries in the region, one particular state, Israel, was specifically being excluded. Indeed, any involvement of Israel, in any shape or form, was being judged as prejudicial to the very continued existence of the coalition. The notion that Israel and any Arab state could fight side by side against another Arab state was considered not only repugnant but also treacherous in the minds and hearts of the Arab masses. It therefore became imperative to keep Israel out of the war. Its protection from possible missile attacks launched by Baghdad had to be ensured by other means. The United States would make certain pledges to Israel, to give priority to an effort to exercise maximum control over the western desert of Iraq, from whence mobile launchers could fire missiles and then speedily disappear. To reassure Israel the United States would take limited action several months later and dispatch a quantity of Patriot antiaircraft missile batteries. In practice these turned out to be, by and large, ineffective. It similarly transpired that the coalition air forces were unable to earmark sufficient resources to operate in the airspace of the western desert of Iraq. Thus Israel was to be targeted by thirty-nine Iraqi missiles during the first Gulf War.

All this was yet to come about; in the meantime the need to secure a measure of understanding and cooperation with Jordan had fast become a burning issue for Israel. After delivering a stern warning to King Hussein on the Iraqi aircraft patrolling the skies so close to Israel's southern border with Jordan, I thought it right to broach the possibility of a meeting between himself and Prime Minister Shamir. The purpose of such a summit would be to try to prevent any use of Jordanian assets or facilities by Iraq and to obtain, perhaps, an explicit or tacit understanding of Israel's needs in certain extreme circumstances. When asked if he was willing to meet with Mr. Shamir, the king replied in the affirmative, but expressed his doubts as to whether Mr. Shamir would take the opportunity, given the total disagreement that the two had experienced during their only previous encounter. I then asked him if he would attend a meeting, were Mr. Shamir to come along, and he responded at once with a quick "Yes!" Upon my return home I met with the prime minister and asked him if he would like to meet personally with the king. The prime minister immediately said he would welcome such an opportunity, but added that he had grave doubts as to whether the king would take the risk of a leak and its effect both on the massive part of his own population and on his delicate relations with Iraq, and with Saddam Hussein in particular. I then said to the prime minister that the king had already agreed and that a meeting could indeed take place.

There was considerable risk involved in the run-up to this fateful summit. The price of failure could be inordinately high since such failure might give the anti-Jordan lobby in Israel an added boost and possibly even hand them a rational adoption of their understandings and policies. In their previous encounter the two leaders had developed a distinct liking for each other and yet, on basic approaches, they were clearly poles apart. Should they meet and then part ways in practical disagreement, such an event might well cast a heavy pall over the future of Jordanian-Israeli relations. Were that to be the expected outcome as the date of their rendezvous came near, would it not have have been wiser to call it off rather than to let it end in dismal failure?

The prime minister and his aides arrived in London a few days before the coalition was to launch its first assault. It was late Friday and two of his closest aides were observant Orthodox Jews who would not and could not be caught desecrating the Jewish Sabbath. The group had to land before sundown because travel was not permitted on the holy day. Apart from them, the deputy chief of staff of the Israel Defense Forces (IDF) was instructed to join the group. This man was General Ehud Barak, later to become Israel's prime minister. The king for his part was accompanied by the head of his court chamber, Field Marshal Zeid Bin Shaker, a former chief of staff and a close confidant and relative of the king as well as one of the most respected figures in the kingdom. Also there was Adnan Abu Odeh—a political adviser of the king, a Jordanian of Palestinian extraction, and a veteran who had occupied many positions in the system. Present as always was Colonel Ali Shukri, the king's trusted aide.

The two leaders meeting on the eve of battle had discussed matters of mutual interest only once before, about three years previously, and had parted in disagreement and yet when they looked into each other's eyes once again, a bystander could not avoid the impression that here were two figures who clearly had much admiration and esteem for each other and had a deep feeling of confidence in one another. They first met with their aides present but soon preferred to sit alone, just the two of them with only one other person present.

Before the proceedings could begin an intricate problem of Jewish religious law—halachic law—had to be resolved. Sensing that this was to be a session where the gravest of issues were to be discussed, the prime minister wanted there to be no misunderstanding in the future as to what had been said or agreed. Hence, the normal request that notes be taken. This was vigorously opposed by both Elyakim Rubinstein, the cabinet secretary, and Yossi Ben Aharon, the director general of the prime minister's office. The two argued forcefully that writing was a desecration of the Sabbath laws and hence could not be permitted. They similarly objected to anybody else writing in their presence and promised that they could accurately memorize the proceedings that were to last for over five hours. When the premier turned to me I told him that in my understanding what was at stake were matters of life and death and, according to the halacha, such subjects took precedence over keeping the strict letter of the law. Indeed, in situations like these the law commanded that it be "broken." How bizarre it must have seemed to the non-Jewish onlooker to witness a discussion of such a nature, in these particular circumstances. The "solution" was also typical. The prime minister ruled in favor of his religious aides, but simultaneously asked me to take notes in a "clandestine" fashion.

From the very outset the issues at stake were crystal clear: Israel had to be assured that Jordanian sovereign territory and airspace would not be at the disposal of the Iraqi forces during the impending hostilities. In view of the events that had occurred in previous months, this could not be taken for granted. The king was immediately forthcoming on this matter and solemnly undertook to prevent the military use of Jordan in any shape or form against Israel. The second issue was much more delicate: Since Jordan could not prevent the use of its outer space by Iraqi ballistic missiles, Israel sought Jordanian understanding and passive acquiescence in the limited and peripheral use of Jordanian airspace, should Israel be constrained to retaliate against Iraqi attacks against Israel. The significance of this was all too obvious. Should the Jordanian air force and ground antiaircraft systems engage the Israeli Air Force there would be no option but to act to destroy Jordan's capacities. An ensuing war, even a very small one, between Israel and Jordan could spell disaster, if it was waged alongside the coalition campaign launched against Saddam Hussein. The king stood firm and refused to agree to the prime minister's demand. He explained at length that he could not be seen to collude with Israel, if Israel felt obliged to attack Iraq. He stated in no uncertain terms that if Israel violated Jordanian airspace, he would give the order to defend and protect the country's sovereignty. It was unfortunately all too evident that Jordan was powerless to prevent Iraqi forces from firing their missiles across its outer space and in this respect it could not defend its "sovereignty," but this state of affairs did not move the king to soften his implacable stand concerning Israel's request for a limited freedom of action.

Notwithstanding the two leaders' understandable preoccupation with the immediate crisis at hand, time was nevertheless devoted to an attempt to peer behind the curtain and to try to discern what the more distant future might look like after the end of the imminent round of hostilities. Even as war was fast approaching, Mr. Shamir took pains to express his belief that one day he would be able to reciprocate the hospitality he had enjoyed by hosting the king on a public visit to Israel. The king, for his part, expressed his fervent desire to see peace come to the region and, in particular, peace between Jordan and Israel. Once again, the two leaders parted without agreement between them. Whereas on the first occasion the two parted ways on the mechanics and terms of reference of a peace negotiation, this time the issue was one of "life and death" and the upshot was that Israel's request and expectations had been rejected.

Of all the comments made at that meeting, one was of particular significance. It was General Barak who said that the upcoming war was to be the very first hostile conflict to be played out since the end of the Cold War. In his view it was essential that whatever the outcome, Saddam must emerge as the one who had lost the war.

Within days, war broke out and the Israeli public prepared itself by activating air-raid shelters and readying gas masks. The immediate threat was that missiles with chemical warheads would be launched against both military targets and the civilian population. All in all, thirty-nine Scud missiles landed on Israel's territory. No military or strategic target was hit. A number of residential houses were badly damaged or destroyed and one civilian died of a heart attack that might have been brought on by one of the missiles. Many of the missiles landed in open fields. They were undoubtedly hopelessly inaccurate. The Patriot anti-aircraft missile batteries that arrived in Israel with their American crews proved almost completely ineffective and were judged to have caused some of the damage to properties. On the face of it, Israel had emerged from the war unscathed.

Alas, this was only one side of the story. The rain of missiles, though limited in number, wrought enormous damage to the morale of the population. A hastily constructed early-warning system enabled U.S. monitoring capabilities to relay messages to an Israeli command post that missiles had been fired. This gave Israel the possibility of warning the public, who then rushed to their shelters and donned their gas masks. As this procedure was followed again and again, public morale sank very low. Tens of thousands of residents of the greater Tel Aviv area, where the biggest concentration of Israel's population lived, hastily evacuated their homes to repair to more remote regions, which were considered either out of range or of lesser priority to the Iraqis. There was also a significant exodus of people leaving the country for the duration. This was an experience never encountered before in Israel's history. In the evenings, Tel Aviv resembled a ghost town with deserted streets and abundant parking space.

In the corridors of power, an intense debate broke out between those who pressed for an immediate Israeli military response and those who advocated restraint. In order to strengthen the hand of those who wanted to hold back, the United States dispatched Deputy Secretary of State Laurence Eagleburger to Jerusalem with the task of acting to ensure the constant presence of a restraining hand. It was all too patently clear that the purpose of the Iraqi attacks was to provoke Israel into retaliation. Saddam Hussein assumed that once Israel hit Baghdad, the vital Arab component in the coalition would be forced to withdraw. The specter of Arab states fighting alongside Israel against an Arab sister state was a sight they could never endure. It was a development that the United States was intent on avoiding and it seemed as if President Bush was ready to invest heavily in seeing that this would never come to pass. It was Eagleburger's mission to meet the prime minister daily and to assure him that the United States and its allies were giving priority to air sorties designed to locate the mobile missile launchers that Iraq was using to direct its Scud missiles against Israel. In order to prevent Israel from exploding in anger, it had to be convinced that the United States was indeed doing its utmost, even though this secondary effort on its part was made at the expense of the principal endeavor that was being mounted elsewhere along the principal lines of battle between the Iraqi and coalition forces. By and large the defense establishment in Tel Aviv, centered around the general headquarters of the Israel Defense Forces did not really believe that the United States was doing its very best to apprehend the missile launchers. This was to be a sore point in any future assessment of what the United States would actually do in any given situation. That experience has reverberated throughout the Israeli system and remains a very powerful consideration when the very survival of the State of Israel is ever discussed as an agenda item.

Yet, there was obviously another formidable side to the equation. Ever since the State of Israel had come into being, one of the more fundamental tenets of its defense policy had been to maintain a deterrent posture vis-à-vis its adversaries. This was considered the point of departure of its overall security position. A counterargument always advanced was that, should Israel refrain from action when directly attacked, its deterrent posture would be irreparably impaired, inflicting permanent damage on the most important bases of Israel's defense and security structure. This powerful argument was championed by no less than the minister of defense, Moshe Arens, the chief of staff, General Shomron, the commander of the air force, and others. There was a second point made— that restraint ran counter to the very ethos of the IDF and that it would take years to restore self-confidence inside the armed forces. Third, some said, the image of Israel relying on the United States for its physical security—either on the American air force operating in Iraqi airspace against static and mobile missile launchers or on the antiaircraft Patriot missile batteries visibly seen on the shores of Tel Aviv—was an image that the citizens of Israel could not stomach, especially since the protective arm of the United States had proved largely ineffective.

The conflicting pressures on Prime Minister Shamir were thus unprecedented and he was to confide in me, many years later in a private conversation, that in maintaining his stand of restraint, he was guided not only by his commitments to the United States (commitments that Washington was unable, operationally, to reciprocate as originally envisaged), but also by his trust in the good faith of King Hussein and his belief that his conduct toward the Jordanian monarch would somehow be rewarded.

One of the important features of the eve of war meeting between Mr. Shamir and King Hussein was that this was a purely local event born out of the immediate mutual interests of the two countries. Given the fact that it was held in Britain with the knowledge of the local authorities, one would assume that the United States was ultimately privy to what had transpired. The United States was to draw its own benefit from this initiative, but it had not launched it and it had not been a party to determining its outcome. In my understanding, there was no meeting of the minds, but there had been a meeting of the hearts. The two principals were seasoned statesmen and were visibly conscious of what lay ahead, and they seemed to draw strength and confidence from each other.

In the days running up to the first Gulf War pro-Saddam fervor reached record heights in the Arab world. Hundreds of thousands of demonstrators filled the main thoroughfares of Cairo, Amman, and Rabat, wildly cheering the Iraqi dictator and identifying with his courageous stand against the United States and the world at large. In Morocco one day, the supreme and reigning monarch, King Hassan II, appeared on television in the morning dressed in military uniform and warned the demonstrating masses not to proceed with their acts of defiance, only to reappear on television that very same evening dressed in traditional garb pleading understanding and conciliation. Traditional and moderate regimes in the entire region were stretched to the utmost and there were genuine fears of revolution in the air. It was precisely at this juncture that Israel was addressing many approaches that asked for its evaluation of the current situation and seeking encouragement and support. If ever Israel needed proof that it had become a regional power, it now received it in ample quantity. Rarely in the past had the eyes of the leaders of the region been focused to such an extent on Israel and its leadership, and seeking its advice. In terms of its longer-term strategic interests, the way Israel was perceived in the eyes of the public at large and the ruling levels in particular was to fashion its regional image for years to come.

The ultimate decision of Yitzhak Shamir to hold fast and not sanction an Israeli independent military operation in western Iraq was the most momentous of his political career. It prevented the collapse of the coalition and the isolation of the United States in the Middle East. It averted a confrontation between the United States and Israel, as well as Israel's possible isolation in the international arena. As we shall see, it created the initial conditions for a sea change in Israel's international standing, the likes of which it had never experienced before. But there was a price for all this: Without doubt, Israel's deterrent image had been tarnished. The uncharacteristic restraint it showed was the first of a series of Israeli actions and nonactions that were slowly and inexorably destined to bring about a change in the manner in which Israel would be evaluated and perceived for years to come. This was indeed an extremely heavy price to pay for a state whose very existence has not been accepted by all the countries in the region to this very day.

The war on Iraq was short and militarily "elegant." Iraq was forced out of Kuwait and the country's freedom, sovereignty, and regime were restored. The armed forces of Iraq were dealt a resounding blow and suffered heavy losses. At the end of the campaign Iraq was a destitute state and its population was economically devastated. The composition of the coalition led the United States to preclude a physical takeover of the country and the toppling of the regime. The notion of foreign troops entering and capturing an Arab capital was abhorrent in the eyes of the Arab partners to the coalition. Thus a speedy cease-fire was arranged and hostilities ended without the demise of Saddam's regime. The assumption appeared to be that the enormity of the defeat and the feeling of shame and degradation would set in motion an internal convulsion that would bring the regime down. This, as we all know, did not come to pass.

So, who won the war? On the face of it there could be no doubt. Kuwait had been liberated and the Iraqi army had been forced to accept a cease-fire. In the years to come Iraq had to submit to an unprecedented regime of inspection and monitoring of its nonconventional capabilities. Its nuclear, chemical, and biological capacities were exposed and destroyed. Its missile delivery systems and the missiles themselves were similarly decimated. The country had to accept a regime of sanctions. Its oil exports were controlled by outside authorities and the proceeds were earmarked for food and medical purchases. Iraq appeared to be prostrate and politically bankrupt. This is how things appeared to be seen in most capitals of the world.

However, there was a different side to this very same saga. Saddam Hussein had stood up all alone against the entire world and the coalition had stopped short of bringing him down. Was he not the most courageous Arab leader ever to have confronted the only true super-power, the United States, and had he not emerged practically victorious? In the understanding of the Muslim masses this was just the way they viewed the outcome of the first Gulf War. In effect Saddam was the first to prove that the United States was not invincible, that a combination of fortitude and cunning could defeat the aims of the only superpower on earth. I think that Saddam showed the way to Osama bin Laden and allowed him to believe in the efficacy of his future endeavors. Within a couple of years the United States was destined to make a quick foray into Somalia, beating a hasty retreat after the bodies of dead American soldiers were mutilated and dragged through the streets of Mogadishu. Little wonder that in the decade to come, Somalia was to become a breeding ground and safe base for Al Qaeda operatives, who took encouragement from what was, in their eyes, a weakening America.

It was in this context that I wish to recall the thought expressed by General Barak at the Hussein-Shamir meeting on the eve of the war: "Whatever the outcome, Saddam must not emerge as a victor. He must be perceived as the one who actually lost it." This did not happen.

The big losers of this war appeared to be the Palestinians. They had thrown in their lot with Saddam Hussein and, in consequence, had exacerbated their tense relations with the moderate Arab statesmen who had championed their cause for generations. Ostensibly, they had very little leverage over either the United States or, for that matter, any other power broker in the region or in the world at large. But in a strange ironic twist of history, they were able to project relevance out of acute weakness and as the sounds of all-out war receded into the background, the United States woke up to sense that their resounding victory over the Iraqi dictator had placed them and their Arab partners in an acutely vulnerable situation. All of a sudden it became vital and urgent for Washington to act decisively and demonstrably to get traction and movement on the Palestinian issue. This rapidly became the litmus test for the United States to prove that it had not become the "enemy" of the Arab nations. And so it came to pass that the apparent losers of the war, Iraq on one side and the Palestinians on the other, each derived such large dividends from their inferior positions. Only Jordan and Israel did not seem to gain much. Jordan was pilloried by the moderate Arab states Egypt and Saudi Arabia, and was deprived of the vital financial contributions it had traditionally obtained from the Gulf principalities. It was virtually under siege and embargo, and American warships patrolled access to the Gulf of Aqaba and boarded every boat en route to the port of Aqaba for inspection because Jordan had become the only naval access route for Iraq. Jordanian-American relations took a steep dive and as the king surveyed the scene, his relationship with Israel took on proportions never observed before.

As for Israel, it would see a very mixed resolution. The defeat of Iraq had drastically weakened the traditional threat from the eastern front, which numbered Iraq, Syria, and others. On the face of it, Israel could expect to receive some recognition if not compensation for the singular restraint it had practiced during the Gulf War. The hostilities had caused Israel heavy economic losses. The key tourist industry had been especially hit and other derivatives had been similarly severely mauled financially. Alas, rather than basking in the sun of praise and material compensation, Israel was almost instantly subjected to strong pressure to get down and work out agreements with the Palestinians, with the Syrians, and even with the Jordanians. Why and how did all this happen?

3

THE COVERT AND OVERT
TRACKS AFTER THE WAR

As the sounds of war died down, the countries of the Middle East woke up to look around and assess the new situation that had emerged from the debris of the death and destruction wrought by the conflicting armed forces. President Bush, who had led the seemingly victorious coalition, was quick to proclaim the advent of a "New World Order" and the spirit of reconciliation that was designated to dominate the scene in the years to come. The evil forces in the Middle East had been supposedly roundly defeated and all that was left was for the powers that be in the world to solidify the new golden era for generations to come.

Within a relatively short period of time, the United Nations, led by the victorious coalition spearheaded by the United States, was able to establish a system that dismantled Iraqi nonconventional capabilities and monitored its future activities in related areas. A sanctions regime was initiated to bring Iraq to heel. Access to Iraq was restricted and ships bearing goods destined for Baghdad were subjected to rigorous maritime searches carried out by U.S. naval vessels patrolling the straits of Aqaba. Iraqi ports were in effect closed down. International air traffic was suspended and foreigners wishing to make their way to the beleaguered country were for the most part forced to do so by land through neighboring Jordan or Syria. Iraqi airspace was largely declared out of bounds for the Iraqis and considerable parts of it, both north and south, became regular patrol grounds of American and British aircraft that took advantage of the opportunity to target Iraqi surface-to-air missile sites and radar installations from time to time. The southern road arteries of Jordan became clogged by hundreds of heavy trucks carrying vital supplies to the Iraqi border.

One could almost hear the sigh of relief from those who had believed that the Iraqi threat was of international proportions. In their understanding, "Pax Americana" had proved itself and as of then, the number-one priority was to list the conflicts that were still outstanding and to launch efforts to adjudicate and to solve them. The Arab partners in the coalition were quick to impress upon the United States the absolute necessity of promoting movement on the Palestinian conflict. The demand fell on receptive ears in Washington and there ensued an American drive to get both sides to the table. Pressure on Israel to agree to an international conference format where the issues would be discussed and decided had been, and was, anathema to the thinking of Prime Minister Shamir and his Likud party–led government. Shamir refused to recognize and therefore to negotiate with the Arafat-led PLO. In the end, after much to-and-fro, a final agreement was reached and a conference was convened in Madrid in November 1991 under the patronage of the United States and the Soviet Union. This was to be the last opportunity for the Soviet Union led by Mikhail Gorbachev to appear alongside its American superpower counterpart. Shortly after that, the Soviet empire crumbled, Gorbachev was removed from office, and the United States was clearly installed as the lone sheriff policing the globe.

The conference convened on October 30 and lasted a couple of days. It was attended by the two principal sponsors, President George Bush and President Mikhail Gorbachev. From the outset, in the detailed invitation, two sets of future negotiations were envisaged as the practical outcome of the conference. One was to be the bilateral track, between Israel and Arab states and between Israel and the Palestinians, with Jordan acting as a "front" for a joint Jordanian-Palestinian delegation. The latter was necessary because, at that time, Israel did not recognize the right of the Palestinians to create a state of their own. The second track was to be a multilateral track designed to deal with regional issues such as arms control and regional security, water, refugee issues, the environment, economic development, and other subjects of mutual interest. The time frames of these negotiations concerning the Palestinians are of significance and interest today, fifteen years after the parties had all agreed to them in advance of the conference. I quote from the invitation:

> With respect to negotiations between Israel and Palestinians who are part of the joint Jordanian-Palestinian delegation, negotiations will be conducted in phases, beginning with talks on interim self-government arrangements. These talks will be conducted with the objective of reaching agreement within one year. Once agreed the interim self-government arrangements will last for a period of five years. Beginning the third year of the period of self-government arrangements, negotiations will take place on permanent status. These permanent status negotiations, and the negotiations between Israel and the Arab states, will take place on the basis of resolutions 242 and 338.

The agreement at the Madrid conference was a multifaceted one; it envisaged a three-track set of bilateral negotiations between Israel and a Syrian, Jordanian, and Jordanian-Palestinian delegation. The bilateral fora began meeting simultaneously in Washington, D.C. Suffice it to say that at the end of the day no tangible result was obtained in any of these meetings or dialogues. The multilateral fora on all the issues set out in the original invitation to the conference convened in a variety of capitals around the world. Gradually enthusiasm for them petered out as the bilateral talks produced no tangible results.

Why was this so? First, the negotiations were conducted under the glaring eyes of the media and, although they did not actually participate in the meetings, the parties more or less rendered a daily account of what had transpired. Second, the conduct of three sets of negotiations simultaneously created a situation whereby each of the negotiating partners with Israel looked over the shoulders of the two others to verify whether any concession to Israel had been made. The obvious result was that no one dared to yield on any matter of substance, lest he be publicly condemned by the others as being compromising and "soft" on issues pertaining to the vital interests of the Arab world. Mr. Shamir lost the general election in Israel in 1992 and the opposition Labor party led by Yitzhak Rabin came to power. The overt negotiation tracks continued to operate for a little while longer. The Palestinians released themselves from the Jordanian tutelage forced upon them by the Israeli side (to the relief of the Jordanians), but apart from that, nothing changed. The negotiations in the Madrid mode appeared to be for all intents and purposes stalemated.

The intense diplomatic effort mounted by U.S. secretary of state James Baker during the aftermath of the Gulf War was, to a large extent, the external façade to a more intimate and candid dialogue that was being conducted by Israelis and Palestinians, as well as by Israelis and Jordanians, through clandestine channels. Whereas the Palestinian "track" was an unofficial one, the Jordanian one was an official one, involving the highest levels on both sides. The Palestinian channels were numerous, and more often than not, it was not always possible to ascertain if those who appeared had the authority or status to represent their side. As for the Israelis who participated in these talks, they were not empowered to speak on behalf of their political masters and the result of this was that there was much confusion and competition among Israelis involved in such meetings. Only at a later stage was a discreet and genuine channel established in what became known as the "Oslo" story. (I was not involved in this channel or in those negotiations. It was a secret backdoor negotiation led by Foreign Minister Shimon Peres that produced the first Israeli-Palestinian agreement, which enabled Yassir Arafat to return to Palestinian soil and set up the Palestinian Authority on a portion of the territories that Israel had taken over in the 1967 Six-Day War. The wisdom and efficacy of this initiative has been at the center of an internal debate in Israel from its inception.)

There were other differences that were important at the time and are worthy of mention. Since the Palestinians were in the formative stages of state-building, they had blinders on concerning all other issues, and took little nor no interest in the wider aspects and implications of Middle East and international relations. If they paid attention to such matters at all, it was primarily in the context of how they could harness outside forces to support them in their quest for independence. Jordan behaved in a completely different manner, viewing its interest and destinies in the much wider context of international affairs. The private and secluded channels of this dialogue provided a unique and fascinating opportunity to analyze key subjects in depth and to look at long-term implications of moves and policies away from the glaring public eye. Alas, although the covert channels were instrumentally successful in launching peace initiatives, they failed to sensitize the politicians to the fundamental threats that were becoming apparent and that were destined to confront the world less than a decade later.

Throughout 1991, in the aftermath of the first Gulf War, the success of the American-led coalition led the Arab members of the allied victory into assuming that they could pursue their desire of furthering the cause of Palestinian statehood alongside a parallel policy of appeasement and leniency toward Muslim religious fundamentalism. Indeed, as far as Saudi Arabia was concerned, this birthplace and original source of fundamentalism sought to deflect its participation in a war against an Arab "brother" by sanctioning and encouraging a major drive into the former Soviet Union's southern Muslim republics of massive funds and numerous clerics. One of the very first external forces to take advantage of the dissolution of the Soviet Union was the Saudi regime. By directing religious and national fervor to foreign channels, it hoped to lessen internal tensions exacerbated by the Gulf War and simultaneously to enhance Saudi and Muslim prestige in Muslim-populated regions, which had until recently been outside the reach of the seat of Islam.

The Saudis did not content themselves by reaching out, beyond the Middle East. They also encouraged fundamental elements throughout the Sunni states in the region, notably in Jordan, whom they faulted for allegedly siding with Saddam Hussein during the war. The support that the Muslim Brotherhood in Jordan received from Riyadh had the potential of destabilizing the Hashemite regime and was therefore a source of deep concern in Amman. Indirectly this aid became, initially, a source of encouragement and strength for the Khammas movement in the Palestinian-occupied territories during a period in the early nineties when the Khammas fundamentalist stream was gathering support in the Palestinian camp.

Traditional Saudi policies over the years had always been characterized by an assumption that the well-being of the realm could be "purchased"—that hostile or potentially hostile elements could be placated and their efforts directed elsewhere, leaving the kingdom of Saudi Arabia safe and sound. The safety and security of the kingdom were always the only consideration and if it caused collateral damage to others, the Saudis were indifferent to this.

Saudi support was sought by the United States for the impending effort to convene a peace conference on the Palestinian conflict. Secretary of State Baker was successful in ensuring the appearance of the Saudi ambassador in Washington, Prince Bandar bin Sultan, at the Madrid peace conference. Yet, strange as it may seem in retrospect, this quest for Saudi attention meant that a dangerous strain of Saudi domestic policy, namely its accelerated drive in support of Islamic fundamentalism, was ignored. Indeed, Secretary of State Baker was effusive in his praise for the wisdom and foresight of the Saudis, as they summoned up the courage that would associate themselves for the very first time, in public, with a reconciliatory peace process. In exchange for this Saudi step which was billed as unprecedented and singularly bold, the Saudis obtained a de facto American acceptance of Saudi involvement in spreading the word of Islamic puritanism throughout the Muslim world. The warnings of moderate Arab leaders in the Middle East that this Saudi policy might ultimately create a volatile situation threatening the stability of the region as a whole went unheeded.

It was not only the United States that ignored the potential of Muslim radicalism. In truth it must be admitted that even in Israel, which was so close to the Arab world and was monitoring every change and trend in its neighboring countries, the precise implication of what was going on did not register on the screens of analysts and decision makers at the time. Religion, as a determining factor in the history of the peoples of the entire region, had not yet been accepted as a key element in modern times when nationalism was believed to maintain center stage. In all, the reporting of secret meetings that took place at the time, indeed throughout the entire decade of the nineties, Arab interlocutors referred to this growing threat from time to time, only to be politely silenced by their non-Arab counterparts. The specter of a war rooted in religion was a development that modern minds would rather not countenance.

The government of the Likud prime minister, Shamir, was adamantly opposed to any contact of an official nature with the PLO led by Yassir Arafat. It similarly refused to sanction any unofficial or clandestine channel of dialogue with the organization and viewed it as essentially a terrorist group that warranted appropriate treatment as such. Nevertheless, it would be accurate to say that Shamir did have indirect means of maintaining an open line to this key piece in the puzzle. He avidly read reports that reached him and he allowed himself to be "served" with information that was not necessarily obtained by the traditional method of running agents in the professional sense of the term. Instead of that, the data trickled in through, shall we say, "contacts," which could be described as agents, except that they were honorable persons functioning in various walks of life, who volunteered their services in the cause of peace.

Shamir, as opposed to other prime ministers, never met these individuals. Given his previous experience both as leader of the prestate Lehi (Fighters for the Freedom of Israel) anti–British Mandate fighting group and as a subsequent division chief in the Mossad, he had an uncanny insight into the inner workings of intelligence and the ways of this vocation. My experience with him was a very unique one. On the one hand, I think I enjoyed his trust and he sent me on numerous delicate missions on his behalf. On the other, he rarely briefed me in detail, and, more often than not, he preferred to invite me to suggest to him what should be said at a forthcoming encounter. Since these briefing sessions were recorded both in shorthand and in tape form, he, like others, had his eye on history no less than on the current conduct of the affairs of state. The result was that whereas in actual fact the prime minister was fully aware of the fact that he was briefing an emissary, in terms of the written protocol he rarely could be caught making a policy statement of any consequence. As he received a report on the proceedings of an encounter he had authorized either he would refrain from any reaction or, if the script was to his liking, he would sometimes say to me, "Well done! You presented our position precisely the way I wished it to be." I cannot recall any occasion when my report met with the prime minister's disapproval. Had this happened, it was clear to me that the method he had adopted to brief me allowed him to choose at any juncture to disassociate himself from what I had said. The protocol of my reporting to the prime minister would reveal little of the prime minister's own thinking. He maintained complete freedom not only of action but also of writing the definitive history of his stewardship.

In this way, the Likud prime minister was able to keep abreast of what was transpiring in the numerous channels and contacts being pursued by unauthorized individuals, while at the same time maintaining a stance of deniability. The prime minister was also able, through these means, to ascertain that the Palestinians were in a state of relative weakness following their identification with Saddam Hussein during the Gulf War. They would have no option but to bow to Israel's condition that they not be allowed to negotiate their future entirely under their own "flag," but under the nominal tutelage of the Jordanians. Mr. Shamir was able to maintain the semblance of refusing to accept the Palestinian demand for outright national recognition, while, at the same time, doing business with them on a practical level.

The basic problem of the secret channels that the Palestinians maintained vis-à-vis the Israelis was that they were numerous up to a point of raising a feeling of uncertainty about their true value and authenticity. Did the emissaries really represent the leadership? Why was it that the chairman of the PLO sanctioned so many dialogues? Was it because he really sought to establish serious contact with as many Israeli walks of life as possible, or was his real aim to cause confusion and to assure himself of the right of deniability?

As long as Mr. Shamir was in power these numerous channels enabled him to pursue his policy of basic nonrecognition of the Palestinians' desire for independence and sovereignty over a part of what was originally the British-mandated "Palestine." As is often the case with Israeli politicians and statesmen, the true roots of their current stands must be sought in the basic positions they formed in their distant past. Even if they sometimes appear to have changed their policies or appear to have veered to positions diametrically opposite to those previously maintained, in the final analysis, these often turn out to be tactical moves dictated by short-term considerations rather than genuine changes of heart. Thus the roots of Mr. Shamir's positions must be sought and found in the the way he voted when the Israeli-Egyptian peace treaty came up for a vote in the Knesset, Israel's parliament. Mr. Shamir cast his vote against approval of the treaty, and in so doing voted against the position of his then prime minister, Menachem Begin. At the time, he was chairman of the parliament and did not fulfill any executive role in the government of the day. However, within the space of less than two years, he was to become foreign minister in the cabinet of Mr. Begin, and a couple of years later he would succeed him to become prime minister for two periods covering more than six years.

Given these salient details, the approach of Mr. Shamir to the covert channel aspect of foreign and defense policy was of much greater significance than that generally associated with his name and his tenure of office. First and foremost, let it be said in no uncertain terms that similar to most of his colleagues in the office, he was imbued with a keen belief of ultimate personal responsibility for the very destiny of the Jewish people. In keeping with this, he felt a sense of "history" each time he engaged in this area of his responsibility, and was very conscious of a desire not only to take the right decisions, but also to make certain that history would judge him rightly and positively. This, by the way, has been a characteristic common to most or all of those who occupied the post of prime minister in Israel's hitherto short history. For Shamir, the covert channels he approved and reveled in were, in my understanding, designed to serve as a major element in his ultimate vindication as a dynamic and innovative leader, belying his image as a dour, uncompromising, doctrinaire politician. Through the covert channels he promoted with kings and Arab and Muslim leaders, Shamir was able to explore new horizons and fresh ideas, without compromising his traditional overt positions. He met King Hussein only three times, and the rest of his dealings with the Hashemite monarch he conducted mainly through the covert channel, but when the peace treaty between Jordan and Israel was signed in a colorful ceremony in the Arava Valley, south of the Dead Sea and north of the twin cities of Israel's Eilat and Jordan's Aqaba, King Hussein demonstratively asked to meet Mr. Shamir there, more than two years after the latter's retirement, and to embrace him warmly and publicly. There were other contacts that Shamir maintained, notably with the late King Hassan II of Morocco. The two never met, but King Hassan developed a genuine respect and trust in Shamir. When the countdown for the first Gulf War began in earnest, Hassan sought the advice and assurance of the Israeli prime minister that, come what may, Israel would not back down in the face of an impending Iraqi attack. As I said previously, pro–Saddam Hussein fervor gripped the Muslim world at the time, and the streets of Morocco's major cities were the scenes of defiant demonstrations, the like of which had rarely been witnessed in the realm. The reassurances that King Hassan received from Shamir served to calm his nerves at a critical point in the history of the kingdom.

The intricate web of covert channels that had been spun and nurtured over the years had served consecutive Israeli leaders extremely well in forging and consolidating the country's strategic assets and capabilities. Little surprise, therefore, that when it came to launching and promoting meaningful negotiations, Israeli leaders preferred the covert routes to the overt ones. It was only thus that Israel could realistically weigh and assess the implications of any step it might take on the road to peace in the context of its overall strategic considerations and interests.

The nature and character of the channel was only one aspect to be considered when assessing and pondering the impact and significance of the covert channel and its effect on events in the region. Another element of paramount importance was the character of the emissary or emissaries chosen by the political level to represent Israel in the covert channel. The different types of representative would have an enormous effect on the outcome of the endless deliberations.

What characterized the Palestinian channel was that, as of the time that Mr. Shamir ceased to be prime minister, the Israeli interlocutors were for the most part persons politically aligned with their principals. It is true that a few of the Israelis were ostensibly what is generally known as "civil servants," but in this case these civil servants immediately became identified and aligned with their political mentor, the then Israeli foreign minister, Mr. Shimon Peres. The immediate result was that the insatiable desire of all the Israeli negotiators was above all to succeed. It rapidly became an overriding necessity to reach an agreement as soon as possible, and in order to do so, it became vital to exclude the professional arms of government not only from the negotiation itself, but also from the very knowledge that any such negotiation was actually being conducted. Thus the purpose and mission of the covert channel underwent a fundamental change. Rather than it being a discreet and reliable way of conducting frank discussions on issues related to the ultimate fate of the nation while maintaining a close professional watch over the basic interests of the state, it evolved into a strategy designed to enable the devoted negotiators to engage in dreams of peace rather than to confront the true facts of life and to grapple with them. The exclusion of the "professionals" was dictated not only by the necessity to ensure secrecy but, nonetheless, by an absolute requirement that the way toward achieving a settlement should not be mired by practical considerations of defense, security, and related factors.

Of the three negotiating tracks in the nineties, there was a single, strong-minded professional element working in the Syrian and Jordanian covert channels. The Palestinian channel, on the other hand, had no genuine, disinterested professional presence. Given the fact that the issues on the security side were dominant and extremely complex, this was ever more incomprehensible. How did it come about that the successor of Mr. Shamir, none other than former chief of staff General Yitzhak Rabin, allowed this to happen? He was known to be a stickler whenever it came to Israel's security interests. He was considered to be the epitome of intelligence analysis and a strategist who had spent several meaningful years as Israel's ambassador to the United States in 1969–1973. He had worked alongside none other than Henry Kissinger, with whom he had developed a singular relationship. If ever there was someone in Israel who must have known the pitfalls of going along the hazardous path of negotiations with the Palestinians without checking every security aspect, it was he. One wonders how all this came about using nothing more than the covert channel.

During the months preceding the surprise announcement of the Palestinian Oslo agreement, I was privy to numerous reports of meetings and negotiations between Israeli figures and Palestinian counterparts, all of a secret and clandestine nature. Some of these reports or rumors reached King Hussein. He repeatedly asked me about them since he was concerned that he would be surprised by an Israeli-Palestinian agreement that would adversely affect his country, a country whose population was more than half Palestinian in origin. Since he was dialoguing secretly with Israel on the possibility of reaching a peace agreement, he believed it only right that he should be kept abreast of developments that had a direct effect on his vital interests. Needless to say, I relayed these fears back to Mr. Rabin, and he demonstratively dismissed them with his customary wave of the hand, instructing me to reassure King Hussein and to allay his fears and suspicions. Being a professional, I was obviously not privy to the "Oslo" channel, which, of course, was in retrospect well known to Mr. Rabin. By the time I had been working with Rabin on this subject, I had known him for at least twenty years. I had worked very closely with him during most of his tenure as ambassador in Washington and had become his closest confidant in the embassy. I had been his special channel for corresponding and discussing the most intimate affairs of state with the then prime minister, Mrs. Golda Meir, and the special relationship I enjoyed with him had long been common knowledge in Washington. Over the years, I maintained contact with Rabin. When he assumed the premiership for the second time, in 1992, I had already been serving as number two in the Mossad and I saw him quite often, either with my chief, Shabtai Shavit, or alone when I acted as head of the Mossad in Shavit's absence.

I had no reason to think that Rabin would ever lie to me or would mislead me on matters of state. It was not in his character, nor was it in line with the nature of our personal relationship. Given his complex relationship with his foreign minister, Shimon Peres, I cannot believe that Rabin would give precedence to that link over his relations with me and would respect a bond of secrecy with Peres, even to a point that would lead him to lie to me. I did not expect him to spill every possible confidence or secret in my ears. I did not expect him, however, to mislead me point-blank.

On the day the Palestinian "Oslo agreement" became public knowledge, I was called to the office of the minister of defense in Tel Aviv to receive instructions as to how to proceed on the Jordanian covert track. Before entering Rabin's office I came across the director of military intelligence, General Uri Sagi. We spoke briefly in the corridor and he told me that he did not believe that Rabin thought that anything would come out of the Oslo track. He assumed it would remain one more clandestine channel of inconclusive and unimportant dialogue, like all the many others that had dotted the horizon over the past year. He was himself taken aback by the outcome, but was politically unable to extricate himself from the web that had been woven by the nonprofessionals who had championed and produced what Rabin himself would later come to describe as a piece of Swiss cheese, where the holes outnumber the actual morsels of cheese.

I never asked Rabin, with whom I had so many minutes alone, if my understanding was correct. This is not the type of question a subordinate poses to his political master. And yet, when the time arrived to enter into the final run-up to the Jordanian peace treaty negotiations, I received indirect confirmation that the assumption of Sagi and subsequently of myself was valid. Rabin instructed me in no uncertain terms not to report to Peres and to take every necessary measure to prevent him from knowing what was truly going on. In comments here and there along the way, I gathered that Rabin assumed that he would be able to repair the damage done in the initial stages of the Oslo negotiations, by spelling out subsequent specifics that would cater to Israel's basic security and strategic requirements. Since the devil was forever in the details, he must have thought that he could thus take care of basic necessities.

Over and beyond the numerous interests and influences which had their bearing on the Palestinian negotiations, there were two, in my understanding, that were paramount and are worthy of mention. On the Palestinian side there was a growing concern for the future of the Palestinian National Movement in the wake of the first Gulf War. Arafat had sided with Saddam Hussein and was therefore counted among the "bad guys" of the Middle East. It became essential to redeem the image of the cause and to make the necessary noises of reconciliation while yielding nothing in terms of substance. On the other side, Israel was under international pressure to do something to alleviate the plight of the Palestinians, as brethren of the Arabs who had fought alongside the coalition in the Gulf War. But there was one more element on the Israeli side that was invisible—the will and personal ambition of certain politicians to succeed. There was no better way to illustrate this than by comparing Likud prime minister Shamir to Labor prime minister Peres. Whereas the former had his eye on history in the broader sense of the term, he preferred to delegate the actual day-to-day work to subordinates and professionals and to bide his time. He certainly was sensitive to his role and place in the annals of his people and country, but being a cautious and suspicious person, he was never in a rush or a hurry to produce instant success, nor did he court populism and instant glory. How different was his political adversary. Peres was by nature an extrovert and as such was that more dashing and the more prominent personality of the two. From the vantage point of Peres, the covert channel enabled him to neutralize any doubts from the professionals and to produce a fait accompli that even the careful Rabin was powerless to delay or even reject outright.

The covert channel had come full circle. Originally designed by its Israeli creators to forge, maintain, and exploit strategic interests of Israel and so many partners who could not do business with it in public, on the one hand, and to facilitate quiet substantive negotiations bereft of attendant drama, on the other, the covert channel now became a vehicle for

arguably more subjective factors. In order to give the process a semblance of professionalism one ingredient was added. The presence and
participation of a legal counsel who would draft the final wording of
agreements obtained between the parties. This addition created a dual
false impression. It gave the parties, and subsequently the public, the
sense that there had been a professional hand in reaching the final understandings and it became the excuse for justifying the absence of other
professional elements as being unnecessary. After all, once you have your
lawyer with you, nobody else needs to be around. The presence of a
lawyer at the outset was, of course, so foreign to the very nature of a
covert negotiation, which was initially designed to free the parties from
having to resort to legal stratagems. One might have thought that a
lawyer would inject a note of caution and hesitation into the discussions.
In actual fact, the lawyer and future lawyers became infected with the
history-making bug and no less than their colleagues on the negotiating
teams they aspired to instant glory. Lawyers became purveyors of rapid
solutions on issues about which they understood next to nothing; they
rose to fame or preeminence solely on the merit of their ability to con-
coct legal formulae attuned to the political necessities of their mentors.
Unfortunately, this was to set the pattern for a chain of painful misfor-
tunes to come.

   The other covert channels (besides those involving the Palestinians)
were a totally different story. The Jordanian one had been active on
and off for decades and many, if not most, of the players had maintained complete anonymity. They did not aspire to or expect that
their identity or their roles would become public knowledge, and in
consequence they were totally free of the burden of assessing and
worrying about their perception by history. From time to time the principals participated in meetings and took initiatives of one type or another. I had gotten to know some of them quite intimately. I felt that, in
their heart of hearts, they did not envisage a real breakthrough. They
saw the Jordanian file as one that was destined to safeguard the fundamental survival interests of the two countries rather than to propel
them toward a formal and open peace. It was because of this that most
of the principals involved felt comfortable to leave the conduct of the
dialogue in the hands of the professionals. There was one exception—
Shimon Peres—who, when he was prime minister and foreign minister

in the four-year period of 1984–1988, relegated the professionals to technical roles and pointedly excluded them from active participation in the substantive discussions he held.

The advantage of the secret channel with Jordan before the signature of the peace treaty lay not only, as stated, in the role it played in the preservation of the mutual interests of the two leaderships and nations. Throughout the years that were turbulent and often prone to regional instability, Israel was able to gain a unique insight into the Arab world surrounding it and to better understand the motives and moods that influenced so many of the events of that period. More often than not, intelligence officers who were privy to the link, and who had access to the exchanges, were themselves influenced by what they heard and with whom they met. These extraordinary meetings were instrumental in fashioning policies for over a quarter of a century.

Compared to the Palestinian and Jordanian channels, the Syrian dialogue was entirely different. Following the end of the first Gulf War, the Syrian leader Hafiz al-Assad reached a policy decision linking the fate of his country and regime with the United States of America. He believed that the road to Washington was the one he wanted to walk, and when it became clear to him that in order to reach his goal he would have to pass through Jerusalem, in the form of a reconciliation with Israel, he was willing to go this route. He set his price for this: the complete restoration of Syrian sovereignty over the Golan Heights up to and including access to the Sea of Galilee. This also determined the approach he adopted on covert channels. He did not object to them as long as they were set up and functioned with the full knowledge and with the desired participation of the United States. It is noteworthy that although this attitude of the Syrian leader limited the value of this means of dialogue, Israel did resort to the use of it over the last decade of the previous century. However, barring one exception, the political level in Israel made sure that the professionals were kept abreast of developments on all the sensitive issues raised and discussed. Indeed, Mr. Rabin when prime minister, in the year before his murder, dispatched his chief of staff, General Ehud Barak, to Washington for secret talks with his Syrian counterpart. He never thought for one moment that on an issue like this, the professionals should be or could be excluded. Perhaps, he was drawing the lessons from the Oslo process, when the professionals had been left out, with the resultant confusion and problems that surrounded the implementation of that accord.

The exception, on the Syrian track, was the brief six-month stint of Mr. Peres as prime minister, following Rabin's tragic murder. He quickly launched into a rapid effort to reach an agreement with Syria. In order to effect this, he jettisoned the seasoned negotiators led by the veteran Syrian expert Professor Itamar Rabinovich, then Israel's ambassador in Washington, and sent his Oslo team to get the business done fast. This time the strategy failed. A series of deadly terrorist attacks carried out by Palestinian terrorists led to a suspension of the American-led talks. Simultaneously, the Syrian leader Hafiz al-Assad concluded that he had better await the outcome of the upcoming elections in Israel, rather than sign an agreement with an Israeli leader who might not be in power in a couple of months. Assad's assessment of the internal Israeli situation proved right. Contrary to most forecasts, Peres lost the election and his Syrian initiative became a dead letter.

Secrecy, in itself, has not been a sure recipe for successful and durable agreements. True efficacy of these channels rests on the motives of those who sanction them and on the motives and beliefs of the actual persons handling the channel. Whereas open diplomacy alone has never been able to produce long-lasting accommodations in the Middle East, secret ones, as we have seeen, have not been a sure way of obtaining the desired result.

4

THE INTERNATIONAL FOCUS OF
LOCAL MIDDLE EAST CONFLICTS

As the efforts to manage or even solve the conflicts of the Middle East gathered steam in the nineties, so did the international fallout of the actions and players of the region. First and foremost of those who were in the front line of this fallout were the states of Western and Central Europe, but they did their utmost to avoid confronting the true issues that were and still are the focal points of Europe's basic dilemmas. The first scene of violent upheaval was, of course, Yugoslavia, where traditional religious and ethnic differences came to the fore and led to a prolonged series of cruel and bloody battles. The world witnessed epic events of ethnic cleansing. We saw mass deportations of hundreds of thousands of people uprooted from their homes, villages, and towns, then forced into exile and conditions of extreme hardship. Seen from the Middle East, the Yugoslavian tragedy rapidly assumed the character of a cultural and interreligious confrontation. Yet, for a variety of reasons, the majority lined up in support of the Muslim victims, and even the United States ultimately stepped into the fray and was the obvious dominant force that caused the defeat of the Serb people of Yugoslavia and the subsequent dismemberment of the state into a group of smaller, separate states based on religious-ethnic majorities.

During this war of the nineties in the very heart of Europe, it became known that there was a very militant and effective Iranian intelligence presence operating alongside the Muslim elements in Yugoslavia. It also became obvious that the enormity of the war crimes of the Serbian leadership under Milosevic could not be matched, either quantitatively or qualitatively, by those committed by the Muslims who were so inferior in their training and equipment. One would have thought that the support given to the Muslims in Kosovo and in Bosnia by the United States and Europe, by none other than NATO itself, would have provided the West with both the capability and the opportunity to deal with the Iranian incursion into Central Europe. Alas, this was not to come about.

What was the rationale that lay behind the policy pursued by the coalition that bombed Belgrade into submission and what did this policy mean for the peoples of the Middle East? Of all the leaders of Israel, only one voiced reservation over the anti-Serbian policies of the coalition—the Likud foreign minister at the end of the decade, Ariel Sharon. Although couched in careful wording, this opinion was met with considerable criticism both inside Israel and internationally, and for a variety of reasons. First, it was thought improper that a leading Israeli statesman would ally himself with a warring side that resorted to ethnic cleansing and atrocities that resonated the world over. After all had been said and done, were not the Jewish people, of all peoples, the ones who were expected to be the first to speak out and unequivocally condemn actions similar to those it endured during World War II? People wondered how the victims of the Holocaust were the almost sole voice that expressed understanding for the regime of Slobodan Milosevic. The second point of criticism was no less telling. Given the fact that none other than the United States was leading the war against Belgrade, was it politically wise or correct for Israel, which relied so heavily on the United States, to cast doubt, even guarded and muted as it was, on the policies of its principal mentor and ally? Although Israel had an interest in the ongoing struggle in the Balkans, it was, after all, a theater of operations outside the Middle East, and therefore Israel might well be wise not to meddle in the affairs of others.

These were valid arguments and they were accepted by the vast majority of the body politic in Israel. Nevertheless, the comments of Foreign Minister Sharon were in line with basic strategic approaches that had characterized Israeli thinking and policies long before he issued his statement and certainly would for the decade to come. The Sharon approach, however unsavory and unpopular, drew its inspiration from one of the basic concepts of Israel's international strategy, namely its necessity and desire to promote and cultivate understandings and alliances with countries and cultures that were non-Muslim or in a state of confrontation or opposition to neighbors who had ties to militant Islamic states or nonstate groups. Thus the Israel of the seventies, eighties, and early nineties sought out and found a fruitful partner in South Africa. In the sixties, it was one of the first to appear on the scene just as Singapore seceded from Malaysia. Within weeks of Singapore's separation and self-declared independence, Israeli security and military advisers were on the scene to help the fledgling nation build its security and defense capabilities. The blueprints of the Israel Defense Forces' officer-training camp that was about to be constructed in the heart of the south of Israel were rapidly flown to Singapore and within a very short period of time the new camp was ready for occupation and training long before its Israeli "sister" came into the world. These were indeed strategic moves designed to create in-depth partnerships with all that they entail.

What distinguished the Sharon gambit was that whereas, in the past, Israel had always steered clear from impinging on U.S. policies and interests, the Serb issue crossed the path of the United States in two key aspects. It appeared to align Israel with the positions adopted by Russia, which was trying desperately to salvage as much as it could of Slav interests in the Balkans, and it depicted Israel as opposing the United States when it was openly at war with the Serbs and their despotic leadership. Little surprise, therefore, that Sharon quietly abandoned his independent stand on the Balkan conflict shortly after he had taken it.

Another interesting case in point was that of North Korea. As the nineties came around, North Korea was rapidly emerging as one of the key suppliers of nonconventional equipment in the larger Middle East. Egypt, an important ally of the United States in the region as of the first Gulf War and a country that had replaced its Soviet-made armor and Soviet-supplied air force with American tanks and modern American aircraft, was continuing to purchase North Korean Scud missiles even up to the very end of the last century. Pyongyang's clients included Iran, Iraq, and Syria, and it rapidly became a major arms supplier, principally in the area of medium- and long-range ballistic missiles.

Toward the end of 1992, the Israeli press gave prominence to a story that I had been in Pyongyang to negotiate with the North Koreans in an effort to stem the tide of the influx of their missilery into the Middle East. The reports had it that I had been sighted on an aircraft leaving Pyongyang for Beijing. The sensational aspect in the report that made it a white-hot news story was that a parallel team of Israeli foreign affairs officials was on board and that the two groups had been operating separately without the one being aware of the other. This was a secondary and insignificant aspect of the issue. The foreign office officials have since written up their versions in both book and media form, and I no longer see any merit in denying the basic fact that such parallel visits did indeed take place. All of the discussions held by the two teams were ultimately communicated to Washington, D.C., after the event. They differed both in the substantive elements of their reporting and, subsequently, in the interpretation and credibility of the Korean positions.

There was, in my opinion, a basic divergence of approaches and views between the foreign ministry professionals and the intelligence officers' attitude to an issue of this nature. The Korean complex had been an item on the international agenda for more than fifty years. The Korean War had been one that had brought the United States, the Soviet Union, and their respective allies into conflict, consequently placing the security of the world in peril. As of the end of that war, American troops had been permanently stationed on South Korean territory and the forces of South and North Korea have been facing each other across a tenuous cease-fire line for decades. Was it feasible or wise for Israel to try to work out a separate deal for itself on the matter that was of concern to it without consultation or due regard for the policies and interests of the United States? Assuming that North Korea might wish to negotiate a separate understanding with Israel, would it not be logical to assume that Israel would have to give its interlocutor something in return and might that not be a "something" that the United States would be loathe to grant Pyongyang? My view has always been that Israel as a sovereign state had freedom of action to launch and develop strategies that would serve its interests and that the more it was capable of doing so, the more it would serve not only its own interests but also those of the free world, of which

Israel has been, and will always be, an integral part. However, when it came to initiatives on the larger international landscape, Israel could not afford to go it alone and to carve out its own separate deals. Not only was this a consideration of expediency, it was also one of practical consequences. After all had been said and done, Israel was heavily reliant on U.S. support and aid both economically and militarily and it was unthinkable that it could act independently on a matter of vital U.S. global interest. One had to question whether or not Israel's capabilities could sustain an independent deal. If so, would North Korea genuinely believe that Israel would indeed go ahead and leave the common front that the United States of America had painstakingly created in its dealings with Pyongyang?

What then could have been the genuine rationale behind a North Korean foray? How would the approach of a foreign office differ from that of what the Israeli media had come to dub as the Shadow foreign office? Over the years, so I believe, there arose a difference of approach that was, maybe, the result of the different cultures of the two disciplines and bureaucratic structures. The "normal" foreign office considered its primary role as being that of promoting foreign and diplomatic policies that would further the immediate aims and necessities of Israel at every given stage. Primarily this was a short-term approach, calculated to obtain the best immediate results in a relatively narrow prism of considerations. Overt reports spoke of a North Korean gold mine that needed to be reactivated, in order to provide the regime with the necessary funds to purchase oil, of which North Korea was suffering a desperate shortage. The notion that in exchange for providing Pyongyang with the expertise it would freeze the supply of Scud missiles to the Middle East was, to say the least, frankly ridiculous. But what was the alternative? Whereas the run-of-the-mill diplomat tended to view international events and developments as an unending series of self-contained happenings, loosely connected but certainly not interdependent, the intelligence officer always looked beyond the immediate present and focused on medium- and longer-term processes dotted along an almost unending course.

There was a semidramatic finale to this episode. Not only did the reports on the Pyongyang talks differ but similarly, the government in Jerusalem was provided with conflicting reports as to America's reaction to the intelligence reports it received on the Korean escapade. The foreign office officials reported that the United States had not expressed any opposition to Israel going ahead; the intelligence officers reported that the United States was opposed to any deviation from the all-out boycott of North Korea that Washington had succeeded in mounting. None other than the Israeli deputy minister of foreign affairs was dispatched to Washington to ascertain what the American position really was. He duly confirmed the intelligence version. The foreign office protagonists were not going to surrender so quickly. They called for a special session to be held by none other than the foreign minister in person. At this meeting they claimed that there had been a conspiracy hatched between the Mossad and the CIA to torpedo the North Korean initiative. They urged Mr. Peres, the foreign minister, to take advantage of an upcoming meeting with Secretary of State Warren Christopher in Vienna, where, so they claimed, the genuine policy of the United States on the subject would be authoritatively revealed. Alas, Mr. Peres came back confirming the intelligence version and the farce played itself out to the bitter end. All that was left was to make sure that history would record that Prime Minister Rabin had forced Mr. Peres to accept the Mossad—the American—policy, a disastrous one, in return for nothing less than Rabin's support for the Oslo Palestinian initiative of Peres. Any future catastrophe that Israel would suffer at the hand of North Korean missiles in possession of hostile countries in the region would thus be attributed to the prime minister's rejection of the brilliant initiative of several foreign office types who, alone, were the true patriots of their country. At the time, I wondered if we could have looked more ridiculous, playing out the farce for our international audience.

The Serbian and North Korean episodes and their reflection on aspects of the Middle East conflict furnish us with examples that serve to highlight the larger, international dimensions of the Middle East conflicts and their roles in shaping and piloting the history of the region as a whole in the thirteen-year period, between 1990 and 2003. On the face of it, neither of the two entities mentioned had a direct stake in the Middle East. Serbian Yugoslavia lay outside the perimeters of the area. Yet once the long-simmering internal tensions in post-Tito Belgrade burst out and engulfed the whole country in a series of bloody, cruel, and inhuman confrontations, aspects of the situation in the Middle East immediately became involved in day-to-day incidents. North Korea was considerably more remote than Yugoslavia as far as our part of the world was concerned, but it rapidly became a priority market for North Korean missiles and other capabilities. Indeed, the endless conflict in the region, interlaced as it was with recurrent major wars, had attracted both national and private weapons manufacturers and agents to do business with states and nonstate groups in the region for decades. The People's Republic of China, Argentina, Brazil, India, Pakistan, and the Soviet Union were only a few of the members of the international community that sought involvement and profit in the region. Thus, for example, an Argentinian involvement with none other than Egypt in a project to construct long-range ballistic missiles naturally directed Israel to focus its eyes not only on Cairo but also on Buenos Aires.

Arms deals hatched and nurtured political and strategic interests and alignments. Hence, the states of the Middle East, and Israel among them, willy-nilly became players on the international scene. The stakes of all and sundry rose as the levels of the conflicts reached ever greater heights. Whereas some of the key states in the region had natural resources, primarily oil, which were vital for the economies and therefore for the very well-being of the nations of the world at large, there were others who were not in possession of such assets and who were consequently at a disadvantage in the eyes and estimate of the outside world. These dispossessed states were hard-pressed to create and maximize alternative assets that could balance those of the others. Israel and Jordan were two examples of countries acting in such a way with dramatically successful results.

Jordan has been singularly deft and creative in translating its initial inferiority into a solid asset. Originally a "buffer state," its apparent weakness made it a prey for its neighbors to the north and south of the country. Inroads from Syria in the north became part of the scenery that any ruler in Amman, the capital of Jordan, had to cope with. Clandestine infiltrations entailing the smuggling of arms to secret cells operating against the regime or groups aiming their sights on Israel gradually resulted in the Jordanian authorities developing an extremely effective security system that has become a centerpiece of the government. Incursions from the Saudi south over countless years breathed fire into violent traditionalist Muslim streams in Jordanian society and forced the Hashemite dynasty to face up to the challenges thus created by carefully mixing resolute security measures with political maneuvers. Iraq, to the east, was originally a "sister" state ruled by a member of the Hashemite dynasty. As of 1958, when the monarch was deposed and murdered, Iraq became a state with multiple interests in Jordan and Iraqi influence in the kingdom rose or waned as regional events took their turns in one direction or another. Israel, to the west, had experienced decades of outward hostility with the Hashemite kingdom, beginning with bloody confrontation during Israel's War of Independence in 1948 and culminating with the 1967 war when Jordan was forced to attack its western neighbor by Egypt (which at that time had a measure of control over Jordan's armed forces). The result was the loss of control of the West Bank to Israel and the establishment of the Jordan River as a major part of the border between Israel and Jordan.

Sandwiched in between all these states and conflicting interests, Jordan was able to forge an internationally strategic asset out of its daily predicaments. It was in the best interest of most parties in the region to maintain this buffer zone in the heart of the Middle East and to prevent those who did not subscribe to this view from advancing toward fulfillment of their aims. The existence of Jordan as a permanent fixture of the region took on added value as the years passed. It became the focus of international attention as violent Muslim extremism, with roots in the Middle East, spilled over onto the international stage. There can be little doubt that had Jordan not existed as an independent entity, the outcome of both Gulf wars might well have been entirely different. This was prominently so, as far as the war of 2003 was concerned. Without the facilities granted to the coalition forces on Jordanian soil it is doubtful if the initial stages of the war could have been characterized by the successes that special forces were able to register. In truth, the strategic support rendered by Jordan can hardly be evaluated in dollars and cents. It was therefore no wonder that the United States invested strategically in Jordan while the countries of Europe have decidedly and prominently supported the kingdom for decades. However, Jordan's strategic location has not garnered the country massive financial aid. Rather, the flow of aid has been measured and at times meager, compared to the investments made in Israel or Egypt, for that matter.

The international dimension of small states like Jordan is one that is too often lightly glossed over. I have often asked myself whether the emphasis I have placed upon this state with a population of three to four million sandwiched in the heart of the Middle East has not been unduly colored by my personal preoccupation and involvement with events centering around Jordanian-Israeli relations. After much reflection, I believe that this is not so. For better or for worse, the destinies of the peoples of the Middle East have been determined for centuries by Great Powers outside the region or by one regional dominant factor, most recently, the Ottoman Empire. Although the emergence of an independent state on the east bank of the river Jordan was not necessarily preordained or preplanned, in retrospect it has served to facilitate an essential equilibrium between conflicting forces that have competed for hegemony for decades. Thus external intervention, in this case, has proved wise and effective.

The alternate side of the mirror, Israel, was not originally part of the Middle East political architecture that the world powers had predetermined to be a national component of the area. When the Jews began to resettle the barren "Land of Israel" in the latter years of the nineteenth century, national independence was not on the agenda. The Zionist dream that was formally launched at the First Zionist Congress held in Basel, Switzerland, in 1897, was not universally accepted or embraced. The now-famous Balfour Declaration, contained in a letter from Lord Balfour on behalf of the British government to Lord Rothschild, in the year 1917, spoke of a commitment to grant the Jewish people a national home in Palestine. The exact meaning of this phrase was to become a subject of controversy for a long time to come and in any event, whatever its authorized interpretation in Britain, it did not reflect international consensus on the issue, let alone any acceptance of the concept by the Muslim population in the region.

When Israel came into being in 1948, it immediately became the focus of international attention, especially from the United States and the Soviet Union, the two international superpowers of the day. This international attention caused Israel to color its regional policies in terms of its international interests and, in this area, the intelligence community, and the Mossad in particular, played a very crucial role. It needs to be said at the very outset that the United States did not take the initiative in trying to harness Israel to play a role in the region that would serve American strategic interests. In the wake of its War of Independence, Israel was thrust into the local scene as a fledgling state devoid of any experience in practicing policies of strategy and foreign affairs. The Soviet Union was quick to seize the initiative not only in launching multiple espionage efforts directed at the newly founded state and its political system. There were, in Israel, political groups and parties who fully identified themselves with Stalin, the Soviet dictator. These were not fringe parties but rather elite levels in Israeli society, including key figures in the defense establishment.

The question whether Israel would align itself with the free Western world in its confrontation with the Communist bloc of nations led by the Soviet Union or prefer to follow a neutralist noncommittal path was one of the very first major issues that the Israeli leadership had to resolve. Within a relatively short period of three to four years, the prime minister, David Ben-Gurion, took the decision to identify Israel with the United States and to purge from the professional levels of the defense establishment individuals and groups that had overt or covert leanings toward Moscow. This primary decision was to be the governing factor in Israel's strategic policies from then until this very day. Once this major decision had been made, a long list of secondary operational derivatives was to follow. In order for Israel to maintain its qualitative edge, it had to forge a policy or, for that matter, a series of policies that would give the state added value on the international scene. Although it was a small country numbering, at first, barely a million in population and burdened, inter alia, with a gigantic task of absorbing literally millions of new destitute immigrants in figures far outnumbering its indigenous population, a major part of its resources had to be earmarked for defense, intelligence and security. In Israel's estimate this area of endeavor had to encompass not only the immediate confines of the Middle East, but also the world at large. Israel was fast to evolve an approach that viewed much of the globe as consisting of essential "theaters of combat." If a country or a people involved themselves in the Middle East, especially if they took sides or contributed in one way or another to the Israeli-Palestinian conflict, Israel could not afford to satisfy its requirements simply by dealing with the threat or the interference entirely in the confines of the region. It rapidly became essential to act and to be visible on the international scene. Israel quickly assumed an international character that by far exceeded the physical and human dimensions of the citizens of the state.

Europe, Asia, and Africa became part of the extended theater of action of Israel's foreign and defense policies.

Of all the arenas, the African was, on the face of it, the least important. After all, apart from Egypt, the continent was remote from Israel in many significant aspects. There has been little cultural interface between Israel and the cultures of Africa. Trade between Israel and the emerging continent has been limited and for all intents and purposes virtually insignificant. From a purely security and defense point of view, there has never been any real substantive involvement of African military units in the Israeli-Arab conflict except for limited contingents of Sudanese forces that fought alongside Egyptian units in Israel's War of Independence in 1948 and an armored element that was dispatched by King Hassan II of Morocco to fight alongside the Syrians in the Yom Kippur War of 1973. Neither of these two interventions was meaningful in the actual conduct of these two wars. The new states of the emerging continent were too weak to contribute politically or militarily to the Middle East conflicts. The only exception was South Africa, under white rule, with which Israel enjoyed a unique relationship that had its roots in specific considerations that were entirely divorced from the continent as a whole.

Why, then, did Israel throw itself into the African fray in the sixties of the previous century? Why were senior defense and intelligence officers dispatched to a variety of states in East, West, South, and North Africa? It was an enormous investment for a small state like Israel, in both manpower and financial resources, and as we look back to those days and compare the investment to the dividend obtained, it would seem that there is precious little left that would even provide faint evidence of what was accomplished over forty years ago. A more profound examination of the events of those days will produce the story of the then ongoing struggle between the West and the Communist bloc led by the now-defunct Soviet Union. The Soviets were being aided by none other than the Egyptians under their charismatic and fiery leader Gamal Abdel Nasser, who harnessed his own political "philosophy" of the "three circles" (Arab, African, and Islamic) to the bandwagon of the anti-Western cause of Moscow. Africa fast became a scene of intense infighting and rivalry with almost all the powers that be, participating in the rush to gain influence and political advantage. In the corridors of power in Dar es

Salaam in the east, as in the palaces of the ruling figures in Accra, Monrovia, or Abidjan in the west, in the streets of Kinshasa, or Lagos in the center of the continent, a bitter struggle was being waged for the future of a continent that had just won its independence but was ill-equipped for a variety of reasons to consolidate or maintain its newly won freedom. It was here that Israel stepped in with its unique youthful approach and flexibility and with its total absence of any colonial legacy. Within a short time—in the space of three to four years—Israel succeeded in positioning itself inside the continent as a vital factor in forming, training, and maintaining the defense and security underpinnings of emerging regimes in many of the key areas in the continent.

What did Israel gain through this investment? First, it was able to stem the tide of Egyptian Nasserist influence in the "backyard" of the Nile valley. These were the days when Egyptian intelligence officers roamed the African continent attempting to consolidate Egyptian political influence under the twin banners of Islam and anti-Western and antidemocratic policies. Very quickly the African policies of Egypt's Gamal Abdel Nasser blended into the overall interests of the Soviet Union and the Moscow-Cairo axis fast became a vehicle designed to win over the emerging independent states of Africa to the side of the Soviet Union. Africa became the breeding ground of intelligence and counterintelligence operations and the training arena for many a young intelligence officer on the threshold of his career. Israel, barely ten years old, was thrust into this emerging and developing world of Africa and Asia, quickly found its feet, and was able to fashion policies and methods that were both novel and extremely beneficial. The U.S. government was able to identify the birth of a partner, albeit a young and junior one, that could, in given circumstances, perform successfully and produce results that a superpower was less capable of doing. Thus, as the Middle East approached the sea change event of the six-day Israeli-Arab war of 1967, Israel and the United States of America were already maintaining an ongoing dialogue on international affairs that encompassed much more than the local events of the area. It was these experiences of the sixties that laid the groundwork for the major change in U.S.-Israeli relations that evolved out of the Six-Day War. From a situation in which Washington maintained an arms embargo against Israel from its very inception until that point in time, the United States was destined to become Israel's principal supplier of arms and its major political mainstay on the international scene. Israel had proved that it was not only a client in need of aid and support but also a partner, albeit a junior one, that could deliver the goods in hard strategic currency.

There was another aspect of the global scene that propelled Israel to the higher levels of international relations—the issue of Soviet Jewry. From the time that the Iron Curtain came down on the Communist bloc of countries led by the Soviet Union, millions of Soviet Jewish citizens were cut off and denied contact with their families and relatives living in the free world. The effort to establish and maintain contact with Soviet Jewry rapidly became a focal point of Israeli policies as of the early fifties of the last century. Israeli officials and individuals entered the Soviet Union carrying written materials, prayer books and papers about newly created Israel and other subjects, and distributed them among the throngs of Jews who wished to maintain their ties with the Jewish people outside the Soviet Union at almost any cost. Given the existence of Jewish communities around the world, first and foremost in the United States, the campaign for Soviet Jewry assumed the character of a worldwide offensive directed at the leadership of the Soviet Union. Although Israel invested every effort in trying to divorce this specific issue from all the other aspects of the Cold War, one could not blame the Russian authorities for treating this specific campaign as part of the overall struggle that was being waged by the West against communism and the communist regimes.

Thus this "battle" for Soviet Jewry that was to be part of the international scene for more than forty years was one more facet of Israel's absorption into the key conflicts of the world. This policy initiative was, in due course, to produce the richest and probably the most significant of returns, when over one million Jews emigrated from the former Soviet Union to Israel in the nineties, adding 25 percent to Israel's Jewish population within a short period of barely a couple of years.

An illustration of the way Israel functioned in those days and of the interconnection between the issues came my way in the mid-fifties. I was then president of the Israel National Union of Students and as such represented my country in the bodies of various international organizations. In the summer of 1956 I traveled to Moscow to participate in a preparatory meeting convened by the Russians to organize a big youth festival that was scheduled to take place the following year. I flew from Israel to Prague, where I boarded a train for a three-day journey to Moscow. The train stopped at numerous stations along the route for fifteen-minute intervals and I stepped off each and every time and recorded what I saw of life in rural Soviet Union. On arrival in the Russian capital I was taken to the newly constructed high-rise student dormitory building of Moscow University, where I was to spend the next few days in meetings over the forthcoming festival. I took very independent positions on many issues related to the festival. At one stage I sneaked out of the building and met with a relative of mine, Sir Isaiah Berlin, who had come to Moscow at the same time to meet with Soviet dissident writers, including Boris Pasternak, the author of *Dr. Zhivago*. Devoid of any professional training, I shook off my "tail" in order not to compromise my interlocutor, who had been traveling on a diplomatic passport. Our meeting, at the home of his aunt who resided in Moscow, was a very tense one, and I returned to the dormitory well after normal hours. In response, the Russians bumped me off the aircraft that was due to fly me to Prague for an international student conference that I was scheduled to attend, forcing me to board the train once again, for another lengthy three-day journey. On arrival at the Czech-Russian border, I was detained by the Czech authorities because of so-called visa irregularities and placed in custody in a wooden hut for twenty-four hours. That was a very minor way of punishing me for my sins. When I subsequently arrived at the conference, I became the focus of considerable interest, and was able to cultivate numerous contacts at the many meetings that I attended.

These were the tense days of mid-1956, on the eve of the Hungarian uprising against the Russians and the bloody riots in Poznan, Poland, also directed against the Soviet occupation. There were also indications in the air that all was not well concerning relations between the Soviet Union and Communist China. My reporting on all these subjects covered scores of pages; I did my best to record everything I saw or heard, having no idea whatsoever why I was doing this, or what purpose it might serve. Years later, I was to learn that my reporting had found its way to Washington and had been evaluated as contributing in a substantial manner to an understanding of those issues that were on the front burner at that time. This digression serves as a small example of the approach of Israel and Israelis to matters of international interest. We have been and are citizens of the world and not only nationals of our country, and thus any event or condition wherever or whenever that even remotely affects us immediately becomes a subject of pursuit.

These background observations are, to my mind, essential to any person desiring to understand the nature of Israel's performance on the international scene in the thirteen years that spanned the period between the two Gulf wars directed against Iraq. At the time of the destruction of the Second Temple of the Jews on the Temple Mount in the holy city of Jerusalem, both tradition and history have recorded that the Jewish people were dispersed to the four corners of the earth. When the time came to restore Jewish sovereign nationhood in the "Land of the Bible," the remnants of exile returned from over seventy countries around the globe, and they gradually emerged from a melting pot to establish both the content and character of the revitalized nation. This unique history was one more key factor in consolidating the approach of the new state of Israel to its place among the nations. Thus melded together both the elements of the nation's two-thousand-year-old history and the immediate concrete necessities of its current strategic interests. It may be said with a large degree of confidence that Israel's involvement in so many aspects of the international scene has been the product of its character, its singular assets and capabilities, and its acute requirements at this point in time in the history of the world.

5

THE PROFESSIONAL LEVEL— A THIRD ELEMENT IN PEACEKEEPING

The aftermath of the first Gulf War—Operation Desert Storm—left the nations of the region gasping for political breath; the defeat of Iraq, its humiliation at the hands of a coalition of states led by the United States and including key Arab states such as Egypt, Saudi Arabia, and Syria, enabled the American administration of President George H. W. Bush to flex its muscles and to get Iraq out of Kuwait, which had previously been invaded and overtaken by Saddam Hussein. But the American success had been obtained at a high price—a wave of anti-American sentiment that Washington was hard put to accept and digest for any length of time. One way of moderating this adverse effect of the war was for the United States to make a determined effort to begin a peace process between Israel and the Arab states, in general, and Israel and the Palestinians, in particular. The Israeli prime minister at the time, Yitzhak Shamir, was a staunch leader of a movement that championed the concept of "the entire land of Israel" and was loathe to enter into a procedure that might result in an eventual partition of the Holy Land. Under much pressure from Secretary of State Jim Baker, he acquiesced in convening an international conference in Madrid at the end of 1991 and in the formation of three tracks of negotiations between Israel, on the one hand, and

Syria, Jordan, and a joint Jordanian-Palestinian delegation, on the other. The Syrian track led to nought; the Jordanian and Palestinian portfolios were handled in covert channels outside the Madrid conference structure.

Much has been said in the past about Yitzhak Shamir and his obstructionist policies. He was often quoted as saying that he hoped that negotiations would last ten years and more, that he would be prepared to lie "for the land of Israel." Yet I found him to be a realist and the latitude he gave me in dealings I conducted on his behalf with leaders of the region indicated to me that he was fully aware of the fact that dialogues have a life of their own and in so many cases result in understandings and even agreements that go far beyond what principals have envisaged when they initially sanctioned this or that "parley."

Before I delve into the intricacies of one set of negotiations with which I was intimately associated and therefore especially familiar, I would like to refer to a few broader insights that relate to the overall picture of conflict and negotiations in the region.

Leaders, sovereigns, presidents, prime ministers, more often than not initiate policies in international affairs on the understanding that they will be in office for the duration necessary to oversee implementation in the letter and in the spirit of their own vision and intentions. So many times this has not been the case. Rather, what has transpired is that successors have taken the initial policies and have transformed them into something entirely different from the original wish of the initiator. During the last decade of the twentieth century, there have been five changes in the premiership of Israel. Each new prime minister has taken the initiative of his predecessor and translated it into a policy divorced from and sometimes diametrically opposed to that of the former leader. The public has voted out four prime ministers after they have served less than the allotted time prescribed by law. Only Ariel Sharon was reelected in a general election and that came about in the subsequent decade.

When Shamir accepted the ground rules of the Madrid conference that was convened under the auspices of the United States and the Soviet Union, he assumed that he would be around long enough to prevent a serious erosion of his basic policies concerning the Palestinians. The United States was well aware of this intention and therefore the administration of George H. W. Bush exerted subtle economic pressure on Israel in the run-up to the general elections held in the country in the early summer of 1992. This was a substantial contributing factor to the defeat of Shamir and the success of Yitzhak Rabin. When Rabin took over the reins of power he used the psychological breakthrough that Shamir had allowed to press forward with policies designed to reach a true accommodation with the Palestinians, the Jordanians, and even the Syrians. Indeed, his game plan envisaged an initial agreement with Israel's most radical adversary, the Syrians, in the belief that if such an agreement is reached, it would remove a major support that the Palestinians enjoyed in the Arab world and would thus weaken the Palestinians' bargaining power in a most substantial way. This did not come about. Instead, Rabin was able to craft an initial, extremely fragile agreement with the Palestinians, the Oslo agreement, which was to herald, so its initiators believed, a five-year-transition period of emerging Palestinian self-rule that was to serve as a positive backdrop for final-status negotiations between the parties, culminating in Palestinian statehood.

Rabin's murder at the hands of an Israeli zealot was the most poignant of indicators that the mood in Israel had changed in the face of a wave of brutal Palestinian terrorist attacks, directed mainly against civilian targets in Israel. Within months a general election ousted Rabin's short-lived successor, Shimon Peres, and brought Benjamin Netanyahu of Shamir's Likud party to power.

Netanyahu, in his turn, tried to take the Oslo agreement, to which he was politically opposed but to which as prime minister of Israel he was formally committed, in a different direction from that envisaged by Rabin. He strove to forge a somewhat amended version entailing an obligation on the part of the Palestinians to restrain terror in exchange for territorial concessions. He coined the phrase "If they will give, they will receive! If they do not give, they will not receive!" This policy did not produce the desired results, and after three years in power Netanyahu was ousted primarily by his own constituency, which believed he had begun making too many concessions to the "enemy."

After Netanyahu came Ehud Barak, of Rabin's Labor party, who launched an entirely new policy, ostensibly aimed at leapfrogging the endless incremental negotiations and going for the jugular—the final status solution to the Israeli-Palestinian conflict, the highlight of which was the negotiation process at Camp David in 2000, presided over by President Bill Clinton with the participation of principals from both sides of the conflict. This was not to be. Within less than two years his political base was entirely eroded and in 2001 an election brought Ariel Sharon to the helm.

The rapid chain of events encapsulated in this thumbnail description evolved at a time that the world as a whole was undergoing a major evolution. Essentially, Israel's successive premiers were trying to stabilize a very volatile situation while each had an entirely separate and mostly conflicting agenda. In such rapidly changing circumstances, the roles of the permanent senior officials in the defense and security field were destined to transcend the normal line of duty. In the internal security arena, it became the rule that only those steps and measures that were approved by the professionals could be deemed legitimate and subsequently worthy of implementation. The Israel Defense Forces (IDF) and the Israel Security Agency (ISA), formerly named the General Security Service (GSS), set the tone. When the political level—the prime minister of the day— went against the advice of the professionals, more often than not the subsequent confrontation on implementation resulted in the statesman succumbing to his subordinates. In those few cases, when the statesman decided to go it alone, against professional advice or, which was more often the case, by simply cutting the professionals out of the picture, the resulting situation created serious circumstances, forcing the political level to fall in line with those who were responsible for the practical outcome.

Thus, in my understanding, there have been three actors rather than the traditional two in the time-immemorial theater of war and peace. There have always been leaders, or rulers, there on the scene. And, of course, there have always been the people who have had varying influence on the train of events, depending on the character of the prevalent regime or regimes of the times. My contention is that, at least in this age, there has been a third element, on occasion an exceedingly powerful element that has exerted influence on the march of history—the professional level that bears the daily responsibility for the peace of the realm. The relative influence of chiefs of staff, chiefs of security, and the intelligence communities has often equaled that of all the other players in the field.

Within the space of thirteen years between 1990 and 2003, four heads of the ISA, the domestic security service, and four heads of the Mossad ran their respective organs of security. One of the four on either side was there for a very limited period of time and resigned because of failure, so that in effect it was three persons on either side that managed their affairs during this very pregnant period in the life of the country and in the fractured history of the Middle East. During that same time span, five chiefs of staff were in command of the IDF. Three of them entered politics very soon after they left military service and one served as prime minister for a relatively short term.

During these years, the defense establishment forged the conditions on the grounds that governed the implementation of the successive political initiatives taken by political masters. Since security considerations have always been dominant in the overall domestic and international landscapes that have shaped the destiny of Israel ever since its inception, the defense establishment professional layer of chiefs of services has dominated the scene and has determined what was possible and not necessarily what has been desirable. In those rare cases where the political level has "gone it alone" and has not invited professional input in advance of policy decisions, the outcome has been, by and large, a failure. One such example has been the Oslo process, where the politicians crafted an agreement, a first ever agreement with the Palestinians, granting them a large measure of self-rule en route to negotiations for permanent status, a euphemism used to avoid, at the outset, the use of the term "Palestinian State." The provisions of the agreement were so imprecise as to warrant their being dubbed a Swiss cheese arrangement, there being more holes than cheese! In the eyes of many, myself included, this was a catastrophic way of decision making; not only was the ultimate aim beyond achievement, but the agreement itself gave rise to more than a decade of strife and thousands of dead on both sides.

In many instances, it was the professional levels that conducted the most meaningful contacts and negotiations with Israel's adversaries. Three ISA service chiefs not only maintained a working relationship with their counterparts in the Palestinian Authority, but also enjoyed the personal confidence of Yassir Arafat, the leader and symbol of the Palestinian National Movement. Simultaneously, the heads of the Mossad were instrumental in servicing the key links of many of Israel's relationships with the Arab world. The best known of these was the decades-long link between King Hussein of Jordan and the Israeli leadership; but this was by far not the only one. This "system" of foreign policy encompassed key countries in the Middle East like pre-Khomeini Iran and Turkey, alongside Muslim states farther afield like Morocco, which not only played a central role in facilitating the very first peace treaty between Israel and an Arab state—Egypt—but also went on to provide Israel with unique sounding boards on the Palestinian issue, leading up to the Oslo breakthrough in 1993.

The nature of these long-standing relationships lent a very special flavor to Israel's policies and ties with its adversaries cum partners. The intimate knowledge that each gained about the others served in many instances to enable the parties to avoid major mistakes and misunderstandings. At the same time, however, this abundance of information and intelligence also resulted, on occasion, in blinding the parties to any real effort to prepare public opinion for contemplating fundamental changes in approaches and attitudes to the conflicts. In truth, this intimacy caused the professional levels to discount or belittle the necessity of catering to the needs and necessities of the populations at large. In the case of the ISA, so many of the emerging political figures in the Palestinian camp had spent years in Israeli jails, it was well-nigh psychologically impossible for the Israelis to transform their way of looking at individuals from viewing them as prisoners to treating them as emerging equals. The condescending attitudes of the professionals rubbed off on the principals, and whereas Israelis often complained that their counterparts had not succeeded in making the transition from armed struggle to statehood—and this was a valid argument well embedded in facts—it was difficult if not impossible for them to turn a blind eye to the daily challenge of terrorism and its heavy toll on life and to negotiate with the Palestinians as if they had become their equals, or even anywhere near that. Indeed, this could well be humanly impossible.

In these circumstances, it was virtually impossible to contemplate a real attempt by the powers that be to launch a sustained effort to get the peoples on both sides of the divide to change their mind-sets and to enter a course of mutual acceptance and recognition. The continued practice of terrorism and violence not only by the Palestinians, but no less by their active supporters and mentors in the Arab and Islamic worlds, naturally focused primary attention on confronting these immediate challenges rather than on other aspects. From time to time, consideration was given to economic factors and necessities, but in comparison to the principal concern the investment in these areas was at best barely minimal. Indeed, in the detailed provisions of the original Oslo accords with the Palestinians there was a section devoted to "peoples to peoples" activities. In practice next to nothing was done, let alone accomplished on this score, and the principal actors on both sides viewed this element as little more than window dressing and wrote the whole enterprise off as just one more exercise in "public relations."

The upshot of all this has been, and still is, that principally on the Arab side there was no real attempt whatsoever to change the climate of rabid incitement and all-out hatred for Israel that has characterized the Arab and Muslim world ever since the State of Israel came into existence. In many instances, the Arab regimes who concluded peace treaties (specifically Egypt and Jordan) or who reached practical understandings with Israel, such as Morocco, Tunisia, Oman, and Qatar, allowed incitement against Israel in the media, inter alia, as a measure designed to permit the "masses" to let off steam and thus to relieve internal pressures created and nurtured for reasons entirely alien to the Israeli-Arab conflict. One of the most striking examples of this dual dialectic approach can be found in the principality of Qatar, which has initiated and implemented policies on the Israeli-Palestinian dispute that have created precedents and novel realities on the ground. Qatar has been in the forefront of the Arab states in the region that have maintained a constant dialogue with Israel, hosting an official Israeli diplomatic representation in Doha and playing host to Israeli cabinet ministers who have visited the country to attend international gatherings. At the very same time, Qatar has played host to Sheikh Yusuf al-Qaradawi, an extreme Muslim fundamentalist, who has championed suicide bombing and who has exhorted the Palestinians and others to resort to this strategy, with deadly results. This is the very same Qatar that plays host to the Al Jazeera television station that has been used extensively by the Al Qaeda and other Muslim terrorist organizations to spread the word of these violent groups throughout the Muslim world. The net result of all this has been that whereas at the senior and top levels of government in the Arab world there has been a steadily growing acceptance of Israel as a reality—and, by some, even as a vital partner in the fight against violence and hate—these very same regimes have nurtured and in some cases have even encouraged popular activities that have run contrary to their so-called strategic policies and interests.

Qatar has been a very special example in relation to additional aspects of the current march of events in the region. It has been in the vanguard of the United States' interests and activities for more than a decade and it has played a pivotal role in providing facilities for the armed forces that have been operating inside Iraq since President Bush launched the war that brought down the regime of Saddam Hussein. The Qatari leadership has had a penchant for initiating moves that can be characterized as "out of the box" and has therefore played the dual role of a dependable ally and a mercurial partner, constantly causing surprises and threatening to upset the apple cart. Whereas the Qataris have played host to a key leader of the Palestinian movement, Abu Mazen, the immediate successor to Yassir Arafat, they have wielded influence over the thinking and outlook of this Palestinian leader far beyond the relative input they might have been thought to have, given the size of the principality and of the population, numbering around half a million citizens, all told. They have tried to prevail on the Palestinians to moderate their positions and to seek working compromises with Israel. At the very same time, Qatar has given safe haven to key figures in the Khammas movement after they were exiled from Jordan, a short time after King Abdullah II assumed the throne of his late and revered father, King Hussein. The proximity of key Fatah and Khammas leadership figures on Qatari soil has made it possible for the Qataris to act, in trying to forge compromises between the opposing Palestinian factions, and to facilitate even tacit understandings with Israel. In 2005, the United States embraced Abu Mazen as a credible leader of the Palestinians and committed itself to supporting this Palestinian leader to parallel its longtime backing of Ariel Sharon and most of his predecessors. This would not have been possible were it not for states like Qatar, which nurtured the likes of Abu Mazen during the long and lean years that preceded the timely demise of Arafat. In passing I must note that in writing less than a year after his death, it is surprising to record how the Palestinians have turned the page and have gone on with their lives, refashioning their instruments of government and consigning

Arafat and his legacy to history, divorced to all intents and purposes from affairs of the present and plans for the future.

In October 2002, the Israeli press published leaks that claimed that I had been to Qatar and had met there secretly with Abu Mazen in an attempt to further understandings between Prime Minister Sharon and the possible candidate for the premiership of the Palestinian Authority. These reports were never really denied. Their appearance at the time was designed to undermine my credibility as a discrete envoy acting in the service of the prime minister. Whatever the intentions of the high-level leakers were, their aims were not achieved and it remained possible for me to operate for a few months more, before I myself took the initiative and resigned from my office of national security adviser to the prime minister. Throughout this period, the Qataris alongside other powerful voices in the Arab world exerted increasing pressure on Yassir Arafat to retreat from his all-out opposition to the appointment of an empowered prime minister. The crucial impact of this stand was an important factor in persuading Arafat to yield where he had hitherto put up a stubborn fight. The concerted effort to force the hand of the veteran Palestinian leader and lead him to concede and agree to the appointment of an "empowered prime minister" alongside himself was ultimately successful as the result of a unique coalition of forces that exerted pressure on him. These included the principal moderate Arab states, Egypt, Jordan, Morocco, and the Gulf principalities—Qatar, Oman, and others. Added to them were the United States, Russia, France, Germany, Britain, and many others. Silent diplomacy prevailed on all of these to accept and champion the concept and the detailed plan of action.

More will be said of this successful initiative later on. In the context of the present analysis, what is important to assert is that the creation of this "bipolar" structure in the Palestinian Authority created the circumstances for the "people" on the Palestinian side of the divide to begin to give expression to their unfettered sentiments and to facilitate a genuine people-to-people process to get under way. The masses were to be given the practical opportunity to identify with someone or a group other than the traditional leader. This happened in 2002 and 2003. Ten years or so after the abortive attempt to launch such a process under the terms of the Oslo Israel-Palestine accord, it was born under the rule of one of Oslo's most bitter detractors and opponents, Ariel Sharon, and it was only made possible by the dramatic turn he took, in forging a new policy of Israel on the Palestinian issue that, in essence, disavowed all that he had fought for during more than a quarter of a century.

6

THE ISRAEL-JORDAN PEACE TREATY OF 1994

The signing of a peace treaty between Israel and Jordan would appear, at first glance, to be a relatively secondary event in the world. The two countries had enjoyed a clandestine relationship for several decades and its existence had long been, for all intents and purposes, common knowledge. Jordan had never been a major adversary of Israel. Its armed forces had never constituted a major strategic threat to the Jewish state and during the Six-Day War of June 1967 it had lost control of the West Bank, including the whole of eastern Jerusalem, and Israel had taken over the entire area and had moved to settle parts of the new territories with no regard at all to Jordanian "sovereign rights" over the "occupied" lands. So why bother with Jordan?

Jordan was a key player in the region despite its comparative weakness. It was a "buffer" state facing across Iraq to the east, Syria to the north, and Saudi Arabia to the south. And at the very same time, it could evolve, very quickly, into a launching pad for either grievous terrorist attacks or full-scale invasion of extremist external forces. It could become the "hinterland" of a hostile Palestinian state or, together with Israel, an island of sanity and stability. A peace treaty with Israel would set the kingdom on a path that would enable it to play a regional role far beyond its normal capacity. That is why I, and many others who had pre-ceeded me, always considered an accommodation with the Hashemite kingdom of Jordan to be an essential segment of the strategic regional architecture that Israel had to pursue.

One spring evening, in the latter part of the month of April 1994, Secretary of State Warren Christopher arrived in Israel from Damascus to report to Prime Minister Rabin on his most recent round of talks with President Assad of Syria. The American secretary of state was completing yet another round of "shuttle" diplomacy and was dining at the prime minister's table at his official residence in Jerusalem. At the end of the meeting, the prime minister asked the secretary if he would meet someone who had recently returned from Amman, the Jordanian capital, and had something of interest to report. The secretary readily agreed and as he was making his way back to the King David Hotel where he was staying, and where the impending meeting was to take place, he was overtaken by tiredness and instructed his aides, Dennis Ross, the Middle East peace coordinator in the State Department, and Martin Indyk, the head of the Middle East desk at the White House, to meet the unknown Israeli and hear what he had to say.

We met late in the evening at the hotel and I introduced myself; I was meeting Ross and Indyk for the very first time and on the instruction of the prime minister I was about to brief my American interlocutors on a recent mission I had completed in the Jordanian capital. The mission had been long overdue; I had delayed a journey twice, once due to an angioplasty heart procedure that I had been obliged to undergo. An 80-percent blockage of my main artery had been relieved three months earlier; when hearing from me that I was to undergo this treatment, King Hussein had offered to fly me to the United States to be treated there; I graciously refused the gesture. Israeli medicine was perfectly capable of seeing to any of my medical needs. On another occasion I arrived in London to meet the king, only to be informed that he had left that very morning for Switzerland, where his mother, the late Queen Zein el Sharaf, had just passed away. Thus the kickoff of what was to emerge as the final and meaningful round of contacts and negotiations was delayed by four months.

The meeting with Ross and Indyk attended by the chargé d'affaires Larocco began with a detailed exposé of mine on the new positions that

King Hussein had taken during several meetings I had had with him and Crown Prince Hassan. The gist of the matter was that contrary to his previous policy, which was that he would like to move stage by stage and to implement each stage separately on an interim basis, he was now willing to move ahead and to enter into a comprehensive peace negotiation that would deal with all the issues on the agenda, including borders, water, military and security provisions, etc. To this end he wished to move away from the Washington venue of the previous rounds of negotiations that had been held under the auspices of the Madrid conference framework. The talks would take place in the region, preferably at some location along the Israeli-Jordanian border, and would be direct talks in every sense of the word. Underlying the king's approach was a sense of foreboding on his part that the breakthrough on the Palestinian track, which had taken him totally by surprise, might lead to a series of Israeli concessions to the Palestinians, and to their leader, Yassir Arafat, who had emerged as a "strategic partner" of Israel following a White House lawn ceremony where Prime Minister Rabin and Arafat had signed a joint "Declaration of Principles" and had publicly shaken hands. The king was particularly concerned about rumors that had reached him, to wit, that Israel was contemplating acceding to a request of Arafat that he be allowed to make a visit to Jerusalem. This was something he could not grasp. Was Israel on the verge of compromising on the holy of holies?

The issue of Jerusalem had been on King Hussein's mind constantly ever since Jordan had been defeated by Israel in the Six-Day War in 1967 and had lost control of the West Bank, including the ancient part of Jerusalem with the Temple Mount and the holy mosques in its midst. In the past he had considered himself the true guardian of the holy places and had invested very heavily in gaining the allegiance of the Muslim clergy and the religious trustees—the Waqf—who controlled the daily affairs on the Temple Mount. There had always been an atmosphere of rivalry and competition on the mount between the different royal houses in the Arab world that claimed to be descendants of the Prophet Muhammad and, hence, charged with authority and responsibility for the upkeep and preservation of the holy sites. Many a time did the king refer to his deep commitment to this mission of his in his conversations with me, and both he and his brother, Prince Hassan, kept very close watch over the daily activities on the Temple Mount. On one occasion, the king decided that the Dome of the Rock needed to be restored and the golden dome gilded in gold once again. To shoulder the cost, the king had sold one of his residences in London, a house on a road named Palace Green, four doors away from the Israeli embassy in London. I must admit that, personally I regretted this particular decision of his since it was there that I had met King Hussein for the very first time and where I was to be received by him on numerous subsequent occasions. It was always fun to prepare to sneak into the residence unnoticed and unidentified just a few yards away from my embassy, which was closely guarded and under constant surveillance.

However, be this as it may, the issue of Jerusalem had not been part of the brief that I carried; what was patently obvious was that in my understanding the king had changed his mind and was now not only willing but also eager to move rapidly to a complete peace agreement with Israel. He was anxious to tackle all the key issues—borders, water, and security—and, what was most important, he intimated to me that he had apprised President Assad of Syria both of his contacts with Israel and of his intentions and had found, so he averred, no objection on the part of his Syrian colleague and sole friend in the Arab world at that time, to these intentions of his. This was a very important revelation because it had generally been thought at the time that Syria was bitterly opposed to the inclination of various Arab states to reach individual arrangements with Israel, thus isolating Syria and weakening its bargaining power vis-à-vis Jerusalem.

As my American interlocutors listened to me and received my detailed report, I noticed that they appeared to be far from enthusiastic. It is true that I added a complementary item that was most pertinent to them—that the whole move could only take off and fly if the United States were to change its hostile policy toward Jordan, lift the blockade that the U.S. Navy was operating against the kingdom off the Gulf of Aqaba, and renew its support for the Jordanian Armed Forces, support that had been withdrawn ever since the end of the first Gulf War in 1991, when King Hussein had pursued a policy of neutrality, with a tilt toward Iraq. But this alone could not account for the reticence that the U.S. envoys were evincing.

The initial reaction was that King Hussein had been there before, that in the past he had supposedly been favorably inclined to embark on the road of peace with Israel, only to draw back at the very last moment. So, as one of the Americans phrased it, the king had a track record of proven absence of credibility and there was no merit to be found in trying once more and risking yet another round of wasted time and effort.

There was, however, a second, more profound consideration that motivated the initial American reaction. I was talking to a couple of very dedicated public servants who had landed in Israel a few hours previously en route from Damascus, where they had been pursuing a tortuous route of peace between Israel and Syria. This was a major American investment. The secretary of state himself had been engaged in shuttle diplomacy between Jerusalem and Damascus for months; the prize of a Syrian peace with Israel was rated the highest in the region. The assumption was that once Syria, the most extreme and intractable of the Arab foes of Israel, would bite the bullet, the entire Arab and Muslim world would follow suit. If the Jordanian track were to be revived at this particular juncture, there was every chance that the Syrian effort would have to be put on ice until such time as the Jordanian angle was taken care of. The Americans sensed that the Syrian prize was within their grasp. The investment already made in this direction was considerable—why risk losing out on this one only to embark on the Jordanian route that was rated doubtful from the outset? There was also a strong residue of dissatisfaction bordering on hostility in Washington vis-à-vis Jordan in general and against the Jordanian monarch in particular, following their stand on the first Gulf War. Some even spoke of a sense of betrayal, of personal betrayal, given the long-standing relationship between President George H. W. Bush and King Hussein from the days that Bush had directed the CIA for a relatively short period in the mid-seventies. Why then, in the face of these multiple considerations, should the United States give precedence to the Jordanian option at this point in time?

Some of the above arguments were voiced out loud; others were much less explicit but, nevertheless, very much in the air. I felt throughout the conversation that I was losing ground in the argumentation and was beginning to lose hope that the move would materialize. Just as I was about to conclude and leave the obviously tired U.S. envoys and allow them a well-earned and essential night of rest, Dennis Ross turned to me and asked me if there was any independent way that he could use to verify that what I was reporting was of true substance. I seized upon this opening and suggested to him that the secretary of state himself telephone the king and ask him directly three key questions relating to negotiations: their venue, his willingness to negotiate borders, and his preparedness to go it alone, regardless of what any other Arab state or element had to say about it. If the replies he received were identical with the points that I had made, then, I argued, we should be in business because a peace accord between Israel and Jordan would be a major advance in securing the "eastern front" and would afford the United States a welcome opportunity to bring Jordan back into the fold in anticipation of the unknown that awaited Washington on the Iraqi issue, which had remained unresolved after the first Gulf War.

To my surprise and, I must add, relief and gratitude, Ross accepted the proposal and within minutes the meeting was over, and I reported on it the following day to the prime minister. I was of two minds as to whether I should apprise the Jordanian side of the content of the discussion and thus prepare the king for the impending approach of the secretary of state. The dilemma was all too clear; if the Jordanians were forewarned, so to speak, the chances of their giving the "right" responses were that much greater. However, if it became known that I had acted in such a manner, the credibility of the response, to say nothing of my own standing as a discreet and intelligent emissary, could be greatly impaired. So I took the middle ground: I told my Jordanian contacts that we had briefed the United States in general terms on the content of my mission and that they, in turn, would be contacting the Jordanian side on the matter. I assured the Jordanians that contrary to the past, when senior Israelis had gone to the United States and had taken the liberty to go far beyond what had actually been discussed and agreed, this time we had kept meticulously close to the brief. Apart from that, I said nothing about the way our talk or talks with the Americans had been held and what reaction had been elicited. I left all this to the initiative and discretion of the powers that be in Washington.

Within days we received word that a telephone conversation had indeed taken place and that the king had responded exactly as I had reported. From that moment on, I knew that we were "in business" and that we could well be on the road to a permanent peace settlement.

Why was a peace settlement with Jordan of such importance to Israel? Why should we believe that the United States would accord such weight to sealing a deal between Israel and what would appear to be a lesser client in the region compared to Syria or Iraq, for that matter? I have already described the strategic positioning of this supposedly small kingdom, acting as a buffer zone in the heart of the Middle East: a buffer between Syria (north) and Saudi Arabia (south), between Israel (west) and Iraq-Iran (east). The role of Jordan as a vital ground that could be used, in extremis, as a staging area or as a safe forward-launching pad was second to none. Moreover, the concentration of hundreds of thousands of former Palestinians living in what were still former refugee camps located in various parts of the kingdom was a key element in the wider picture related to the permanent solution of the Israeli-Palestinian dispute. Jordan's long common border with Israel made this issue especially delicate, one could even say volatile. If Israel could get a peace treaty with Jordan even if it formally left the refugee issue open (including the most explosive question of settling the question of their "right of return"), we would have made progress in diffusing one of the main festering wounds that had been wide open for close to fifty years—ever since the State of Israel came into being. For many years there were Israelis, some very prominent, who advocated settling the entire dispute by substituting for the Hashemite regime a Palestinian one. The slogan "Jordan is Palestine" was, at one time, adopted by none other than Prime Minister Ariel Sharon and I thought, as did at the time my political master, Yitzhak Rabin, that a peace treaty would lay this bogus option to rest. Jordan was a vital component in ensuring Israel's security and the sooner the permanent status of this concept could be put in political concrete in the form of a peace treaty, the better. That is why a seemingly minor item on the Middle East agenda assumed such greater proportions and significance.

Within weeks, on May 19, 1994, Prime Minister Rabin met with the king in London to agree on the parameters and the modalities of the negotiations. The talks would be held at a point on the Israeli-Jordanian border, about fifty kilometers north of Eilat and Aqaba; they would be direct and bilateral, without any third party participation, and would be cast as a serious attempt to produce a final peace treaty. The United States would be kept informed by both sides and a technical mechanism was set in motion to effect this transfer of negotiations from what was the original Madrid conference framework to the new bilateral model. It was also agreed that Israel would impress upon the United States the importance of assisting Jordan both economically and with military hardware, thus restoring the original tone and content of the relationship which had soured as a result of the Gulf War.

The positive signals emanating from Washington produced a flurry of statements issued by Jerusalem and Amman, stating that direct talks between Israel and Jordan were to begin in mid-June 1994 at a point north of Eilat and Aqaba. The dates coincided with the planned visit of Secretary of State Warren Christopher in the region. He was scheduled to conduct talks in both Israel and Jordan and, as time progressed, a first public visit of an Israeli leader, Foreign Minister Shimon Peres, to Jordan was suggested and agreed between the parties. This was to be a public event, widely covered by the media, and Peres enthusiastically plunged into preparations for the event and, as was so often the case with him, he seemed to keep the prime minister in the dark concerning the plans and initiatives he was about to launch. However, before this could come about, one additional hurdle had to be overcome.

Everything appeared to be on track: The venue for the direct negotiations had been agreed, the agenda mutually accepted, and the United States appeared to be signaling that its policy toward Jordan was about to change and revert to the way the relationship had been conducted over many decades. But all these were no more than words, utterances, and King Hussein was in need of concrete proof that his courageous step of authorizing direct talks with Israel was going to pay off; in particular it was essential for him to obtain quick relief for the Jordanian Armed Forces who had been starved for equipment and spare parts since the Gulf War. After all, the security and armed services were in many aspects the very backbone of the regime and if these were disaffected, this could spell serious trouble in the kingdom. Hence, King Hussein requested and received an invitation to visit Washington in June 1994, and it was his assumption that he would be warmly received and duly rewarded for the courageous step he had taken.

At his request, I was dispatched to be present in Washington and to assist behind the scenes, if this became necessary. As he began his round of talks in Washington, the king was in for a very rude awakening. He was complimented on his bold decisions concerning Israel, but was told by the officials he met that Jordan would not receive any aid of any kind whatsoever, economic or military, before he signed a peace treaty with Israel. The upshot of this was that he would have to return to Jordan empty-handed and to face the military, telling them that he had an empty bag. This could spell disaster for the regime and for him personally. I met with the king more than once during the first couple of days of his visit and he intimated to me that it might well be that I had been deliberately misled to assure him that he would have a successful visit or that I myself had been hoodwinked into believing that this would be so. It so happened that the Israeli ambassador to the United States, Professor Itamar Rabinovich, had flown home to attend the wedding of his daughter, and I therefore requested and was granted authority to go directly to the State Department and to deal with them on these issues. At a meeting with the peace process coordinator, Dennis Ross, I strongly argued the Jordanian case and, inter alia, supported their request for a squadron of F-16 fighter aircraft, thus upgrading the Jordanian air force considerably. In the heat of the conversation, Ross turned to me and said, "Tell me, Efraim, who are you representing here? Israel or Jordan?" Without thinking twice, I blurted out, "Both!"

Another round of meetings did not produce any better results. On the eve of the final meeting, with President Clinton himself, I again saw Ross and he assured me that he would do his best to turn things around. He asked that the Jordanians submit their essential requirements in a short one-to-two-page memo for the attention of the president. I passed on the request, only to learn the following morning that they had sent in a document containing scores of pages! There was nothing I could do about it. In the late afternoon I received a call and went over to see His Majesty; a beaming monarch received me and told me of the extraordinary meeting he had just had with President Clinton. The president met with him, holding not one single sheet of paper; as soon as the conversation got under way it became obvious that he had read the Jordanian brief from cover to cover and had absorbed every small detail in it. He gave his guest satisfactory responses to most of the requests and within a very short time the business part of the day was over. The two principals were then joined by the queen and the first lady for lunch at the White House. The atmosphere was excellent and the president used over an hour of the time in an attempt to persuade the king to buy Boeing aircraft for his Royal

Jordanian civilian air company and thus to replace the Airbus fleet that they had!

Before proceeding, it is necessary to clarify some aspects of the uneasy relationship between the prime minister and his foreign minister as seen through the eyes of a senior civil servant. The prime minister was well aware of the modus operandi of his colleague; it had led him to instruct me to refrain from reporting to Mr. Peres without being briefed in great detail as to what the man should be told. The prime minister was clearly knowledgeable concerning the attitude that the king had cultivated toward Peres ever since the abortive attempt that Peres had made in 1987 to launch a peace initiative in London at a secret meeting he had held with King Hussein. The accounts of the discussions between the two, as related by the two principals, varied. This was to repeat itself in November 2003, when Peres paid a secret visit to Amman and then publicly disclosed his trip in a television appearance in Israel a day later after his return. Hussein had made his view of the person abundantly clear when he repeatedly signaled Rabin that if Peres were privy to the intimate discussions between the principals, he felt that the whole endeavor would be in jeopardy.

From King Hussein's vantage point, any event entailing the participation of Mr. Peres was more of a public-relations exercise than one of substantive content. Such events had their value; they served to begin conditioning the Jordanian public to a possible rapprochement with Israel and they could pass without the personal participation or involvement of the king or the royal family, for that matter. Hence, the Peres-Christopher meeting was destined to take place without it being an opportunity for policy revelations.

Needless to say, this was not how Peres viewed the event. For him this was a golden opportunity to wrest control once again of the process and lead it to its ultimate happy end; thus he would not only achieve the principal aim of cementing peace between the two countries, but would also remove memories of his previous setbacks on this vital issue.

A few days before Christopher landed in Israel, a message came in from Washington to the effect that King Hussein was ready to meet Prime Minister Rabin in public for the very first time and that the meeting would be convened in Washington on July 25, 1994. Rabin decided to turn the forthcoming event into an opportunity to upgrade the relationship between the two countries even before a formal peace treaty was signed. He instructed me to prepare a draft document that would include language to the effect that the state of war between the two states had been terminated and to detail a series of practical steps that would be taken in the direction of normalization. One such step would be the inauguration of border crossings that would be open for tourist and other traffic; another would be the inauguration of telephone communications; other similar moves were contemplated.

A day before the meeting between Peres and Jordanian prime minister Majali on the eastern shores of the Dead Sea, in the presence of Secretary of State Warren Christopher, I was in Amman with the draft in my hand, going over it word for word with Crown Prince Hassan and, after that, with His Majesty himself. Except for some minor changes, the document remained intact, and I must admit to a sense of pride when the work appeared to have reached its successful conclusion. Evening came and I was preparing to report to the prime minister prior to catching a short night's sleep, when all of a sudden the king's trusted aide came to see me to tell me that after additional thought, His Majesty had decided that the document had to include a paragraph relating to Jordan's role in the city of Jerusalem. I almost literally lost a heartbeat! I told my interlocutor, Colonel Ali Shukri, that I had no mandate whatsoever to negotiate on Jerusalem or on any aspect of it and I intimated that I might well be "hung, drawn, and quartered" if I returned to Israel with such a message. The response I got was firm and unequivocal—either the section was included in the document or the whole peace endeavor would go to ground.

The Jordanian text was worded as follows:

> The two countries reconfirm the historic responsibilities of the Hashemite Kingdom of Jordan in the Islamic holy place in Jerusalem, and they reaffirmed their commitment to render the city, a city of peace and hope for all believers.

As we were negotiating the texts, representatives of Foreign Minister Peres were meeting with their Jordanian counterparts, entirely oblivious of an impending, yet unannounced meeting between the king and the prime minister. The Israelis negotiating the parameters of the Christopher-Peres-Majali meeting were pressing for a substantive session that would end with a list of practical measures agreed between the parties. I was receiving real-time reporting on these parallel talks and, on instruction, counseling my interlocutors to leave all these issues for agreement between the principals; it did not need very much to convince them to reject the overtures on the other channel. This approach was identical with their own attitude and they wished to leave substance to His Majesty himself.

It was Tuesday, July 19. On Wednesday I made my way back to Israel, genuinely fearful of the wrath of Prime Minister Rabin over the Jerusalem paragraph. I met him in the presence, as usual, of my chief—Shabtai Shavit, who supported the effort throughout this period—and he read through the document and commended me for the thorough work accomplished. As he reached the paragraph on Jerusalem, he read it twice and then said that he thought the wording was not satisfactory; he told us that he would consult on it with a couple of people, whose names he did not mention, and would get back to us in a few hours. A few hours passed and we were summoned by the prime minister who gave us a different wording, which, he said, would also conform to what had been told to the Palestinians on the Jerusalem issue. I told the prime minister that I would send the correction through the existing channel. "No way," said the prime minister. "You are dealing with the most sensitive of issues; you must go back to Jordan tomorrow, ask to see the king personally, and give him the text that I am proposing." Our meeting ended as the media was reporting on the historic meeting of Foreign Minister Peres and Jordanian prime minister Majali on Jordanian soil. The secretary of state was there to consecrate the ceremony. None of those present knew that within a few hours there would be an announcement on a first overt meeting of the principals.

I dutifully traveled to Jordan again on Thursday, July 21, and as I left I received a call from the prime minister suggesting that the venue of the forthcoming meeting between himself and the king be somewhere in mid-desert along the Israeli-Jordanian border. The prime minister knew by then that the U.S. "sponsors" had invited the two leaders to Washington. The prime minister thought that it would look strange that the two would have to travel all the way to the United States in order to meet each other in public when they could easily do so "almost within walking distance!" I met the king around lunchtime; he was dressed in army fatigues, wearing a black army beret, and virtually beaming with joy and satisfaction. I gave him the text that the prime minister had approved, which read as follows:

> Israel respects the present special role of the Hashemite Kingdom of Jordan in Muslim Holy Shrines in Jerusalem. When negotiations on the permanent status will take place, Israel will give high priority to the Jordanian historic role in these shrines.

Prince Hassan added a sentence, as follows:

> In addition the two sides have agreed to act together to promote interfaith relations among the three monotheistic religions.

I then proposed to His Majesty that the venue of the forthcoming meeting be moved from Washington to the region and he readily accepted this. Both His Majesty and the Crown Prince insisted that the text agreed upon would be kept entirely secret until the two actually met; there was a very short list of "need to know" persons drawn up and any addition had to be approved by one of the principals. We agreed that the master copy of the document be kept in Jordanian custody, believing, unfortunately rightly, that they were better equipped to preserve the secrecy of its contents.

As I prepared to depart, I learned that the day before, after the Peres-Majali meeting, it had been decided that a senior American official would leave the secretary of state's party and repair to Amman, where he would ask to meet with the Jordanian leadership to suggest a text of a joint document that the leaders would jointly make public when they met.

The American draft was in many aspects similar to that which we had drafted together with our Jordanian colleagues. To the surprise of the American diplomats, they were told that most of their suggestions had already been incorporated in a draft that the parties had approved between themselves. However, when the Americans asked to see the paper, they were politely refused and told that it was not possible for them to even see it, let alone obtain a copy, because this was what had been agreed upon between the parties. In the days to come, this hide-and-seek game was to become a matter of growing irritation on the part of many would-be actors in the approaching drama.

There were, however, a couple of elements in the American proposal that differed substantively from what had been agreed. The Americans proposed that the public statement contain a commitment of the parties to develop steps and mutual actions to counter threats of terrorism and to reduce the threats that "conventional and nonconventional weapons pose to the security of both sides." This was wording that we could never accept, but in any event there was no need to argue about it because the agreed text was final. Another element that the Americans wished to incorporate in the declaration was a provision to promote exchanges of visits by military and security experts, sharing military information. There was also a suggestion to develop a "subregional conflict center," where information could be shared to help reduce threats to security. The signature of a military and security protocol between the parties was also proposed as an overt item in the declaration. Luckily, again, there was no necessity to deliberate on these proposals; there is no doubt in my mind that neither we nor the Jordanians would have thought it politically wise to trumpet such issues in public documents.

I returned home and reported on the following Thursday that the mission had been successfully accomplished; all the points raised and/or amended by the prime minister had been satisfactorily resolved. In the evening, all hell broke loose! We were hastily summoned to the prime minister, who happened to pass by our building en route to a meeting he was about to attend. Apparently Washington had reacted furiously to the decision to move the venue of the meeting away from the United States. "This is unheard of," it was said. "You expect us to pay the full costs of the wedding and you do not understand that the least you can do is invite us to host the ceremony!" There was nothing that anyone could do in these circumstances; we agreed to return to the original plan, and when I contacted my Jordanian friends, they told me that they had also accepted the inevitable. We would all travel to Washington.

Secretary of State Christopher was winding up his short tour of the region with a brief stop in Israel; he met with Prime Minister Rabin and obviously asked to see the joint document that had been prepared. Mr. Rabin knew that a similar request in Jordan had been politely refused. Did he or did he not show the document to Secretary Christopher when they met in a for-eyes-only session? I, for one, will never know. What I can say is that at that very juncture, the United States was not given a copy of the declaration.

I traveled to Washington over the weekend; several prominent Israeli journalists were on the aircraft and a few knew me. They asked whether I knew anything about a joint declaration and I told them that I was going on other business. None of them knew at the time that I had anything whatsoever to do with the "Jordanian Portfolio." On my arrival in Washington, the Israeli ambassador asked to see me urgently. He was not privy to all that had transpired and was in contact with one of the Jordanian princes of the Royal Court, and the two were trying to "negotiate" arrangements and contents of the forthcoming meeting. I avoided him as long as I could and when I met him eventually, he already knew that there was a text and asked to receive it; I told him that I did not have the text and that it was "in Jordanian hands." We would all have to await the arrival of the principals.

Sunday, July 24, on a sunny bright morning, the official Israeli Air Force Boeing 707 aircraft landed at Andrews Air Force Base, near Washington, D.C., with Prime Minister Rabin and his entourage on board; after much hesitation, he had invited Foreign Minister Peres to join him on this mission, but not before the issue of Peres accompanying the prime minister had been aired in the media at length. Ambassador Rabinovich was, of course, on hand to greet the visitors, as were senior U.S. State Department officials. By that time, the existence of the "Washington Declaration" had become public knowledge and there was a clamor from all angles to get a copy of the document; Rabinovich told me at the air base that a State Department official was on hand to receive a copy in order to duplicate it into several hundred copies and distribute them as embargoed items, to be released for quotation after the White House ceremony that was scheduled to take place on the lawn the following day. Shortly after landing, the ambassador spoke to the prime minister and asked him to instruct me to give him a copy. The request was turned down, and the morning passed without a copy being passed out.

The prime minister convened a meeting of those close to him, including the head of the Israeli delegation for negotiations with Jordan, Elyakim Rubinstein. This was the first time he had been able to see the document that I had drafted with the Jordanians and he was understandably unhappy about this. As he read the document he came to the paragraph which read:

> The long conflict between the two states is now coming to an end. In this spirit the state of belligerency between Jordan and Israel has been terminated.

Rubinstein expressed deep dissatisfaction with the use of the term "belligerency." As he was a lawyer by profession, a future attorney general and Supreme Court judge, a veteran participant in the original Camp David negotiations between Egypt and Israel in 1979, his opinion carried weight with the prime minister. Rubinstein hastened to consult with a couple of Israeli experts in international law, who, of course, supported his position. The prime minister turned to me and instructed me to request an urgent meeting with the Jordanians to get the text changed. At Rubinstein's demand, the word "belligerency" would have to be changed to the word "war." It was the state of war that was being terminated, not the state of belligerency. I argued most vigorously that we had agreed on a text and had also agreed that it was final, that once we opened the text for changes we could expect amendments from the other side as well and there might be no end to this. It was of no avail. Rubinstein was a good personal friend of mine and we had worked well together on the Jordanian Portfolio for several years. I could well understand that he felt hurt that he had been cut out of this chapter of the process.

I had to concede. An atmosphere of foreboding quickly spread among the few who were in the picture of what had transpired. I called my Jordanian contact and asked him to come over to see me urgently. He came in under the identity of an Israeli delegation member and thus a host of security procedures were avoided. He met with a group of us and received a detailed dissertation on the issue at hand. I sat there silent and glum; I began fearing for the worst: Could it be that the whole move would end in a fiasco with the prime minister having egg on his face? My Jordanian friend looked at me several times during the meeting, exhibiting genuine disbelief. Had we not agreed on a series of understandings on this document? What was happening here? Was this a last-minute attempt to grab one more element of peacemaking, knowing that the king could ill-afford a botched diplomatic peace enterprise?

My Jordanian friend left and promised to come back to me some time later in the day, after he had consulted with His Majesty. A meeting had been scheduled between the prime minister and Secretary of State Christopher for five o'clock in the afternoon; as the clock ticked away, I was becoming fearful that all was lost. Around 2:30 P.M., I received a call and was asked to come over to a hotel where some of the Jordanian delegation were staying. My Jordanian friend was there; he told me that he had consulted with Prince Hassan and others, notably Aun Hassauna, the head of the Royal Court, an international lawyer of considerable repute, who was later to become a justice on the bench of the International Court of Justice in the Hague. Like Rubinstein, his legal counterpart, he was not in the know about this document until that morning, but unlike Rubinstein, his reservations were not confined to one solitary item. He had amendments on nearly every item in the text. As we went from paragraph to paragraph, we reached the key amendment. Hassauna did not accept the proposed change since, he argued, the term "belligerency" had been used in all the legal documents relating to the state of affairs between the two states. However, he had an amendment of his own to add to the paragraph. The text should read, he said, "The state of belligerency between Jordan and Israel *will* be terminated rather than *has* been terminated."

I realized that if we did not stop here, it would spell the death knell to the whole effort. Hassauna was in Amman and he was being consulted on the phone as my friend was speaking to me. At this juncture, I threw the papers in my hand on the table and told my friend that I could not proceed any further and that rather than go on, I would prefer to terminate our meeting and report back to my prime minister that I had failed, plain and simply. I was asked to wait; my friend left the room to consult with His Majesty and the Crown Prince, who was in Amman. A quarter of an hour later, he came back, saying that His Majesty proposed that the text remained unchanged; in any event, I was told, in Arabic, war and belligerency were translated as the same word, *kharb,* and it was possible that His Majesty would say something openly in his address at the ceremony to set the record straight. I returned to the hotel and reported back to the prime minister. Rubinstein continued to argue that the arrangement was legally insufficient. I claimed that the document that was being signed was not the peace treaty itself and that if he wished, he could certainly change the text when the time came to approve a full peace settlement with Jordan. Time was running short. Secretary of State Christopher would be coming in to see the prime minister in less than thirty minutes. Rabin instructed me to get ironclad assurances from the Jordanians that the king would, indeed, make a public statement as I had been told.

I called my friend, who had repaired to King Hussein's residence on the Potomac, and asked him to give me a formal assurance that His Majesty would indeed make public mention of the end of the state of war—*kharb*—as requested. I received an affirmative response. However, I felt that this was insufficient, to convince Prime Minister Rabin that all was well. I did not terminate the telephone conversation but continued to explain that our credibility was on the line, that if, God forbid, this item was omitted, it would spell disaster for the relationship. A few seconds later, I suddenly heard the voice of His Majesty on the phone; apparently he had been listening in on the conversation. "My friend," he said in his deep, profoundly unmistakable voice, "you can assure the prime minister that I will be making this element entirely clear when I speak tomorrow and I shall state very clearly that the state of war has come to an end." A couple of minutes before the arrival of Secretary of State Christopher, I rushed to the suite of the prime minister and reported the telephone conversation verbatim. All now seemed to be set for the ceremonies of the next day.

The secretary came and left; it had been a courtesy call, a gesture of welcome and nothing more. The text of the Washington Declaration was still a closely guarded secret; no person in the administration had seen it and we were less than twenty-four hours away from the appearance of President Clinton, Prime Minister Rabin, and King Hussein on the White House lawn. The situation was becoming virtually untenable. Here we had a host, no one less than the president of the United States of America, who was about to preside over a major diplomatic and international event—a breakthrough in the relations between two warring states—and on the night before the event he had not yet been briefed by the parties as to what it was that they were about to say or do!

This could not continue any longer; it was agreed that at nine o'clock that evening I would meet Martin Indyk, the head of the Middle East desk at the White House, together with my Jordanian colleague at the

Hay Adams Hotel, within a stone's throw of the White House. There we would formally hand over the text of the Washington Declaration and thus enable the White House both to brief the president, so that his speech could be prepared, and to give the document its final format.

That evening, the ambassador held a reception for the prime minister, his party, and other invitees at the residence. I could not help recalling the numerous times I had been to the house ever since I had arrived in Washington about a quarter of a century previously, as a young "diplomat" in the embassy under the then ambassador Yitzhak Rabin. I had spent four formative years there under Rabin and his successor, Simcha Dinitz, and in retrospect, I felt that much that I had learned during those years shaped both my outlook and my diplomatic modus operandi. I had come, so to speak, full circle, and here I was at the side of Rabin, now prime minister, and I, deputy chief of the Mossad, the author of a document named no less than the Washington Declaration. In common with the tradition of the service and the State of Israel, I assumed that my role would remain secret, but this did nothing to minimize my sense of pride and fulfillment that evening. The evening was tense and uneasy; in one corner of the room sat Mr. Peres, the foreign minister of Israel, a person who had striven so hard over many years to clinch a Jordanian deal, with no idea whatsoever as to what was going to happen or to be said the following day. In another part of the room I was sitting waiting for the evening meeting at the Hay Adams Hotel, trying to relax and pass the time away. A leading Israeli journalist, Emmanuel Rosen, tried to get me to talk about the event, and I replied that essentially I was quite a dull person, with very little worthwhile knowledge from a journalist's point of view.

The time had come for us to go, and Eitan Haber, the prime minister's chief of staff, left the room with me to attend the meeting with Indyk. Only on my return did I learn that Rabin had eyed me on my departure as he was briefing a group of Israeli journalists. He had pointed his finger at my receding figure and said something to the effect that they should look at me since all that was going to happen was my doing alone, that others might wish to claim credit but that it was my doing alone, period. Needless to say, the item hit the headlines of the Israeli media the following day; my professional cover had been irretrievably blown and I was exposed as never before. I then realized that I would probably have to leave the service before very long, that my Mossad career had probably come to an end, and that I would have to think where my future might take me. I never dreamed then that less than four years later I would be back in the Mossad, this time as its chief, in circumstances that would be linked—how not?—to events in Jordan.

July 25 began uneventfully. Everything appeared set for the ceremonies; an hour before the first of two ceremonies, Elyakim Rubinstein and I went to the executive wing of the White House to make sure that the declaration had been handled properly. As we went through the text we found, to our surprise, that the text on water had undergone changes and that there had been substantive alterations inserted by one of the Jordanians. We immediately told the White House official, David Sutterfield, that a correction had to be made. He refused to do so without Jordanian consent, and rightly so. But the Jordanians were unavailable, since they were on their way to the ceremony. We were lucky in that two, and not one, ceremonies had been planned. The declaration would be made public only during the second one. In the intervening pause between the ceremonies we met again in the White House, and the Jordanians agreed to reinstate the original text. Due to the lack of time, I inked in the change in my own handwriting and both I and my Jordanian colleague initialed it. The principals signed the declaration, oblivious of the fact that on one of its pages, a written correction had been inserted.

By pure chance I was seated in the second row of the ceremony directly behind Mr. Peres. Before it began he turned to me, greatly irritated, and asked if at long last he could see the text of the declaration. I told him truthfully that I did not have a copy in my possession. He reacted very angrily and I felt he did not believe me. By that time I had heard of the publicity that Prime Minister Rabin's revelation concerning my role had received in the Israel media; in that light, the ire of Peres was more than understandable.

As President Clinton was reading out the Washington Declaration he came to the section on Jerusalem; no sooner had he finished reading that passage when Mr. Peres turned back to look at me, only to say that this wording was, in his words, "a very big mistake." More provocative than that was the reaction of the director general of the Israeli foreign ministry, Uri Savir, a good friend of mine, who said to me, immediately after the end of the ceremony, that the section ran contrary to what had been promised to the Palestinians on Jerusalem. "Contrary to what?" I asked in response. What exactly had been promised the Palestinians that this section contradicted? I received no reply and was left wondering, to this very day, what it was that the Palestinians had been promised on the most delicate of subjects, that of Jerusalem, that the Washington Declaration appeared to contradict.

The three speeches of the principals at the ceremony were works of art. Rabin read his prepared text slowly and carefully, yet it was clear to me that he was full of emotion as he spoke. President Clinton was as eloquent as ever, but in my view, it was King Hussein who "stole the show," as he stood there speaking without a note in his hand, as if he was extemporizing as he went along. He appeared to have committed a prepared text to memory; whether this was so or not I did not know, but it seemed as if every sentence had been well thought out in advance. When he came to the point of the state of relations between Jordan and Israel he said in Arabic, loud and clear, that the state of war—*kharb*—had come to an end. A deafening and spontaneous round of applause greeted the simple statement and it became the punch line in the reporting in the media throughout that day. The king had delivered handsomely on his promise to us, and he had done so in the generous tone and content that he was so often capable of summoning, when he so wished.

After lunch, with all the pomp and circumstance over, I went to my room and tried to relax. I knew there was still much work to be done; the peace treaty had not yet been achieved and there were many obstacles that still had to be overcome. I felt a sense of loss that Crown Prince Hassan, who had toiled so much and so effectively, was not in Washington, but this was not possible due to the absence of the king from Jordan. I called him and expressed my appreciation of everything he had done to make this event possible. He was a rock of steadying moderation and good sense all along the way and I felt we would need his wisdom and firm hand in the days ahead. I was about to doze off when I received a call to appear at once in the suite of the prime minister. As I made my way I tried to imagine what new problem had arisen. I entered the room and found the prime minister all alone with a glass of whiskey in his hand; he offered me a glass, which I at first declined but then accepted. He told me that he had asked me to come over in order to thank me for my service on this issue; he said that it was my doing and that without me it would not have been possible. He said he would be having a private meeting with King Hussein later in the day. Only the queen and Mrs. Rabin would be there and he asked that I join them; and, indeed, several hours later I attended that meeting, which was a very happy and emotional occasion.

I had been preparing to go home with the prime minister in his official aircraft, but this was not to be; one of the agreements related to the declaration was that the United States would grant Jordan debt forgiveness to the tune of around seven hundred million dollars. This necessitated congressional approval and Congress was about to begin its summer recess within days. The Israeli embassy in Washington led by the ambassador swung into action right away to lobby Congress to approve the move. However, the king requested the prime minister to let me remain until the issue had been finally resolved. My return to Israel was delayed for five days and I departed on the royal aircraft of King Hussein, who traveled to London for a short holiday.

The declaration in itself did not change attitudes and sentiments on the ground in Jordan. I received a vivid illustration of this as we were flying to London. The king was in excellent and high spirits and was celebrating a tremendous success. He was well on the way to obtaining widespread debt forgiveness; the blockade on his southern port, Aqaba, was being lifted by the United States; his Armed Forces were going to receive not only sorely needed spare parts but also upgraded equipment, including a first squadron of F-16 fighter aircraft. Above all his relationship with the American superpower had been restored to where it was before the first Gulf War. All this had been accomplished within the span of three months. He now wanted to celebrate and began telephoning friends from his airborne satellite telephone; at one stage he asked to speak to the prime minister. I made the arrangements and when Rabin got on the phone the two leaders had a very pleasant conversation. The king handed the receiver to me and I was expecting to hear a few final words of courtesy. No way! Rabin was angry. According to the agreement as laid out in the Washington Declaration, we were going to inaugurate two border crossings between Jordan and Israel, one in the south and one in the north. These were to serve both local traffic and tourism. The Israeli side had moved to implement this provision at once, only to find that the Jordanians had chosen a point somewhere in the desert up north from Aqaba-Eilat, the idea being that the crossing be as distant and as obscure as possible. Rabin told me that this was, of course, entirely unacceptable to us. The whole purpose of these crossings was that they be easily and comfortably accessible, especially for the tourist trade. He told me to raise the matter with the king and to get it resolved as soon as possible. I spoke to His Majesty at once and it was obvious to me that he was in no way aware of this decision and did not support it. He gave immediate instructions from the aircraft and the crossings venue was settled. It had been clear from the outset that it was going to be an uphill battle to change the mind-sets of the Jordanian population on the Israeli-Arab issue; it was going to take years to get the people to think and feel otherwise than they had for generations.

There was still a long way to go before a final peace treaty could be concluded. Of this, more will be said shortly. But one little last vignette related to the Washington Declaration seems to me worthy of being recounted. As already stated, one of the important features of the declaration was the agreement of the United States and others to grant Jordan massive debt relief and thus set the Jordanian economy back on track, following a disastrous few years exacerbated by the years following the first Gulf War. In Washington, the procedure was put in motion in the last days of July 1994, just before Congress recessed for its summer vacation. I had taken leave of the king when I reached London aboard his royal aircraft, and shortly afterward my wife and I departed on what I thought was a well-earned holiday in Ireland. In those days, portable—cellular—phones were a relatively rare species and this was certainly so as far as international calls were concerned. Thus, when I left, I undertook to call in every couple of days to my office to make sure that nobody really needed me in my absence. Several days into my trip, as we reached the town of Kilkenny, I called in to Israel, only to hear that a grave crisis had arisen over the debt-forgiveness issue. A Jordanian residing in a New Jersey city had murdered his American wife and had fled to Jordan with his two children. He was a member of a prestigious tribe in Jordan and had taken refuge in the heart of his tribe land. The family of the slain wife had made this a public issue and was demanding the extradition of the purported murderer and, above all, the return of the two children, American citizens, to the United States. A prominent U.S. senator for New Jersey, Frank Lautenberg, was up for reelection that year.

The matter rapidly became an election issue and the senator was asked to use his clout with Israel to get the Jordanians to send the man and the children back to the States. Lautenberg, a prominent Jewish leader of the past, began exerting pressure on his Israeli friends to do what they could, but to no avail. It transpired that there was no extradition treaty between Jordan and the United States, and that therefore, legally, there was no remedy for the American family.

Tension rose and the senator sent his personal aide to Amman to pressure the local authorities, but this had not produced the desired result. In desperation, the senator had informed the Israeli ambassador and others that if the man and his two children were not surrendered somehow or other to the United States within a very short specified time frame, he would publicly chain himself to the railings of the Jordanian embassy in Washington, D.C., where he would hold a press conference to denounce human-rights abuses in Jordan; at the same time he would exercise his right, that of any individual senator, to delay the debt-forgiveness legislation for an unspecified length of time. All of this was related to me at a local phone box from where I had put in a call; I was asked to "resolve the issue" or get on a plane and fly back home right away.

I immediately got on the phone to Amman, and after lengthy conversations with the Crown Prince and others, a formula was devised whereby the three persons would be flown to Europe, handed over to U.S. authorities, and then transported to the United States. The crisis was over; debt forgiveness proceeded to its successful legislative conclusion and Senator Lautenberg was reelected.

7

THREE MONTHS TO A FINAL TREATY

The days following the euphoric event in Washington provided a rude awakening for all concerned in the peacemaking efforts that were now gathering pace. Plenary sessions and working groups of the two sides were making little or no progress in getting things moving in the right direction. The issues of borders, water, defense, and security were mired in a maze of intractable detail. Jordan was demanding a complete return to the 1967 borders between the two countries and on the face of it, this would entail the transfer of land from Israel to Jordan south of the Dead Sea to the tune of more than 380 square kilometers—more than the area of the entire Gaza Strip. Moreover, along the Arava Valley, stretching from the southern tip of the Dead Sea to the ports of Aqaba and Eilat, a string of villages had sprung up and they had become a center of agriculture and flower growing—the pride of Israeli agriculture. In order to secure water resources for some of these settlements, Israel had bored water wells quite deep into Jordanian territory, and it was exceptionally difficult to see how the powers that be in Amman would be capable of digesting continuing Israeli exploitation of this vital source of life and economy.

In the past, Jordan had rejected any arrangement that would entail "leasing" land to Israel; politically, this was totally unacceptable to His Majesty since it would be construed by the extremists in Jordan as an act of betrayal and forfeiture of sacred Arab soil. When Foreign Minister Peres had met with the king in November 1993, in what was initially agreed to have been a secret meeting, he came away to tell Prime Minister Rabin that he had succeeded in obtaining the Jordanian monarch's approval of a lease that would grant Israel the land it had appropriated over the years. Subsequently, King Hussein strenuously denied having made any such concession. Indeed, his account of the exchange between himself and his Israeli interlocutor had him rejecting the proposal instantaneously and outright, leaving no room whatsoever for any negotiation on the issue.

The Washington Declaration did not resolve these issues; it created a positive climate for peace-treaty negotiations in that it relieved Jordan of enormous burdens that it had been carrying ever since the Gulf War. A very difficult bout of negotiations lay ahead and the prime minister feared that if the discussions were unduly prolonged, the process could well run out of political steam, and ultimately end without achieving the desired result; time, and not only meaningful content, became of the essence.

As the negotiating teams resumed their talks in the wake of the Washington ceremonies, I sensed that an air of distrust and suspicion was creeping into the minds of the Jordanian principals. It was true that the Israeli side had demonstrated its capacity to effect a dramatic turnaround in the strategic position of the Hashemite kingdom of Jordan; this was undeniable and clearly proven. Yet in the past, King Hussein felt that he had, on occasion, been misled by his overenthusiastic counterparts who in their eagerness to demonstrate rapid results had, in his understanding, compromised him in no small measure.

In order to fathom the true nature of this deep-seated mistrust, it is useful and relevant to turn back a moment to reconsider the events of November 2, 1993, when Peres had paid a secret visit to Jordan and came back to tell the prime minister that he had succeeded in extracting from His Majesty those concessions that made the final run to a peace treaty a mere "piece of cake." I have often thought about whether this string of events was nothing more than political gossip or if it went to the heart of the art of negotiations. After mulling over the issue, I have chosen to recount the sequence, because it is, after all, a minichapter in the history of the region and because it was, at one time, part of a pattern of behavior, worthy of being accurately recorded. It is in this vein that I have allowed myself this discretion.

As already told, a day after the secret meeting of the king and Mr. Peres in Amman, on November 2, 1993, the latter revealed the fact that it had taken place in a public television interview on state television. How did the meeting come about? Shortly after the historic meeting between Prime Minister Rabin and PLO leader Yassir Arafat on the White House lawn in September 1993, it transpired that King Hussein regarded the exercise as close to an act of political betrayal on the part of his erstwhile Israeli friends in the Israeli Labor party. For years they had been dialoguing and seeking ways and means of effecting an overt relationship between Israel and Jordan; in this they had not succeeded, but despite the many setbacks, the king had reason to believe, or so he thought, that come what may, he would not be deserted. In the eighties he had met Mr. Peres several times in the residences of Lord Mishcon, a prominent lawyer and eminent supporter of the British Labour Party, who was a friend of both men. These meetings had not produced the ultimate results and when the Oslo agreements between Israel and the Palestinians suddenly came to light, the king turned to Mishcon, his friend and lawyer, for advice and comfort. Mishcon, a most honorable man, kept his channel to Peres open and when subsequent initial effort to get Rabin and the king to agree on a peace move floundered, and a virtual stalemate in the relationship arose, Peres approached Mishcon to suggest to His Majesty that he, Peres, be invited to Amman, to launch an ambitious regional economic conference to be attended by the most wealthy nations and private enterprises in the world. The idea was that the atmosphere of economic advance and opportunity engendered by such an initiative would impact on the political situation and would make a peace treaty more or less a foregone conclusion.

King Hussein received this request from Lord Mishcon less than two weeks after he had had a very unsatisfactory meeting with Prime Minister Rabin, which was leaked to the media owing to a series of genuine mishaps surrounding Rabin's travel arrangements; he had planned to fly back from Eilat, the southern port of Israel, under cover of darkness, but a technical failure delayed the aircraft and as dawn arose, the inhabitants of the city saw his plane on the tarmac. Within minutes the secret of the nocturnal meeting was out. The king's deep-seated belief in the "conspiracy theory" of Middle East history led him to assume that the leak was intentional; after all, for so many years His Majesty had iron-clad proof of successive rounds of true conspiracy, of which he was a victim.

Thus, when the Mishcon message came to Amman, the king decided to delay his response to his friend in London, and he sent me a message asking me to receive the advice of the prime minister as to how to respond. I dutifully forwarded the request to the prime minister, who, it transpired, was not "in the loop" of this move. He elected to ask his foreign minister to "brief" him on this fresh step. Peres, so I was told, responded angrily, accusing the king of a breach of confidence; here was he, Peres, making a delicate maneuver through a personal and private friend, and the king had chosen to reveal the whole scheme of things to none other than Rabin, who was at one and the same time Peres's prime minister, archrival, and political competitor!

The decision taken was that I would accompany Peres on his secret trip and would serve as the rapporteur of the talks. Beyond what has already been said and written on the discussions held that day in Amman, I do not see any merit for embellishment. What I can affirm is that the November 2 meeting did not produce a peace treaty, since one of the items in the joint concluding paper stipulated that discreet negotiations on solving the many outstanding issues would take place at a specific venue inside Jordan.

Three weeks after the meeting I received a message requesting that I come over that very same day to meet with the king. He was in Alexandria at that time on a visit to Egypt, and he was due to land in Aqaba that evening. I went to Jordan and was flown in an aircraft of the royal squadron directly to Aqaba, where I was immediately received by a very agitated and angry monarch. He told me the following story: A few days after the November 2 meeting, an American official passed to the Jordanian foreign ministry a copy of a letter from President Clinton to King Hussein in which the American president expressed delight that Israel and Jordan had agreed to sign a peace agreement. Since His Majesty was scheduled to travel to the United States in January 1994 for a medical checkup, the president suggested that he seize the opportunity to have a

White House peace-treaty ceremony; the signed original of the letter was to follow by the diplomatic bag. The king said that he was astounded; he had not agreed to a peace treaty and he was obliged to reply to the president and to set out in detail what the actual sequence of events had been. The reaction in Washington had been one of skepticism and, at least partial, disbelief. The result of all this was that his credibility had been put in doubt, both toward his own professional staff who had not been even faintly aware of the secret discussions and contacts between us and toward the American leadership and public-service levels, who now doubted more than ever before that the king was a reliable and serious negotiator. Why was all this done to him? asked His Majesty. What had he done to be repeatedly exposed both to his own trusted staff and to the few who still believed him in Washington, D.C.? He also said that he had received a message from Yassir Arafat claiming that Israel had granted the Palestinians a special status in Jerusalem. How could Israel have done this behind his back? Was Israel not aware of the special role that the Hashemite house had in Jerusalem?

We stayed up the better part of the night and at one moment His Majesty decided to relieve the atmosphere and invited me to see a Tom Clancy movie with him at his private screening room in the Aqaba palace. He was so emotionally upset with the way things had gone for him in that month of November. At one moment that night the king asked me what Mr. Peres had told me on the issue of leasing part of Jordan's occupied land to Israel. This matter had been discussed in a for-eyes-only encounter. I replied that given the circumstances, I believed it would not be appropriate for me to tell him what Peres had said to me; if he, the king, wished to tell me what he had said, I would report it faithfully to the prime minister. Thereupon, I was told that Peres had raised the subject and had requested a lease on the land and he had received a flat no.

It was most unpleasant to be in the middle of such a situation and sandwiched, so to speak, between the two Israeli leaders; and yet there was no doubt in my mind how I should act. The prime minister was the ultimate source of authority and it was to him that I owed total loyalty. As the hours went by, I pondered my position. When I ultimately returned to Israel I would have to report back to Mr. Rabin, who, in turn, might well confront Peres with my report. It would end up with my word against his, and I was at the time a civil servant, deputy head of the Mossad, and by any yardstick, a junior to the veteran Israeli statesman. How could I insulate my position and reduce my vulnerability? After much thought, I determined that the only way open to me was to request the Jordanians to give me copies of their exchanges with Washington and a copy of the Arafat letter to His Majesty on Jerusalem. I raised the matter with the Crown Prince when I flew back to Amman, en route for home, and a few hours later was provided with the necessary copies of the documents.

On return home, I met with Rabin and before entering the room was told that he was very tired and could only spare twenty minutes for a quick review of my mission; the meeting lasted one and a half hours and he listened attentively without batting an eyelid.

The story, as I said earlier on, might be classed as somewhere between personal reflection and history, but I felt it should be told because it illustrated the frailties of human nature, the ambition of politicians and statesmen, their rivalries, jealousies and desire for recognition and adoration from their constituencies. Did the final outcome prove that history always marches on, regardless of the momentary weaknesses of the figures that strut its stage or, as I am led to believe, that often history is the victim of the drawbacks of human nature? In the end it is every individual observer who must reach his own personal verdict on this crucial element in the annals of civilization.

Back to our narrative, admittedly dictated by considerations of proportionality and expedience. The summer of 1994 wore on and the negotiating teams were getting nowhere. A new ceremony loomed on the horizon, and it was the inauguration of the southern border crossing point just to the north of Eilat and Aqaba. It took place in September and was a very colorful one. Prime Minister Rabin was there together with Foreign Minister Peres and others. On the Jordanian side it was Crown Prince Hassan who was the senior Jordanian personality on the scene. Immediately after the midmorning event, King Hussein hosted a lunch at his Aqaba palace for the Israeli delegation. Rabin and Peres were at the table, accompanied by three other personalities, and the rest of us lunched elsewhere on the palace grounds. Halfway through, I received a message and was asked to proceed to somewhere behind the palace building, where I found Prince Hassan in a state of great agitation.

Apparently, Mr. Peres had spoken to both the king and Prince Hassan and had been told that the negotiations were not making any progress. On the spot, Peres proposed that Prince Hassan and he travel secretly to Turkey, where they would board the yacht of his friend Dan Abrams. There, away from the limelight, they would work out the peace agreement without the interference of individuals who might have been, to Peres's mind, less-than-desirable participants. The king felt embarrassed by the proposal and was at a loss as to how to respond and requested that I consult with the prime minister and give him the latter's guidance. I managed to corner Rabin as the meal was ending and quickly related to him what I had heard—his reaction was swift and unmistakable. "Kill it!" he said, and the determination in his voice left no doubt whatsoever as to what he thought of this fresh enterprise.

Toward the end of September, Rabin took his first "civilian" flight to Aqaba. The negotiations had continued to bog down, and in order to create a better atmosphere, he wanted to receive Jordanian consent that a joint airport be constructed to serve both Eilat and Aqaba, and that there would be two entries and outlets enabling both Israeli and Jordanian nationals to make use of the facility, without each having to enter the "sovereign" territory of the other. The model chosen for the airport was that of Geneva, which serves France and Switzerland simultaneously. A joint group went there to study the arrangements and facilities. Given the conditions of the terrain, it was thought that the runways of the existing Aqaba airport were better suited to serve the new facility. It also became apparent that most of the personnel at the airport would be Jordanian and the prime minister believed that this was a definite plus from a political point of view. The Jordanians were hesitant, notwithstanding the obvious advantages they would enjoy, so the prime minister instructed me to raise the matter privately with His Majesty, during the nocturnal trip to Aqaba. After hearing the details, King Hussein gave his blessing to this novel project which, so we thought, had not only practical value but also symbolic importance. Nothing came of all this; the Israeli minister of transport, Mr. Kessar, objected to the whole scheme because it would lay off around fifty people employed at the airport of Eilat. He refused to countenance consideration of alternative employment and in this he was, in my opinion, supported by the Eilat municipality and the local trade union council. Thus a visionary enterprise foundered on the rocks of traditional Labor-party vested interests. Rabin had been a great states-man in leading the fractured nation to peace and historic compromise, but he was powerless to overcome the vested interests of the trade unions who were still, at that time, one of the mainstays of the Labor party.

As time went by, the cumbersome negotiating machinery of plenary sessions and numerous subcommittees was taking its toll and the powers that be on both sides resolved to take a shortcut in order to reach a speedy and successful conclusion of the exercise. It was agreed that select members of the two delegations would convene in the Aqaba residence of Prince Hassan in secrecy and over a few days would hammer out a peace treaty that would address all the issues on the table. The Jordanian delegation brought along an expert in international law, Australian-born Professor Crawford of Cambridge University, in the United Kingdom. He was the tutor of the Jordanian legal expert, Aun Hassauna, the head of the Royal Court, who much later would be appointed to the bench of the International Court of Justice in the Hague. Crawford was equipped with his own personal laptop and in no time he became the rapporteur of the entire exercise and his laptop was used by him to record the authori-tative version of the peace treaty draft. Discussions on borders, water, and a host of other issues were intense during those few days, and at the end, the differences had been sufficiently narrowed down to enable the negotiators to report to the principals that the time was ripe for a summit meeting to iron out the remaining outstanding points.

Before this could come about the issue of the territories that Jordan de-manded to be restored to its sovereignty had to be settled. The lawyers could not produce a satisfactory formula. It was clear that most of the land that had been taken over south of the Dead Sea would have to revert to Jordan. As elsewhere recorded, the size of this chunk of territory was larger than that of the Gaza Strip, but what would be the destiny of the settlements that had sprung up over the years in the Arava Valley south of the Dead Sea and all along the border? One such settlement, Tsophar, was cultivating considerable tracts of land, which, from the air, resem-bled a tight fist thrust deep into the territory of Jordan. Moreover, culti-vation of the fields was made possible only by the utilization of water that was being obtained from new wells that had been bored in Jor-danian territory even farther to the east.

The final status of these territories could not be that of a land lease.

There had to be a unique arrangement the like of which had hitherto not existed and this, of course, provided a challenge to the lawyers who always preferred to bend reality to the established rules and norms rather than to strike a new path of imaginative jurisprudence. Questions like, "How will entry into the fields be controlled?" "Will the farmers have to carry passports all the time?" or, "If a murder is committed in the fields, which law enforcement authority will conduct the investigation and, in consequence, which court of law will try the defendant?" were discussed in all seriousness by legal experts of both sides. In the end the arrangements for this area and for a parallel zone in the north were finalized. Prime Minister Rabin's instructions were that whatever the fine print, the villages in the south must be assured of their continuing cultivation of all the soil they had been tilling to date.

But how long would these provisions be in force? When would the time come for them to be renewed, or, in any case, reviewed? The negotiators on the Jordanian side had no mandate to commit themselves to a time frame, and I was therefore instructed to proceed to Amman and to raise the issue with the king himself. We met over the lunch table in the guest house of Prince Hassan and besides the host, His Majesty was accompanied by the head of the Royal Court, Aun Hassauna. The atmosphere, as usual, was cordial and informal, but it was clear that the issue on the agenda was one of the more difficult ones in the negotiations. I broached the subject after an hour or so of talk and described in vivid colors how the settlement area in the south had become a showcase of the Zionist dream of much of Israel's renowned flower-growing enterprise. The flower exchanges and markets of Europe had recognized the Israeli flowers for years as outstanding and exquisitely beautiful products, and we did not wish this branch of our economy to be damaged by the impending peace treaty. Such an eventuality could cast a heavy shadow on what was about to be achieved, and serious efforts should be made to avoid such an unfortunate development. Before responding, the king turned to the prince, and invited him to make a comment. Prince Hassan began by saying that the last thing he wished was to uproot the flower groves in the south. After the issue had been raised and had assumed the proportions it now had, he had traveled to the south to observe what was going on and to examine the terrain. Peering into his binoculars, he was able to see a great number of "slit-eyed people" working on the land;

very few others were to be seen. Was this the Zionist dream that I was talking of? the prince asked. In effect those he saw were laborers who had been hired in Thailand and who had come to work in Israel. Each Israeli farmer was allowed to employ four such farmhands. Was it this that we were now discussing?

I replied to the best of my ability and, in essence, stated that this was indeed the translation of our dream of reclaiming the deserts; it was an Israeli enterprise and initiative, and scores of Israeli pioneers had gone south to brave the scorching sun and the difficult desert conditions to build farms and to restore soil that had been wasted there for centuries. The fact that the settlers had brought in foreign labor did not detract from the pioneering nature of their deeds. Only after I had held forth at length did I spot a twinkle in the prince's eye; he was teasing me and, as always, I had fallen for the bait and he was enjoying himself listening to me defending my positions!

The time had come to address the main problem—the time frame of the temporary arrangement that had been thrashed out. The king turned to me and asked whether I thought that five years was reasonable. I shook my head from left to right, so he offered ten; this time I responded verbally, saying that this was too short a time to allow people on the ground to accustom themselves to a condition that would resemble the relations between Belgium and the Netherlands. The king went up to fifteen and as I shook my head once again he said twenty. By this time Aun Hassauna was beginning to show signs of growing agitation and as I indicated that we had not yet reached the right number, His Majesty said, "Twenty-five," whereupon Hassauna veritably exploded, urging His Majesty to go back rather than forward. I immediately realized that we could go no further and concentrated my effort on securing the twenty-five-year limit. At a given moment, His Majesty said that it would be twenty-five and that was it. Thus did we secure a quarter of a century of continued exploitation of the land in the south together with the use of the water obtained from the wells in exchange for additional water that Israel would allot to Jordan in the north.

All was set for the final negotiations, and on October 18 the prime minister and a large party of officials and senior military officers came to Amman for the final negotiations. Work went on throughout the night. The final lines were drawn and approved on the maps; the water issues were resolved by the principals and a host of other subjects were attended to. Toward early morning, it was all over and His Majesty asked, "What next?" Rabin replied that they would have to sign the draft treaty and then proceed to make arrangements for the public ceremony. His Majesty paused, and at that moment I sensed that he felt the enormous weight of the responsibility he was shouldering and the risk that he was taking. He could not but recall the death of Egyptian president Anwar Sadat who had been gunned down by Egyptian Islamic extremists only a few years after he had taken the bold initiative of reaching out to Israel and traveling to the Israeli capital of Jerusalem. In truth, I could not know what actually went through his mind at that specific moment, but he asked for a break. As he left the room Rabin quickly called me over and said to me, "Run after him, and do not leave him alone. He must not have time to rethink; this could spell disaster!" I did as I was told and followed His Majesty into a facility nearby, where we were alone for a few minutes. His Majesty drew in a deep breath and asked me what my thoughts were. I said that this was a historic moment, that he had risen to the highest levels of statesmanship, and that although there were obvious risks it was "now or never." The unique combination of him and Rabin might never be repeated. A little while later, His Majesty indicated that he would proceed, and I went back to report to Rabin that I thought all would be well.

The two principals met again, spoke on the phone to President Clinton, and informed him about the final agreement and invited him to come over to be present at the signing ceremony that was scheduled to take place a week later. The tired negotiators went away to catch a few hours' sleep in the rooms of Hashemiya Palace where they had been up all night; the arrangements were then made for a signature ceremony on the draft that was scheduled to take place toward evening. A large contingent of Israeli media people was due to fly in to cover this event. This was, for many of them, a "first," and they were, I was told, thirsting for the occasion. As I began to survey the preparations I sensed that something was wrong. At first I could not put my finger on it until it suddenly dawned on me: The king himself was not going to sign the document and he was going to delegate this to his prime minister. I reported on this at once and the prime minister was beside himself with anger. After all that he had gone through, was the king going to devalue the final act by not affixing his own signature to the treaty?

I was sent to raise the matter at once. The response was that the monarch would not sign a provisional agreement, and I was led to believe that he would do so at the Arava ceremony, which by now was already assuming the proportions of an international occasion to take place in the open air, with literally thousands of participants.

The prime minister ultimately accepted the sequence that had apparently been worked out. The provisional document was signed by the two prime ministers, with His Majesty standing behind the two and beaming with clear satisfaction.

The next few days leading up to the final act were full of action. At one point, the prime minister ordered me to travel to Amman to ascertain that there were no further last-minute surprises. I thought this a bit of overkill and thus quite unnecessary. Yet orders were orders, and when I arrived and met with Prince Hassan, he told me that the king would not be signing the treaty. Once again it would be Prime Minister Majali who would be affixing his signature on behalf of his country. I telephoned Jerusalem on my mobile phone and the reaction was such that everyone in the room could understand what the gist was of what had been said. I was led, more or less, to understand that I had botched the whole project and that it was up to me to solve the matter. There was a hint that the prime minister might cancel or postpone the whole enterprise until the problem had been solved.

My Jordanian interlocutors explained to me that His Majesty was barred by the constitution from signing a peace treaty or any treaty with a foreign country, for that matter, until the document had been discussed and approved by parliament. Professor Crawford, from the Aqaba negotiating round, had been consulted on this and had affirmed this interpretation of the constitution. Moreover, Prince Hassan, who was discussing the issue with me, said that if we insisted on the signature of His Majesty, the consequence would be that he, personally, was making his peace with Israel, but that the state of Jordan was not committed to the treaty. This would have a very negative effect on the exercise as a whole; it would mean, on the one hand, that the people of Jordan, as opposed to the monarch himself, were not a partner to the entire process and that, on the other hand, the king would personally exposed as an individual, who had made his private peace with the erstwhile enemy—Israel. I asked to see His Majesty, but the request was turned down. He was too busy to meet with me and I well understood that he was signaling that nothing could change his position.

After much discussion, we put together a package, which, so I believed, would give satisfaction to both sides and would cater to the substantive necessities of both Israel and Jordan: The Arava ceremony would proceed as planned and the peace treaty would be signed by the two prime ministers and President Clinton, as a witness and a de facto guarantor of the peace. The treaty would then be brought for ratification before the parliaments of Jordan and Israel. Subsequent to this, His Majesty would pay a first public visit to Israel, landing on the Israeli side of Lake Galilee, and would give Prime Minister Rabin a signed letter stating that the treaty had been ratified by the appropriate authorities in Jordan. Thus the king's signature would appear on an official document related to the peace treaty, all the relevant organs of government in Jordan would be on board regarding the treaty, and Prime Minister Rabin would openly host His Majesty on Israeli soil.

Prime Minister Rabin approved the formula and we were dead set for the final act. Or were we? It had been agreed by us and the Jordanians that regarding the signature of the draft document, no change would be made in the details of the ceremony or on any related issue without mutual consent. Less than twenty-four hours before the ceremony, I received a call from the Israeli foreign ministry telling me that they had agreed to a change in the procedure and that at the request of Russia, there would be an additional signatory to the treaty in the role of witness and it would be a representative of Russia. I told my friends in the foreign ministry that they had no authority to approve changes in the ceremony without my consent and that this also required Jordanian approval. I expressed surprise and immediately called my Jordanian colleagues. Marwan Al Qassem, a close adviser of His Majesty, spoke to me and said that they had indeed accepted the Russian request. "You will need the Russians in your negotiations with the Syrians," he said to me. I told him he need not worry about us and our negotiations with the Syrians. There was an American partner to this and it was not possible to make changes of this nature without consulting with Washington.

When the Americans were told of this last-minute development, reaction from the White House was swift. President Clinton would sign the treaty only if he were the sole signatory. If others would sign, then Secretary of State Christopher would be the most senior American to sign the paper; there was even a faint intimation that the president, who was already on his way, might turn around and head back for Washington. This position was doubly enforced when it became clear that Russian president Yeltsin would not be attending the event himself, but that Foreign Minister Kozyrev would be on hand carrying the title of personal representative of the president. The United States was adamant, and in the end President Clinton was the sole person signing officially as a witness. Following the act of the three signatories, the two prime ministers and the president, others were invited to sign the treaty on the side: Kozyrev signed, as did Foreign Minister Peres, Secretary of State Christopher, and the German foreign minister, Klaus Kinkel, who represented the European Union.

I continued to remain in contact with the powers that be in Jordan for many years after the act of the treaty and to enjoy the confidence of both sides of the divide, regardless of the personnel changes that came about as the years went by. Yet one "prize" eluded me. Mr. Rabin wished me to serve as the first Israeli ambassador to Jordan and this desire of his was welcomed top-down in Amman. However, this was not to come about, and I was not appointed as ambassador. For several months the post remained vacant and the media in Israel published reports that I was to all intents and purposes non grata in Jordan due to my being a Mossad officer. This was patently untrue, but the campaign persisted. At one stage I suggested to Rabin that I go and see Peres. At the meeting Peres was blunt and clear: He said that if I were appointed, I would be the envoy of the prime minister and he would be out of the loop to all intents and purposes. This was a state of affairs he could never accept. In light of this, I withdrew my candidacy for the post and prepared to leave the Mossad in October 1995.

Peres had second thoughts, and, at the instigation of the prime minister, offered me an ambassadorial appointment in one of the six embassies around the world. After some thought, I asked for the position of Israeli ambassador to the European Union. This was granted and I went around to make my farewells. A large reception was scheduled to take place on November 8 at the Mossad headquarters and Prime Minister Rabin was scheduled to be there and to honor me on the occasion. Four days before the event, Rabin was brutally assassinated and, of course, I attended his funeral in Jerusalem. Needless to say, the reception was cancelled. Nobody, least of all myself, was in any mood to celebrate. Mr. Peres succeeded Rabin as prime minister for a brief six months and then lost the general election to Benjamin Netanyahu. How providential it was that I never made it as ambassador to Amman; I could never have served as the personal envoy of Peres there, and what is much more significant, I could never have played a future role in saving the peace treaty a few years later in circumstances yet to be told.

The interplay of personalities as depicted in this restricted tableau of the Jordanian file is, to my mind, representative of so much that has happened in this part of the world, as events played themselves out on the stage of history in ways reminiscent of days and eras gone by. It was this preoccupation of mine as a forty-year-career intelligence officer, my fascination with human nature and human behavior, that led me to the best of my successes and to the worst of my failures. More anon.

8

REMEMBERING LEADERS
AND THEIR COUNTRIES

The description of the advent of the Jordanian-Israeli peace treaty high-lights the essential ingredients necessary to produce a breakthrough in policy between nations. It demonstrates the need for principals com-mitted, basically, to achieving a break with the past and possessing a vision that transcends the present. It demonstrates the need for a small and select group of senior public officials at the executive level who are determined to see an enterprise or endeavors through to conclusion. It also shows how these senior officials function as originators of op-tions and ideas, as well as shock absorbers who prevent the total col-lapse of dialogues in the face of disagreements and, at times, major confrontations.

The truth needs to be stated unequivocally: More often than not there has been very little love lost between the principals and they have often, in private, been not only critical but also scornful of their interlocutors. The egos of the players involved, the respect and deference they showed to each other, and the constraints placed on them by their domestic constituencies are only a few of the issues that have fashioned the march of history throughout the ages. It is only appropriate and relevant that attention be given to some of these before we proceed with relating the sequence of events.

Yassir Arafat, or Abu Amaar, as he was also known, was without doubt a key figure in the decade that transformed the world and set it on its new trajectory. At the turn of the nineties, the Palestinian independence movement had reached one of its all-time lows. Arafat had tilted during the Gulf War in the direction of Saddam Hussein and, having ended up on the losing side, was in no position to launch a successful campaign against Israel or its ally, the United States. And yet, despite this initial disadvantage, there was a deep reservoir of sympathy for the cause of the Palestinians in Washington, D.C. There were those in the administration of President George H. W. Bush who were conscious of a vicious backlash against the United States, which had swept through the Arab and Muslim world in the aftermath of the victory of the American-led coalition that had defeated the regime of Saddam Hussein, but left the entire political edifice in Baghdad intact. Spurred on by the Arab allies of the United States in the coalition it had put together, the American administration initiated the Madrid conference, led it, and succeeded in promoting three negotiating tracks: the first between Israel and Syria; the second between Israel and Jordan; and the third between Israel and the Palestinians appearing under a Jordanian umbrella.

The relatively weakened state and status of the Palestinian movement produced a spate of efforts to create a new political process. After a change of government in Israel in the summer of 1992 and the ascendancy of Yitzhak Rabin to the premiership in Israel, it became possible to give a fresh start to Israeli-Palestinian reconciliation. For Yassir Arafat, this was a golden opportunity. He was able to envisage a move from exile in Tunisia, and a return to a part of Palestine that had been taken over by Israel during the Six-Day War of 1967. Arafat and his organization were not combatants in that war; the war had been fought between Israel and three Arab states—Egypt, Syria, and Jordan—and the territories that Israel had then "liberated" or "occupied" (depending on one's political views) had been administered up to that time by Arab states and not by the Palestinians themselves. Those Arab states had not granted independence to the Palestinians, and indeed, the latter had at that time been much too weak and disorganized even to contemplate any form or semblance of self-rule of any kind. The results of the Yom Kippur War of

1973 gave the Palestinians no option at all. When they began amassing in Lebanon, in the second half of the seventies, and carried out acts of terror against Israel, Israel entered Lebanon in 1982. The practical outcome of this and the exile of the Palestinian leadership to Tunisia propelled the Palestinian leader away from the inner circle of the Middle East. That Arafat was able over so many years to lead his people and to almost literally force the Arab world and the powers that be in the world at large to recognize the validity of the cause he personified was, without doubt, a singular success equal to very few achievements reached under similar circumstances. In the final analysis, though, his was a failed leadership. Many have already written about him from various vantage points. I would like to approach my estimate of Arafat from the vantage point of an intelligence officer.

It was only after the Six-Day War of 1967 that Arafat and his Palestinian Liberation Organization came to the fore as a factor to be reckoned with in the Middle East equation. It is pertinent to recall that the 1967 war was, among other things, a confrontation between major world powers. Israel was supported up to a point by the free world, which included the United States, while the Egyptians and Syrians, Israel's principal opponents, had been armed to the hilt by the Soviet Union. In one sense this was a war fought on international terms by proxies and the resounding defeat of the Arab side was, at the same time, a major setback for the Soviet Union. Russia, the leading component of the union, had a formidable interest in the Middle East that stretched back to precommunist times and, as such, any reversal of fortune like the one experienced in 1967 was evaluated, rightly, as a strategic setback.

In 1967, how did Arafat perform on the international scene and how did his performance affect the national cause that he was espousing? A short while after the Six-Day War, the government of Israel approved a decision, whereby the territories that had fallen into Israeli hands in the wake of the war would be considered as cards in a future negotiation, to be, in effect, traded for peace with the Arab world, including, of course, the Palestinians. This olive branch, extended to the Arab states and by implication to the Palestinians, was rejected by them because it included, of course, the acceptance and recognition of the State of Israel and its right to exist. The existence of this government of Israel decision is public knowledge, although seldom quoted. What is less known is that

during the year following the war, a great effort was made by Israel security agencies to track down and to apprehend Arafat, who was hiding
inside the territories and constantly on the move. Within a short time
before the end of the war, armed resistance had already been launched in
the territories, especially in the West Bank, previously under Jordanian
occupation, and armed squads engaged in combat with Israeli forces and
often gave them a serious run for their money. In the end all these groups
were killed or captured, but Israel had, on occasion, suffered grievous
losses, including those of high-ranking officers. Parts of the West Bank
became known as the "land of pursuit" because they had become the
scene of many a battle and many an encounter.

Contrary to common knowledge, the desire to establish contact with
Arafat was not entirely motivated by the need to put an end to the violence that had begun to take its toll. There was a parallel move, set in
motion, to meet with the Palestinian leader in a conscious endeavor to set
in motion a substantive political dialogue between the two warring sides.
This initiative that was approved at the highest political level of the day
made no headway whatsoever. It was summarily rejected by Arafat, who
was bent on leading an armed struggle. Palestine was destined to be re-
deemed in death and blood and from the end of 1968, for a period of
twenty years, this was to be the only policy of Arafat on the "Palestinian
issue."

The late sixties and early seventies would become formative years for
Arafat. He was clandestinely bundled onto an aircraft in Cairo in 1968
and traveled with Egypt's pro-Soviet president Gamal Abdel Nasser to
Moscow where, among other activities, he was to meet with senior Soviet KGB officers who would maintain contact with him from that time
on. He would never become an "agent" in the technical professional
sense of the term; but he would be serviced by his handlers and would,
through them as well, acquire a deep love of, and obsession with, espionage and intelligence. He would learn how to "play" with information,
how to make use of genuine intelligence in the service of his cause, how
to trade intelligence with foreign services and obtain benefits in return,
and how to engage in disinformation and take it to the ultimate bounds
of absurdity.

Over the years, the leaders of the region took their measure of him
and unanimously branded him as a compulsive liar and as a person who

would never honor a commitment and rarely would have anything but contempt for his peers. This latter attribute quickly became mutual.

He had a weird preoccupation with money and funding. He himself largely led a spartan life, but he reveled in dabbling with enormous sums of money and in amassing assets the world over, ostensibly to support and fund the struggle.

With the passage of time, he shunned every attempt to reach a real resolution of the Palestinian plight and he blocked almost every attempt to establish a credible and reliable channel of dialogue between himself and the Israeli adversary. Indeed, he had many channels with generations of Israeli political figures and their aides and he did, on occasion, use these channels for relatively brief periods of communication. Yet, inevitably, these supposedly "safe and secure" channels were abused by him whenever he thought this would serve a momentary purpose of his. Time and time again, he resorted to fantasy, in order to achieve his goals, and although it was obvious on more than one occasion that he was disseminating pure, unadulterated falsehoods, he was not deterred from resorting to this stratagem repeatedly. Two unrelated incidents are worthy of mention in this context.

In May 2001, a deadly terrorist attack took place in a Tel Aviv nightclub close to the seashore of the city. Twenty young Israelis lost their lives that evening at the Dolphinarium club, and the following morning, on holy Saturday, the Israeli cabinet convened in an emergency session to discuss the situation and to decide on an appropriate reaction. The German foreign minister, Joschka Fischer, was by coincidence visiting Israel at the time and he, alongside other world leaders, joined in a diplomatic effort to restrain Israel, on the one hand, and, on the other, to galvanize Yassir Arafat into some kind of action designed to lower the level of terrorist activity directed against Israeli civilian targets and the civilian population of the country. Arafat countered the pressure that was building up against him by uttering the claim that the terrorist act was no less than an Israeli provocative operation perpetrated by the Mossad, which I was heading at the time. The obnoxious accusation was not a one-time lapse of the senses. It was repeated again and again by Arafat in all his meetings with the media and with foreign dignitaries. The utter absurdity of this claim was, needless to say, devoid of any fragment of evidence, which in any case did not exist, and did not remain a solitary statement of this kind.

Several months later, an Israeli cabinet minister, Rehavam Ze'evi, was murdered by Palestinian assailants in a prominent Jerusalem hotel, where he used to stay when in the capital of Israel. It was on October 17, 2001, and I happened to be traveling outside Israel to meet a leading Arab statesman. My interlocutor immediately told me that he assumed that the act had been that of an extreme terrorist group in the Palestinian camp. Ze'evi was known for his right-wing views in Israel; he had headed the National Union Movement, the most right-wing element in the cabinet, and his particular group within the union advocated the transfer of Palestinians living in the West Bank to Arab states where they would be settled and rehabilitated. Arafat immediately let it be known that this was yet another provocative act executed by the Mossad, at the time, again, under my command. This time, Arafat did not content himself with leveling the general accusation. He used a trip to Europe that he had laid on previously to describe to his listeners exactly how the whole operation had been carried out. It so happened that by sheer coincidence I traveled that week through Europe and met many of Arafat's interlocutors. From stop to stop I was treated to ever more detailed accounts of the operation that I had supposedly masterminded. There was no end to the embellishments that were added, stop after stop, and it fell to me to refute every one of the details and the heinous fabrication as a whole.

The repulsive nature of this particular accusation was compounded by the fact that the murdered minister happened to be a person whom I knew very well and with whom I had worked on several occasions when he served as a general in the Israel Defense Forces at the time I occupied operational positions in the Mossad. He was a highly respected and valued officer. He had been promoted to the rank of full general on the very same day that Ariel Sharon had received his promotion. He was a very thorough and meticulous officer and it was an honor and pleasure to work alongside him. As a cabinet minister I saw him very often and, as a matter of fact, usually found myself seated next to him at the end of the cabinet table; we talked very often during the long hours of cabinet sessions and although I was miles apart from his political views, I found some of his practical suggestions on purely operational issues stimulating, at times very original. Ze'evi or "Gandhi," which was the nickname whereby he was commonly known, served several years as a member of the prestigious parliamentary subcommittee on intelligence and the intelligence services, and I could always count upon him for support when I met the committee and reported to it on the activities of the Mossad. To remotely associate me with the death of this man, a friend, and a colleague, was for me a travesty of basic human decency.

But beyond that personal aspect of the issue at hand, I tried in those days to fathom the thoughts and emotional composition of a man, a political leader who was the anointed symbol of an entire national movement and who was able to resort to stratagems like one just described, which were at one and the same time debased and ridiculous. Did, or could, Arafat really believe that what he was saying had any truth whatsoever to it? If he knew that what he was saying was indeed utterly false, how could he ever expect to be accepted as a credible partner for any serious dialogue of any kind? I often raised this subject with my Arab interlocutors, who invariably responded by saying something on the order of, "Are you telling me about Arafat's lying and prevarications? This is nothing compared to what I have to tell you!" Indeed, Arafat had reached a degree of infamy in the circles of leadership in the Arab world that was an all-time record. There was, of course, a second interpretation of Arafat's behavior, that he actually believed that what he was saying was true; this, of course, had different consequences, primarily that he lived and functioned in a world of fantasy and that he therefore did not relate in practical terms to life the way it was. The practical outcome of this line of analysis would have to be that one could not negotiate with a person who was divorced from reality.

And yet, in some respects, Arafat was a very practical and pragmatic leader. He knew the relative value of every figure surrounding him and exhibited an uncanny capacity to play individuals and groups against each other, and thus to assure his survival at the helm of his movement. And he had a singular capacity to amass funds and to dispense them personally in order to buy loyalties and support.

The only time I saw Arafat face-to-face was when I served as Israeli ambassador to the European Union with my embassy located in Brussels. It was in the winter of 1997, and the then Israeli foreign minister, David Levy, was about to pay a periodic visit and to have a meeting with the council of foreign ministers of the European Union. At that point in time the relations between Israel and the Palestinian Authority were going through one of their recurrent spells of rupture. The European Union decided to step into the breach and to invite Arafat to come to Brussels, where the Europeans would engineer a joint appearance of himself and Foreign Minister Levy at the council meeting. I was instructed by the minister's office to oppose the initiative. Levy was scheduled to have his own meeting with the plenary of the foreign ministers and here was Arafat who was about to jump on the bandwagon and to enjoy the spot together with the Israeli statesman. In the end, a compromise of sorts was worked out. Arafat and Levy each appeared separately at the council of ministers and we agreed that a separate meeting between Arafat and Levy would be held under the auspices of and with the participation of the officials of the Union.

It was at this separate meeting that I met the man for, what was for me, the first and the last time. The meeting began with some words of introduction by the host, the foreign minister of Luxembourg, which held the rotating chair of the Union during that six-month period. Foreign Minister Levy was then given the floor and he launched into a very detailed exposé, speaking in Hebrew which was translated simultaneously into English and French. It was a very cold day, the rooms of the Union were, as they often are, considerably overheated, and gradually several of those present began to doze off and to sink into a pleasant, carefree sleep. Most prominent among those who were dozing off was Arafat, and when Levy concluded his exceptionally long discourse, a strange silence reigned in the room. Nobody took it upon himself to awaken Arafat and invite him to express himself. After a short silence, Nabil Sha'ath, the Palestinian Authority foreign minister, took the floor and responded to the words and thoughts of Levy and after a relatively short while a general discussion developed over a number of practical issues that had become bones of contention between the two opposing sides in the Middle East. One such pair of issues was the desire of the Palestinians to reactivate their airport in the Gaza Strip that Israel had rendered inoperative due to its use as a channel for smuggling arms into the Strip and their demand that they be allowed to construct a deepwater port off the town of Gaza that could serve the Palestinians for the import and export of goods, thus relieving them of the necessity to use Israeli ports as the sole access to the Strip. These two projects were favorites of the European Union, which had undertaken to fund key elements of the two showcase enterprises.

Discussion on the projects went on in an atmosphere of what appeared to be a genuine attempt at cooperation and, inevitably, the question of monitoring the goods arriving in the proposed port and checking them security-wise to prevent the entry of war materiel of any type took center stage. At this point, the Union representatives announced that the government of the Netherlands had earmarked the sum of twenty-five million dollars to finance the purchase of the necessary equipment to ensure effective monitoring. Arafat, instinctively, literally jumped up in his seat and, in a rapid stream of words, was heard saying in English: "Twenty-five million dollars! What twenty-five million dollars? How twenty-five million dollars?" It was clear that he had no idea what subject was being discussed, but the moment his sleeping ears caught the mention of the sum of money, he was as alert as any person could be!

What surprised me at that meeting was not only the outburst in itself but, no less, the way his Palestinian subordinates and collaborators took the event in their stride. It did not upset them at all. This singular preoccupation with monies and worldly assets was a well-known trait of the Palestinian leader. The channeling of E.U. funds to the Palestinian Authority to unofficial or semiofficial accounts was a bone of contention that often troubled many an honest official of the Union. Arafat used to approach Union officials or influential European foreign ministers from time to time with requests for "emergency funding" to the tune of twenty or twenty-five million dollars here and there. I recall on one occasion, being in the office of one of the senior commissioners of the union when he received a call from a leading European foreign minister. The latter launched into a castigating condemnation of the way the commission had handled a very recent request of Arafat for "emergency" funding. "Surely," said the respectable minister, "you must have understood that this type of funding should not have been transferred to the normal accounts. Arafat has complained bitterly about this and we must find a way of arranging matters." The commissioner asked the minister for a few minutes' pause and then turned to me and politely asked me to excuse him because he had to attend to the matter at hand. I left, of course, but not before my host had unburdened himself and had expressed his exasperation at the way he was being forced to cooperate in these matters.

What Arafat lacked in the end was a true understanding of the basic rules of conduct in international affairs, an ignorance that was to result in his being totally and finally discredited as a credible interlocutor. The first rule was, and will remain for a long time to come, that a political master, a head of state or prime minister or leader of a national movement, must never lie to the president of the United States. All Arafat's falsehoods and prevarications did not disqualify him as long as he made certain not to entertain such behavior vis-à-vis the United States and its president. Arafat was specifically caught red-handed when he disclaimed knowledge of, let alone complicity in, the purchase of a shipment of high-quality arms in Iran and their dispatch on board a ship named *Karin A;* the boat was apprehended on the high seas about five hundred nautical miles south of Eilat by the Israeli navy and it was brought with its crew to Eilat, where the shipment was put on display for all to see. The Israeli intelligence community was able to gather the information on this adventure of the Palestinian Authority in good time and to provide the navy with the highest-grade information, enabling it to make a perfect catch. Israel was able not only to apprehend the shipment in 2001, but also to pass the intelligence to the United States in such a convincing manner as to not only prove the case of the caught ship and its cargo but also to highlight Arafat's deliberate misrepresentation of the facts. A subsequent admission wrung from Arafat in the form of a letter from him to Secretary of State Colin Powell could not undo the irreparable damage caused to the image and standing of Arafat in Washington. Both had been shattered beyond repair.

The second basic rule that all players had to learn in pursuit of their policies was that no one can survive if he tries to exploit the president of the United States. This was a bitter lesson that Arafat learned after he had twice used the president of the United States for his own gain. The first time was at the Camp David conference in the summer of 2000, and the second was when President Clinton came to the Middle East in the twilight of his reign in a final effort to effect a mutual reconciliation between Israel and the Palestinians. Sending President Clinton back to Washington with empty hands was an act of sheer political stupidity for which Arafat paid the ultimate political price long before he died. He was, thereafter, dubbed by all—including his closest colleagues—as an obstacle to peace.

Of the traditional leaders of the Arab world—President Mubarak of

Egypt, King Hussein of Jordan, and President Assad of Syria—each had had his experiences with Arafat that led him to regard Arafat as an impediment to any progress of any kind in the region. Assad severed his contacts with Arafat when the latter decided to go his own way and to negotiate with Israel, secretly and separately. Arafat was boycotted to all intents and purposes by Damascus until he died in Paris, a lonely, almost abandoned leader. As far as President Mubarak was concerned, Arafat constituted a threat to the security of the state and to the stability of the Egyptian regime in that he led his people on the path of violence, and thereby aroused the nationalistic emotions of the general populance in Cairo and throughout the whole country. Arafat's theatrical performances embarrassed the Egyptian president on many an occasion, but the latter nevertheless felt bound by a commitment to the Palestinian cause, which was a source of identification for the Egyptian people as a whole. And yet a moment of truth came about in April 2002 when the level of Palestinian violence against Israel and Israeli civilians reached unprecedented proportions. The Israeli cabinet, meeting on the morrow of Passover night to discuss the consequences of a particularly brutal attack on a hotel in Netanya, a popular tourist seaside resort, approved a massive operation of the IDF, who immediately entered the Palestinian Authority territory in the West Bank and launched attacks designed to break the back of the terrorist network functioning throughout the area. Pressure on the Palestinians reached extreme proportions and Arafat countered, inter alia, by calling upon the Arab masses in the Arab states to rise up and to demonstrate in the streets of Arab capitals in order to mount pressure on Arab leaders to suspend or even sever their relations with Israel. And, indeed, the streets of Cairo, Amman, and other capitals witnessed violent demonstrations, even resulting in a few dead; this was one step too far for President Mubarak. The peace treaty that his predecessor, the late, assassinated Anwar Sadat, had concluded with Israel was considered a strategic asset of the state of Egypt and whatever the strains that characterized the Egyptian-Israeli relationship during the signing of the treaty on the White House lawn in Washington, D.C., from time to time, no responsible Egyptian figure would think otherwise of this key component in Egypt's overall strategy. An attempt by a third party, especially Arafat, to subordinate Egyptian key interests to the desires of the Palestinians was not only doomed to be rejected, but also was destined to cast a shadow, a very dark shadow, on Egypt's approach to the Palestinians.

This move by Arafat, at the height of the Palestinian-armed *intifada* against Israel, dealt an almost fatal blow to the Palestinian national cause. It created a unique opening for Israel to engage the Egyptians in meaningful discussions on the future of the Palestinian saga. It gradually created a climate of serious cooperation between Israel, Egypt, Jordan, and many other Arab and Muslim states on the concept of promoting the notion that the Palestinians needed to produce a new leadership, to institute wide-ranging reforms in the structure of both their security services and their civilian organs of government.

Another leader of the region who had a similar reaction to Arafat was King Hussein of Jordan, whom Arafat had attempted to overthrow in August–September 1970. He never forgot the clear moves by the Palestinians to assassinate him and his family. After the peace treaty between Israel and Jordan had been signed, the Palestinians spared no effort to prevent tripartite trade relations from developing, let alone flourishing. In this case, it became apparent, again, that the Palestinians would go to any length to sabotage Jordanian attempts to gain advantage from the new circumstances. Indeed, on many occasions, the Palestinians tried to force Israel to choose between them and the Jordanians, and these predicaments were not always easy to solve.

IT IS TIME NOW TO TURN TO EGYPT'S ROLE IN THE MIDDLE EAST, ITS MA-jor figures, and how its participation was viewed on both the regional and the international scene. Egypt has always cast itself in the role of a regional power. Straddling the continents of Asia and Africa, its interests have reached deep into the dark continent in the south and southwest. It has aspired to leadership of the Arab world and to a central role in the community of Islamic nations and, as a major littoral nation on the southern shores of the Mediterranean Sea, it has claimed a key position in determining the political, economic, and cultural future of the countries and cultures surrounding the sea. This long list of aspirations understandably has shaped the character and content of Egypt's modern leadership. Beyond Egypt's "Pharaonic" posture, the new leadership of post-regal days envisaged Egypt as performing, inter alia, on the international scene. Egypt in the eyes of Nasser, Sadat, and Mubarak was cast in the role of a world player, which, on the one hand, was capable of mustering significant support in the international community for causes, and, on the other hand, had to pay the price of membership in this club of select nations. Indeed, the more junior the member in the club, the greater the "fee" that had to be paid in order to continue to benefit from the advantages of such a membership.

In this respect, there has been a resemblance between Israel and Egypt in the method each adopted in their approach to basic strategies. This became especially evident after Sadat assumed the presidency and almost immediately began steering Egypt away from dependency on and identification with the then Soviet Union. Following the Yom Kippur War of 1973, the Egyptian leadership openly turned to the United States and recognized it as the sole serious broker in the Israeli-Arab conflict. All the other players—the Soviet Union, the European Union, and all the other leading nations of the world, as well as the U.N.—were relegated to a secondary status. Egypt was the first Arab state in the region that signed its peace with Israel. It was the first state that chose and enjoyed the privilege of having the signing ceremony take place on the White House lawn.

President Mubarak, who succeeded the murdered President Sadat, a man who literally lost his life in the cause of peace with Israel, took this concept of Egyptian policies several steps further. He led Egypt to stand beside the United States in two successive campaigns directed against an Arab state—Iraq—and he placed his country firmly on the side of Washington and the free world in its gigantic struggle against international Islamic terror. These steps were far from technical or ceremonial. The successes of the international intelligence community in its battle against terrorism would not have been possible without the active support of Egypt. The cooperation that Egypt extended to the United States in facilitating interrogations of major terrorist suspects, apprehended by American agencies and then transferred to Cairo for debriefing, has now become public knowledge. The process labeled "rendition" was a means of avoiding the necessity to resort to the traditional procedure of extradition that would most likely be inapplicable in the case of these particular individuals. By doing this, President Mubarak had the courage and conviction to resort to steps that were extremely unpopular in his own country and to provide the violent extremist Islamic elements in Egypt with added reasons to propagate hate and destruction from within. At the same time, the singular contributions that Egypt rendered to the most profound security interests of the United States cemented a bond between the two countries that would serve Egypt well in the years to come.

This was not the only price that was paid in the pursuit of this strategy and its concomitant policies. Although the peace with Israel was officially billed as a fundamental interest of Egypt, the regime nevertheless not only allowed but often encouraged a public vilification of Israel to rage constantly in the press and in the electronic media. The demonization of Israel and its leaders, particularly the prime minister Ariel Sharon, took on enormous proportions, and all Israel's requests and, at times, demands that this campaign be halted remained unsatisfied. The glaring contradiction between the overt and the covert relationship was keenly felt by myself and by others close to me who performed similar missions. Whereas behind closed doors there was much mutual understanding and interest, and a great deal could be and was accomplished, the hostile atmosphere from without often reached the boiling point.

I believe the major turning point came at the height of the tension engendered by the Palestinians after the IDF entered the cities and areas of the West Bank in the spring of 2002. The demonstrations in the streets of Cairo, incited by the Palestinians as a movement and by Arafat, in person, sounded an ominous warning note in the corridors of power on the bank of the Nile. The Palestinians demanded that Egypt take visible action against Israel on the bilateral level, that the Israeli ambassador in Cairo be asked to leave, and that the embassy be closed or considerably restricted in manpower. Years before, Egypt had withdrawn its ambassador from Israel in protest against Israeli activities in the region, but the embassy was left to function under a chargé d'affaires with a big and active staff. Now the moment of truth had arrived. Would Egypt take action or not? I well remember those days and recall thinking that if the Egyptians succumbed to Arafat's demands, there could be no end to further demands and what could be, in effect, political blackmail. After several days of deliberations, a statement emerged from Cairo couched in terms that necessitated repeated perusal and interpretation. The Egyptians had elected to sit on their hands and to take no action whatsoever. I believe this was the ultimate watershed in the whole equation. President

Mubarak had decided not only to reject the brazen Palestinian demand to make sacrifices—Egyptian sacrifices—in the Palestinian cause. He had identified a threat to Egypt and to Egyptian interests in the moves initiated by Arafat, and from that moment on, he had accepted the basic premise that the future of the Palestinians was dependent on a leadership change and on a set of reforms that would propel the region as a whole and the Palestinians into a new and promising era.

It would take another three years and the demise of Arafat to obtain an overt manifestation of this dramatic change in Egyptian policy. President Mubarak would continue, during that period, to refrain from sending a new ambassador to Israel and his press would continue to rail against Israel as never before. He would also resist suggestions that he meet Prime Minister Sharon, for the first time, and he would refuse to release an Israeli Druze citizen, Azzam Azzam, languishing in an Egyptian jail after having been sentenced on a charge of espionage that was devoid of any basis. (Not until 2005, after the virtual end of the Palestinian uprising, would Azzam Azzam be released, as Egypt assumed a growing role in the implementation of Israel's disengagement plan.) And yet, as stated, the Rubicon had been crossed in the spring of 2002. President Mubarak had accepted that Arafat was an obstacle to any progress. Although he differed with Israel on some of the methodology that was to be used in order to achieve the practical result on the ground, close aides— in particular General Omar Soleiman, the supreme head of the Egyptian intelligence community—swung into action with the aim of obtaining the desired result. Arafat, born and bred in Egypt (and not, as his self-serving legend would have it, in Jerusalem), had come full circle. His traditional mentors were now set to divest themselves of him.

KING HUSSEIN WAS ANOTHER PROMINENT FIGURE IN THE MIDDLE EAST conundrum. His reign spanned forty-six years and all the wars between Israel and the Arab world, except for Israel's 1948 War of Independence. During this exceptionally long period of time he entered into alliances of sorts with all the countries surrounding him and he knew ups and downs in the relationship with every one of them. He became, as years went by, a consummate player on the board and developed a knack for sensing when to change course and when to replace one alliance with another.

This unique sense stood him well, except on one occasion, the first Gulf War, when he "tilted" in the direction of Iraq led by Saddam Hussein. His secret understanding with Prime Minister Shamir was crucial at the time in saving the kingdom and the dynasty. His recognition of this rendered him eternally appreciative and grateful as of then. The detailed description of the denouement of the Jordanian peace with Israel clearly illuminates the sovereign's qualities and capacities. More need not be said.

THINKING REGIONALLY, I ALSO REMEMBER HAFIZ AL-ASSAD OF SYRIA. Like President Mubarak, he reached the top through a military career ending in a stint as commander of his country's air force. Both he and Mubarak had received training in the Soviet Union. Yet, unlike Arafat, neither leader became obsessed with intelligence and manipulation of information. Assad developed a strategic relationship with the Soviet Union. He was the recipient of billions of dollars' worth of advanced equipment, aircraft, surface-to-air missiles, armor, and electronic warfare systems. When Sadat parted ways with Moscow in the mid-seventies, and before he flew on his dramatic and historic visit to Jerusalem, the capital of Israel, the Egyptian president came to Damascus and made an offer to his Syrian colleague to accompany him and to do a deal with Israel together. Assad declined; he preferred to stay with his Soviet mentors and to achieve, through them, what he termed a strategic balance with Israel. He assembled an impressive array of support to complement the massive Soviet aid he was receiving. He struck a deal with North Korea to purchase Scud-C and Scud-D surface-to-surface missiles and obtain from Pyongyang a production line for this modern-day equipment. He hosted Pakistani and other individuals who had expertise in the field of nuclear warfare and he also developed his own home-made capacities in the chemical warfare field. Following the Khomeini revolution in Iran, Assad cultivated a strategic link with the Shiite regime in Tehran and permitted it to use Syria as a transit area for channeling aid and weaponry to the nonstate Shiite Hizbollah force in Lebanon, deployed along the southern area of Lebanon, close to Israel. Assad also sanctioned activities of the Hizbollah directed against Israel and tacitly cooperated in allowing this movement to create and maintain an international terrorist network spanning five continents of the earth.

It was Assad's hope that the combined weight of all his efforts would give him the necessary leverage he needed in his relationship with both the United States and Israel.

Assad played his cards on the international scene in a very astute manner. When it came to purveying terrorism, he cleverly appeared to distance himself from active practice of this form of "combat." In the seventies and eighties, he still maintained an independent capacity in this arena, and senior officers of his, not surprisingly emerging from the air force, were in command of this branch of activity, but his visibility on the larger landscape appeared to evaporate and in the nineties he seemed to restrict his dabbling in terror to the Lebanese scene and to the provision of safe haven and facilities for a group of the more extreme Palestinian groups, including the Khammas and the Islamic Jihad movements. With these carefully crafted strategies in his possession, Assad devoted the greater part of the nineties to negotiating with Israel in various shapes and forms through the auspices of the United States. Successive American secretaries of state (Baker and Christopher being the most prominent) carried out prolonged shuttle-diplomacy missions between Jerusalem and Damascus, and President Clinton himself became involved in a supreme attempt to finalize a deal between Israel and he who was considered its bitterest of foes. The "prize" that eluded the negotiators was not purely a Syrian-Israeli peace. The view held at the time both in Jerusalem and in Washington was that if Syria were to come in, the entire Arab world would follow suit. Assad, who was conscious of this view held by his interlocutors, exploited this to the full and proved to be a tough negotiator and an unyielding one. What often gave me personally much food for thought was the way the Syrian dictator, for that is what he was, had succeeded in using the Soviet Union and its massive aid as a lever in his dealings with the United States. This was a testament not only to his singular capacity to manipulate international support to his advantage. The fact that Moscow continued to maintain a sizable military advisory presence in Damascus during all those years and the decision of the Russian leadership to continue supporting Damascus, albeit at a reduced scale, seemed to prove that Assad had assessed his Soviet mentors correctly. In the absence of better alternatives, they had to settle with what they had and, to some extent, on the conditions set by the client rather than on those of the supplier.

As Jerusalem had long realized, Assad was the master strategist of the region. He was able to put together a performance, the like of which none of his equals was able to match. And yet, when he died, he left his people, his country, and his Alawite minority tribe without the coveted prize—restoration of the Golan Heights to Syrian rule—the greatest goal he had set for himself. How did this come to be and why, in the final analysis, was his a failed leadership?

Much of the solution to this question lies on the Israeli side of the equation, which will be examined a little further on, but there are elements which have to be identified and recognized relating to the way Assad ran his policy. One cannot avoid a comparison between the Egyptian and Syrian approaches to the subject of a peace treaty with Israel, since both had international and regional components. Playing the international card, Egypt came to the United States, a country still in the midst of the Cold War with the Soviet Union, bringing a precious gift: a strategic decision to sever the link it had fostered over the years with Moscow. Egypt broke with the Soviet Union and then proposed, in effect, a new relationship with Washington based on a common strategy in the region. It complemented this move with a historic decision to seek and obtain a peace with Israel, braving the bitter criticism of much of the Arab world, which crystallized into an almost ten-year boycott of Egypt in the Arab Middle East. Syria's policy and tactics were markedly different.

Syria maintained its relationship with Moscow and also fostered its link with Iran, lending this latter aspect of its defense and foreign policy special significance. It resisted repeated American and Israeli demands that it curtail the activities of Palestinian and other terrorist groups on its territory and, although it joined the U.S.-led coalition against Iraq in the first round of the Gulf War in 1991, it not only refrained from repeating this performance in the second round of the war in 2003, but actually extended the use of its territories and open borders with Iraq to the insurgent and Iraqi forces battling against the United States. It is probably true that Bashar al-Assad, who succeeded his father, gave limited support to the United States in the struggle against the Al Qaeda brand of terror; but such support as was given was concentrated, limited, and certainly far from the all-out effort contributed by Egypt at the exact same time.

Conflicting strategies produced totally different results. Syria retained all its traditional assets and bargained to relinquish many of them in exchange for a peace with Israel and acceptance by the United States. Egypt severed itself from its past, more or less unconditionally, and was rewarded with both a peace with Israel and a strategic relationship with the United States, encompassing the refurbishment of all its armed forces and the receipt of state-of-the-art modern weaponry, together with economic aid on a regular yearly basis. The Egyptian approach appeared to involve a high element of risk. Ostensibly, one could imagine a situation arising wherein the Sadat initiative would end in failure. This was, by far, not in the realm of fantasy. And, yet, once the die was cast, it was realistic to assume that neither the United States nor Israel could afford, politically, to leave Egypt ultimately high and dry.

Thus, in the final analysis, it would be true to say that the strategy of Hafiz al-Assad, of playing "safe" and holding on to every asset until a deal was done, worked to Syria's disadvantage. If the ultimate aim of Assad was to realize his dream of restoring the lost Golan Heights to Syrian sovereignty, then the path he chose to realize this dream was ineffective. However, if the underlying aim of the Syrian Alawite minority leader was first and foremost to preserve his dictatorial regime, then the path he chose was essentially the right one. In holding on to his bargaining chips to the very end, he was able to build tactical alliances with Iran, on the one hand, and with the Hizbollah, the violent Shiite movement, on the other. With this strategy, he found two allies prepared to sustain Syria, underpin the support of the masses inside the country for a rabid anti-Israeli stance, and thus ensure the perpetuity of the regime. In the final analysis, only political masters like President Sadat, King Hussein, Yitzhak Rabin, and Ariel Sharon, leaders who were conscious of their historic responsibilities and who were prepared to challenge their domestic constituencies, succeeded in leaping across the chasm and bringing a new dawn for their peoples.

· · ·

THERE WERE ADDITIONAL ACTORS WHO PLAYED THEIR ROLES BOTH ON the international and on the local scene, several of them belonging to the periphery. One such figure was King Hassan II of Morocco, who ruled his country with an iron fist for decades. At a very early stage in his reign he realized that his survival could not be assured simply by brute force inside his realm. As I said earlier, he knowingly created and nurtured his bond with Israel, and was subsequently able to position himself as a safe and secure host for the initial delicate and fruitful contacts between Israel and the Arab world, first and foremost with Egypt. His foresight and uncanny grasp of human nature enabled him to absorb the Algerian incursion into his country in the sixties, an incursion that included direct Egyptian military participation on the Algerian side, and to move on, in the seventies, to host Egyptian secret emissaries who came to Rabat to meet their Israeli interlocutors. But King Hassan set his sights much higher. He cast himself in the role of one of the most senior and prestigious figures in the Muslim world, a direct descendant of the Prophet Muhammad, and as such aspired to play a key part in the resolution of the issue of Jerusalem. To this purpose, Morocco assumed the chair of the Jerusalem committee of the Arab League and afforded an opportunity rejected by Israel, to place the issue of the status of the holy part of Jerusalem on the international agenda rather than on the agenda of the Israeli-Palestinian dispute.

This issue of Jerusalem, probably one of the more intractable ones in the Israeli-Arab dispute, has been a subject of endless emotional debates in Israel and in the Muslim world. When the United Nations' assembly approved the plan to partition Palestine into two separate states, it also approved a plan to internationalize the city of Jerusalem, thereby giving it a special trusteeship status. It will be recalled that the Arab world rejected the resolution and went to war against the newborn fledgling state of Israel. Israel, on its part, rejected the notion of "internationalizing" Jerusalem and when the War of Independence came to an end and a cease-fire was declared, the cease-fire line went through the city and confirmed the status of a divided city between Israel and Jordan, which was cast in the role of the occupying power of the West Bank of what had formerly been Palestine. The war of 1967 put an end to this anomaly and Jerusalem became a "united city, the capital of Israel never again to be divided," in the words of successive Israeli prime ministers on both sides of the political divide. Walls and obstacles separating the various quarters of the city were torn down and under the guidance of the legendary mayor, Teddy Kollek, an enormous effort was made to unite the city with its disparate populations. With the passage of years, with the advent of the Palestinian Authority and the insistence of the Palestinians that any permanent settlement would have to include recognition of Palestinian sovereignty on the holiest of holies—the Temple Mount—in the center of the Old City of Jerusalem, more and more plans were aired as trial balloons entailing the repartition of the city into two parts, the Israeli part and the Palestinian part.

How should the destiny of the "holy basin" in the heart of the Old City be determined? Certainly from Israel's vantage point, it would like to hold on to the entire area in the tradition of the ironclad policy that all the prime ministers of Israel have enounced since the end of the victorious Six-Day War. But if this turned out not to be feasible in the end, would it not be in Israel's interest to promote a settlement between Israel and the Muslim world rather than between Israel and the Palestinians alone? Would this not neutralize the temporal sovereignty aspect of the entire issue and would not the outcome be to Israel's advantage? I often thought about this in the years when King Hassan II was in the saddle of the Jerusalem committee of the league. Maybe these thoughts were premature. It could well be that we will resort to this approach when the appropriate time comes.

In the eighties and nineties, Morocco assumed the role of a "political Mecca" for Israeli politicians from many walks of life. People prided themselves on being invitees to the royal palaces and competed between themselves on the number of times they had been received in audience by His Majesty. He maintained dialogues with both the right and the left on the political spectrum of Israel and considered himself a father figure of the hundreds of thousands of Jewish immigrants who had left his country and who had gone to Israel to set up home. On the other side of the equation, he invited Yassir Arafat countless times to meet with him and for years tried to prevail on him to enter into a meaningful political intercourse with Israel. He studiously tried to avoid grandstand diplomacy. He acceded to a move by Shimon Peres in 1986 to invite him to Morocco for talks on setting up a channel between Israel and the PLO. He was embarrassed to discover, to his clear chagrin, that the Israeli guest arrived on an Israeli Air Force aircraft with a bevy of top Israeli media figures at his side. Peres was, at the time, a partner in a national unity government alongside Likud leader Yitzhak Shamir, and ultimately was, in my opinion, incapable of delivering what his emissaries had promised before he arrived. The event ended in a near fiasco. The visit became public knowledge before it had come to an end. Peres and his entourage were asked to leave earlier than planned and were more or less summarily expelled from the country. King Hassan went on live television to explain his initiative and to admit his failure to obtain success. He had paid a price for his bold step. Syria suspended diplomatic relations with Morocco in protest against the Peres visit. In calculating the pros and cons of the move, King Hassan felt he had paid a steep price related to his status inside the Arab world and had received nothing in return. The departure of Peres and his large retinue was sweetened when they discovered that just before takeoff King Hassan had seen to it that the aircraft was stocked to capacity with the choicest products of Morocco's famed cuisine and wines. I kept a bottle of choice wine as a memento of the visit for many years. When, ultimately, I opened the bottle, I discovered that it had gone sour. Only the beautiful bouquet remained as a sad memory of what might have been a real breakthrough.

Following the signature of the first Israeli-Palestinian agreement in Washington in 1993, successive Israeli prime ministers of the Labor party became welcome public guests of King Hassan in his splendid palaces in the country. However, when Prime Minister Rabin was savagely gunned down and murdered in 1995, the king did not avail himself of the opportunity to attend the funeral alongside scores of heads of state and high-level representatives of the Arab and Muslim world. Even President Mubarak, who had constantly refused to visit Israel for years, came to Jerusalem. In his decision to stay away, King Hassan unhappily demonstrated the limits of his capability at political maneuvering both inside his own country and inside the Arab world.

ANOTHER PLAYER ON THE FRINGES OF THE DISPUTE WAS SAUDI ARABIA. This country, the seat of the holiest of Islamic shrines, in Mecca, had for years played a subtle role in the affairs of the region, both by virtue of its vast oil resources, without which the Western industrial world could not function, and due to its preponderant role in the religious life of every Muslim individual on earth. The Wahhabite-purist strain in Islam, born, bred, and nurtured in the Arabian Peninsula, was by character a formidable foe of Judaism (and Christianity), both of which it claimed to replace in the field of monotheistic faiths. Recognition of the State of Israel by Saudi Arabia entailed a tremendous admission of a profoundly religious character. Thus it is only natural that such a sea change was very late in coming.

The first overt indication that such a change was at all possible came in 1991, when Saudi Arabia sent a representative to the Madrid conference convened by the United States and the Soviet Union to set the guidelines for negotiations on the Israeli-Arab conflict. The person chosen for this role was the legendary Saudi ambassador to the United States, Prince Bandar bin Sultan, a figure well known internationally with very close ties to ruling circles in Washington. Saudi Arabia was destined to play a series of roles in subsequent years behind the scenes and to contribute to the efforts of the United States, especially on the Syrian track, but all these endeavors ended in futility. For reasons already enumerated, the Syrian track did not materialize and hence all the attempts of auxiliary persons and entities to facilitate the process came to nothing.

The turning point in Saudi policy came in the spring of 2002. Its roots lay without doubt in the events of 9/11, when the fruits of Saudi neglect of the violent traits in purist Islam came home to roost with unprecedented vengeance. It was a very rude awakening and one of the immediate consequences of that terrible event was a wave of anti-Saudi sentiment in the United States and in the Western world. It became clear that Riyadh would have to invest heavily not only on the domestic terrorist scene but no less on the international arena. However, it would be wrong to attribute the dramatic change in the Saudi approach to the Israeli-Arab dispute solely to the necessity to accomplish a public-relations face-lift. When Saudi Arabia revealed what later became known as the Saudi plan or Saudi initiative in a press interview given by Crown Prince Abdullah to Tom Friedman of *The New York Times,* the very fact that the Saudis had resorted to an initiative of any kind was a subject of considerable surprise. It was so contrary to the deliberate abstinence of the House of Saud from any direct involvement in the conflict. The initiative, in its original form, was vague on many accounts and lacked precision, which, I thought at the time, was beneficial to all concerned. I was one of those who immediately urged Prime Minister Sharon not to reject the move out of hand and to simply state that he would not comment on a press interview and would await further elucidation and clarification. An Arab summit for heads of state was about to be convened in Beirut, Lebanon, and I suggested to the prime minister that he openly propose traveling to Beirut and confronting his Arab peers then and there. After consulting with others he did indeed come out with just such a statement. It was met by ridicule by some and by sheer amazement by others. In any event no invitation to Beirut arrived in Jerusalem and what I believed was a historic opportunity to galvanize the entire region into a mode of reconciliation passed by, unrequited.

THE SPRING OF 2002 WAS A PERIOD PREGNANT WITH INITIATIVES AND painful decision making. The *intifada* terrorist wave of suicide bombers was mounting weekly and sometimes daily, Arafat was exhorting the masses to look forward to the day when a million martyrs would converge on Jerusalem, and Israel was beginning to think that a massive operation would have to be launched at the West Bank in order to bring down the level of violence. At one and the same time, it was dawning on the powers that be in Riyadh, the capital of Saudi Arabia, that, should the current tensions aroused by the Palestinians continue to mount, a serious threat might develop to the stability and very integrity of the kingdom. If the youth of the cities would take to the streets in support of their suffering Palestinian cousins, if religious anti-Israeli fervor were to scale new heights, Crown Prince Abdullah began to think that the foundations of the regime might begin to tremble with consequences catastrophic to both the kingdom itself and the entire region of the Persian Gulf. The Saudi move was in no way motivated by a freshly discovered sympathy for Israel. Prince Abdullah continued to harbor a very deep antipathy to Israel and in particular to Jewish presence at or affinity to the Temple Mount. He would make his feelings on Jerusalem clear again and again every time that he met with foreign and especially with American interlocutors. What had moved Prince Abdullah to change course was his growing conviction that the survival of his regime, of his dynasty, necessitated movement toward a settlement between Israel and the Palestinians sooner rather than later, and that in any event, the level of violence would have to be reduced drastically, before the pot boiled over and it became too late.

WHAT WAS THE ROSTER OF ISRAELI LEADERS THAT CONFRONTED THE Arab world in the thirteen years that spanned the two Gulf Wars and their aftermaths? How did each of the six prime ministers of this thirteen-year period perform both as regional figures and as players on the broader international scene? I have referred to several aspects in relation to a few of them in previous chapters; it is now appropriate to attempt to put together a "score card" for every one of them and to indulge in a comparative study involving a few of them.

The first of the figures was Yitzhak Shamir, of whom much has already been said. He was a cool practitioner of international diplomacy and he played his cards extremely close to his chest. Contrary to common belief, he attached great importance to the image that Israel projected both within the region and toward the world at large. He was an avid reader of political biographies and autobiographies, and I remember traveling with him at one time to a foreign country and finding him studiously trying to master a big volume devoted to General George Marshall. He mastered the opus and read it from cover to cover. He never boasted about anything, let alone about his hunger for books, and if one would ask an average Israeli citizen how he evaluated Prime Minister Shamir, I doubt if anyone would even remotely mention this side of him. It should be remembered that Shamir was the person who went to Madrid and thus set the political process rolling in the nineties. He had little trust in his Arab interlocutors but was, of course, strict in observing every commitment that Israel had undertaken toward the Arab side ever since the War of Independence.

Yitzhak Rabin was cast in a totally different mode. His entire upbringing was military and yet at a comparatively early stage in his career he was exposed to the political interface between physical force and the other aspects of power locally, regionally, and internationally. At one time he told me that he would always remember an event that occurred when he was serving as an officer at the head of the Northern Command in the mid-fifties.

At a given moment, a crisis arose between Israel and Syria over the explosive issue of water. Syria had decided to divert one of the three tributaries of the Jordan River which flowed in its territory. Had this move been allowed to be completed, Israel would have suffered an acute short-age of water, which was, and is, always in short supply in the country. To thwart Syria's aim, Israel resorted to force and its long-range artillery opened fire on the diversion team and on its military support. A very tense situation arose and it was compounded by the fact that Syria had by then become a client state of the Soviet Union, which had begun to supply Damascus with military equipment. Rabin was, of course, in command of the operation but was surprised to find that none other than the minister of defense, David Ben-Gurion, traveled up north and spent the entire day at his side in the forward command post in order to moni-tor events at close range. Rabin said to me that this had been a unique ex-perience for him. Fearing a possible escalation and a deterioration leading to involvement with a superpower, Ben-Gurion wished to be on the spot and to handle any possible development hands on.

Rabin learned that even the smallest of incidents could mushroom into a major confrontation and he was therefore a stickler for details. His leadership was built not only on his self-confidence, but also on his con-stant need to gain and sense the support of his subordinates. I remember one particular day when I was serving as deputy head of the Mossad. Rabin had approved a very daring operation overseas and my chief had departed at the head of the force. I was left behind as "duty commander" at headquarters. I received a telephone call from the prime minister's mil-itary secretary telling me that the prime minister had decided to cancel the operation and that I was to pass the word to my chief. Having been aware that an enormous effort had been put into this endeavor, I asked whether there was any point in coming over to see the prime minister to convince him to allow the operation to proceed. I was told that there was no way that he would change his mind, so I went ahead and passed the message to the field. An hour later, I received a call summoning me to meet at once with the prime minister. I asked if he had changed his mind and the answer was definitely negative. "Why the summons?" I asked. The prime minister wanted to explain to me personally what had caused him to make his decision. I replied that it was really unnecessary to waste the prime minister's time. When my chief returned, we could hear the reasons together. The prime minister insisted that the meeting take place and I spent over half an hour with him, as he expounded at length on his reasons for calling off the operation. At that given moment he sought my support and understanding and this was, in my eyes, a singular quality of leadership, which I came to admire and to try to emulate.

Rabin's leadership was characterized by his great emphasis on every small element in the matters he dealt with. The well-known dictum that the devil is in the details was a rule he kept strictly. His military career had so often taught him that even the best of plans could go awry. He knew of the danger in what Clausewitz called "friction": forces rubbing up against each other, causing each and every one of them to change direction. He knew that friction had to be taken into account in political planning and implementation, no less than in operational circumstances. I can never forget those instances when I experienced the Rabin theory in practice. One evening in the mid-nineties, I remember being called into headquarters around two A.M. to attend an exercise of two of the Mossad's most experienced and renowned operatives. They were scheduled to leave within a few days on an exceptionally dangerous mission and Rabin had decided that he wished to be present at the final exercise and to monitor every stage in the planned activity. He arrived on time after a grueling day, but this did not prevent him from staying on for about one and a half hours as the model was gone through, step by step. By virtue of his presence, he naturally assumed responsibility in advance not only for the decision in principle, but also for the minutiae involved in the operation itself. This was, indeed, a very rare exhibition of responsibility, as practiced at the top of the ladder. It was a rarity in general but also, in particular, an exception as compared to others who occupied this loftiest of positions.

Around that time the Khammas terrorist organization had kidnapped an Israeli soldier, Nachshon Waxman, and held him as a hostage, demanding the release from an Israeli jail of the leader of the movement, Sheikh Ahmed Yassin. Rabin refused to accede to the demand and authorized the mounting of a special-force operation to free the captive soldier by force. The attempt failed, notwithstanding the near-perfect intelligence that had been gathered to support the assault. Waxman died at the hands of his captors and the attacking unit also incurred loss of life. This had been a very bad day for Israel, and yet Rabin insisted on chairing the dramatic press conference, announcing the sad news, beginning the gathering by simply stating: "It was and is my responsibility."

In matters of peacemaking as in affairs of war, Rabin was, as has been said, a stickler for details. He had his visions, he made his historic decisions that changed the course of events in the region, and had their effect on the international scene, but he nonetheless devoted so much of his time and energy to reinvigorating his leadership through seemingly small acts in small limited circles. In so doing he exhibited a rare quality of humility, painfully absent in so many other figures who strutted the stage. He was all too conscious that at any given moment, something might go wrong at the very last minute, and he therefore was wary of being overconfident and scornful of his adversaries. He never underestimated his adversaries and was careful not to romanticize the achievements of his diplomatic endeavors. I have more than reason to believe that to the very end there was no love lost between him and Yassir Arafat. Arafat would claim feelings of brotherhood between him and Rabin, after Rabin's assassination. His use of the word "brotherhood" had no basis in reality. Rabin did not view Arafat as a close partner and companion in their joint pursuit of peace. There were no feelings of brotherhood as Arafat would claim. In private, Rabin railed against the manner in which Arafat clowned his way along the path, against his total absence of credibility, and against the corrupt nature of his administration. In this he differed from his Israeli partner, Shimon Peres, who tended to become emotionally enamored with the venture he had championed to the extent that all the subsequent obstacles on the path to fruition and implementation appeared to the latter to be small easily surmountable pebbles along the main highway to peace and everlasting security and prosperity.

I have never made a secret of my admiration of Yitzhak Rabin and of his approach to the issues of the day. There is one more aspect of his political testament that I have considered as a guiding rule. Whenever he engaged in a project or in a diplomatic move, even when he did so wholeheartedly, he was always conscious of the absolute necessity of developing and sustaining an exit strategy, should his effort end in failure. He never wished to put all his eggs in one basket, and was anxious at all times to preserve and nurture additional options at the same time as he pursued a chosen one. In the definition of a renowned man of ideas and history, Sir Isaiah Berlin, he was both a hedgehog and a fox at one and the same time. He possessed the tenacity of the first and the wisdom of the latter.

Shortly after his death, after a brief interregnum of a few months with Shimon Peres as prime minister, a general election in Israel in the summer of 1996 brought Benjamin Netanyahu to power as a surprise victor over the experienced and seasoned Shimon Peres. The contrast between Netanyahu and Rabin was all too apparent. Their policies were totally different, but this was not the element that captured my attention. Netanyahu was relatively little known to me when he became prime minister. I had already served as ambassador to the European Union for six months and had been thrust into the forefront of defending and propagating the policies that Netanyahu had initiated in his relations with the Palestinians and the Arab world at large. He was depicted as a hard-liner, as a person set against compromise, and as such was regarded with much skepticism bordering on hostility by the leaders of the European Union. In the Arab world there was one personality who greeted him with a sigh of relief. It was none other than King Hussein, who was not only mourning the death of Prime Minister Rabin but also regretting the accession of Shimon Peres. For Hussein, the reelection of a Likud prime minister was a welcome change, given the alternative.

Netanyahu moved very quickly to establish a close working relationship with the monarch of Jordan. Things went remarkably well until the day Netanyahu sent his political counselor to Amman to confer with senior Jordanian officials on current affairs. The visit was reported in the media as a routine event. Several days later a severe clash between Palestinians and Israelis occurred close to the Temple Mount of Jerusalem. The mayor of Jerusalem had sanctioned the opening of a hitherto closed tunnel under the Temple Mount, close to the revered Wailing Wall, one of the holiest of sites of the Jewish religion. The Wall is the remaining relic of the Temple of God that had been built by the ancient kings of Israel more than two thousand years ago. The action taken by the mayor, and approved before or after the act by the prime minister, was viewed as a blatant attempt to upset the extremely delicate status quo that had prevailed in the "holy basin" since Israel had taken control of the whole of Jerusalem and the West Bank in the wake of the 1967 Six-Day War. The outcry in the Arab world was shrill and without doubt disproportionate to the gravity of the specific act committed. For King Hussein, the situation was compounded by the fact that only a very few days before Netanyahu's aide had been in Amman, and as a result of this the word spread that the king had been privy to the intention and had given his approval to the initiative taken. In the eyes of King Hussein he had been set up by Netanyahu and this precipitated a rupture in the relationship. Every attempt by Netanyahu and his close aides to renew contact with the Jordanian sovereign was rebuffed by the king, whereupon I received a direct request on behalf of the prime minister to make contact with Amman and, if necessary, to go there in order to try to get things back on track once again. I did as requested, and within a couple of days I paid a secret visit to the Jordanian capital and was able to obtain the consent of His Majesty to receive two envoys of Netanyahu and thus to reactivate the vital link between the two principals at the highest level. I had requested that my mission be kept secret. I believed that in order to preserve my capacity to act when necessary, it was essential that my role not be made public. Unfortunately, my mission was leaked to the press and thereupon I was publicly reprimanded for making an unauthorized journey outside my area of jurisdiction. I was told, through the press, that my mission in Brussels would be terminated after its first two years and that I would not be granted the normal extension of a third year that was customary in cases such as mine when appointments were made outside the regular foreign service.

The way Netanyahu performed at that time was indicative of some of the more basic traits of his administration. He was, and is, an unusually intelligent person, who has mastered the art of government with relative ease and who is exceptionally gifted in utilizing the media, particularly the electronic media, to his advantage. He was gifted with a lightning grasp of international and domestic affairs and whenever I dealt with him, including during the time when I served under him as director of the Mossad, he exhibited an uncanny ability to absorb endless details and to assemble them together into a coherent pattern of facts and thoughts. This was both his strength and his weakness. His repartee was so instant that he more often than not beat every person around him to the punch line. And when this happened, there were not always those around who would dare to counsel a pause, an afterthought, before a decision on this or that was taken. He became the man with an instant solution to a problem or a predicament.

And yet, when confronted with a real issue, with a "flap" in operations, he did give unstinting backing to his subordinates although they, for their part, did not always provide him with the support he was enti-tled to expect. A few months after he appointed me as director of the Mossad, I experienced a flap in operations—two men were apprehended and arrested on the island of Cyprus and the "affair" immediately be-came public knowledge. Coming less than a year after my predecessor had resigned, due to two mishaps, this third event was greeted by the customary criticism and derision of the lords of the media. I came in for my expected share of the blame; the division chief whose men had been detained submitted his resignation, which I regretfully accepted, and this was published with the expected public disapprobation. The prime min-ister came in for his own share of dissatisfaction with his performance. He was discredited for not gaining proper control of the Mossad after all the gaffes that it had caused. One could have expected that, in circum-stances such as these, a prime minister would have clamped down on the intelligence service that had repeatedly embarrassed him. But this did not happen. I received the full support and backing of my political master and was able to proceed with every operation I deemed necessary. This was a measure of leadership that I could not help but admire. The prime minister was risking much by giving me his unqualified support. Had he not done so, the damage wrought could have been irreparable. A possible dismissal of mine would have been the least of the losses. The Mossad, Israel's vital secret foreign arm, could have been dealt a blow from which it would take years to recover. That Benjamin Netanyahu grasped the significance of this threat and was personally willing to stand in the breach was, and is, to my mind to his eternal credit.

Netanyahu was, and is, a real master of the media. He often exhibited a use or—if you wish—a manipulation of this arm of society that was second to none. I was to be a player in such a drama, when he decided to appoint me head of the Mossad in order to resolve an acute crisis that had arisen and that had resulted in my predecessor tendering his resigna-tion. It was February 1998, and I was winding down my duties as am-bassador to the European Union. One afternoon, I was making my way home on the highway from Luxembourg to Brussels and my cellular phone rang. The military secretary to the prime minister was on the line. He told me that the prime minister was about to telephone me and to of-fer me the position as head of the Mossad, which I had left a couple of years previously as deputy chief of the agency. I was told that this was an offer I could not refuse. When the call came through and Netanyahu made me the offer I responded by saying that this was a matter upon which I had to consult my wife. "Where is she?" the prime minister asked somewhat impatiently. I told him that she had gone to a museum where she was incommunicado; I promised to call back that evening, in a few hours' time. When, eventually, I called back, I said to the prime minister that the offer was extremely flattering but that I would like to meet with him before making my mind up. Since I knew that he would be making a visit to neighboring Germany in two days' time I suggested that we meet there to talk about the matter face to face. "Impossible," said Netanyahu. This was an urgent appointment that had to be made without delay. He asked that I fly to Jerusalem the very next day and meet with him immediately on arrival. I naturally agreed but asked that the media not be alerted to the offer until we were able to meet. I was told that the prime minister would do his best to meet my request, but success could not be guaranteed. Within minutes, a leading commentator on Israeli State Radio released the "scoop" of my impending nomination.

I arrived in Jerusalem the following day and met the prime minister for a lengthy session. He had decided to appoint a hand-picked deputy chief, the outgoing commanding officer of the Northern Command, General Amiram Levine, and he was expecting me to groom the man as my successor after an unspecified period of time. It became necessary for me to meet Levine, whom I hardly knew, personally, in order to ascertain if the two of us could work together as a team. This was immediately arranged and Netanyahu demanded my prompt reply. It was seven o'clock in the evening and Netanyahu was about to leave his office and go home. I asked for an hour or so for reflection. "No way," said the prime minister. The response had to be forthcoming here and now! I could not understand why the matter was so urgent. After more pressure I gave an affirmative reply. It was a couple of minutes before eight o'clock, the time for the daily prime-time evening news on state television. Within minutes the newscast was interrupted with a dramatic announcement that the prime minister was about to hold an unscheduled television press conference. The prime minister appeared and told the public at large that he had appointed me as the new head of the Mossad. He also announced the appointment of my deputy. It became known at once that he had consulted the leader of the parliamentary opposition,

Ehud Barak, the minister of defense, and several former chiefs of service and their endorsement was unanimous.

That same morning, the Knesset had convened to elect the state president for the coming five years. Incumbent president Ezer Weizman was being opposed by Shaul Amor, a member of the prime minister's Likud party. The campaign had been intense and the prime minister's coalition had been exerting a supreme effort to get their candidate elected. The vote was close and Weizman was reelected by a narrow majority. This was, of course, described in the media as a serious political defeat for the ruling Likud party and, by inference, for the prime minister. Needless to say, seconds after the press conference, attention was entirely diverted to my appointment and for the rest of the evening it became a centerpiece of commentary, with all and sundry lauding both the choice made and the orderly and responsible way that the prime minister went about it. The following morning my appointment was the main headline, with the presidential contest relegated to second place. This was the only occasion that such an appointment was made public by any prime minister personally and in such a dramatic fashion. Not for a split second did I think that this procedure had been chosen to afford me such an exceptional honor!

Netanyahu was succeeded by Ehud Barak as prime minister. I had known him for many years and did not anticipate any problem working under his stewardship. I was so wrong. Barak was considered one of the most brilliant minds in the country. He had served in the army for thirty-five years and had risen to become chief of staff. He had also served for several years in military intelligence and I had worked with him on several operations, successfully. As prime minister, he behaved so differently from the way he had in the past. I enjoyed his complete confidence and he did not interfere in any way in my decision making. And yet he became so suspicious of everybody surrounding him, he kept all his civil service subordinates at arm's length, did not really confide in them, and thereby created an atmosphere of deep mistrust between himself and them and between themselves. He came to power a little after a year after I had taken over the service, and my deputy, who was expecting to succeed me, was gradually becoming impatient and was anxious to obtain a decision assuring his orderly and rapid succession. This situation gave rise, understandably, to mounting tension inside the Mossad, and true to human nature, there were those who were already "placing their bets" on the man of the future. Barak appeared to be slow in making his mind up. When he had originally assumed the premiership, I had offered him my resignation as I believed he had the right to wish to work with someone who enjoyed his complete confidence. He had rejected this offer outright, but I knew full well that the succession was looming over the service just a little more than a year after I had been appointed in a crisis situation. The uncertainty was gnawing at the foundations of the Mossad, and I thought that Barak should indeed make up his mind as soon as possible. My deputy was in a somewhat greater hurry than I was. He met the prime minister at his own request after several postponements and delays. Indeed, Barak was notorious for his timetables. He rarely saw anybody on time and I recall waiting more than two hours in his office before being ushered in and greeted with the question, "Is there anything urgent on your agenda?" On more than one occasion, I said, "No!" and suggested that I leave, but I learned that I was in excellent company and therefore did not take it personally.

Weeks went by and Barak said nothing. Press rumors were rife that I was about to leave, until one day, Barak invited my deputy in for a personal meeting that was to take place within a couple of days. He said nothing to me and I concluded that the die had been cast and I was about to depart. I called in my deputy and started speaking to him about an orderly transition, which he accepted of course, and when the time came, with the meeting scheduled for the early evening, I went home and began preparing my farewell message to the troops.

It was getting quite late and my deputy called to tell me that he was waiting and was being told that the meeting might take place as late as eleven o'clock at night. Time passed and no word from Jerusalem. At close to midnight I decided to go to bed and was talking to my wife about our possible plans for the future when close to one o'clock I received a call from the prime minister's office telling me that he wanted to talk to me. Well, they had problems setting up the communications and a half hour later Barak called me to tell me that he had had a very serious conversation with my deputy in which he had told him that he did not wish me to leave at this stage. The deputy had said that he saw no point in waiting around and had decided to resign. Barak asked me to treat the departing general with all the necessary sensitivity, given the sterling service he had given to his country. Barak asked me to stay on indefinitely and was profuse in his praise of me. I must admit that, given the time frame and circumstances of our conversation, I think I responded very coolly. He had surprised me, that was certain, but why do it that way? It was vintage Barak.

There was one other occasion that I cannot forget. Shortly before he went to Camp David to meet with Yassir Arafat, in a brave attempt to obtain a sincere settlement of the Palestinian conflict under the auspices of President Clinton, he had sent me a handwritten letter lauding the successful completion of a very daring operation of the Mossad. I will readily admit to unabashed pride when the letter came. The Camp David attempt ended in failure and within a few months Barak would be out of office, after the shortest tenure of an elected prime minister. I was home that evening and received a call from the prime minister's office telling me that the prime minister wished to speak to me. I had never spoken to a prime minister when out of the country on delicate matters for reasons of communication security and tried to explain this to the staff there, but to no avail. They insisted that this was his wish and expected me to comply. The prime minister was on the line shortly afterward, speaking to me minutes before he was about to board his aircraft en route to Israel. He went straight to the point and entered into a detailed description of the discussions that he had conducted in Camp David. He invoked the memory of Sir Isaiah Berlin, to whom I was related, and who had been a prominent figure in the world of philosophy, political thought, and history during the twentieth century. He was also known as one who had served in the British embassies in Washington and Moscow during World War II and whose reports on the American scene were read studiously by Prime Minister Winston Churchill and his closest aides. Berlin was a renowned professor and teacher at Oxford University, a president of the British Academy, and a highly respected figure among the elite of Israel for close to fifty years. His counsel was sought by many and he was a great expert on, among other subjects, Russia and Russian affairs. Barak knew of him and was an admirer of his works and he was one of the few who were privy to my relationship with him.

Barak began by mentioning Berlin's name and his extreme devotion to the cause of Israel and Zionism, with particular emphasis on Jerusalem. He then went on to tell me how far he had gone in accommodating Palestinian sensitivities only to discover that his interlocutor Arafat not only refused to meet him halfway, but denied that Israel and the Jewish people had any historic or other stake in the holy city of Jerusalem and specifically the Temple Mount. I tried to respond to Barak and to enter into a dialogue with him on what he was saying, but he cut me short and instructed me simply to listen to what he was saying. It was a very long and detailed monologue and, when it was over, the prime minister simply hung up before I could say anything at all. I was left wondering what this was all about, only to conclude that the whole exercise might have been intended primarily for additional ears and that I had simply been chosen as a technical instrument to get the message across to unnamed others. I never asked about it again and preferred to leave any solution to this mystery to my imagination.

It was this occurrence and others, involving other leaders, that taught me over the many years of service that there were times and situations when officials and officeholders were assigned roles in intricate scenarios and maneuvers without being alerted to the true nature of their mission. I recognized that this was a legitimate privilege of political masters and that this was, on occasion, an essential tool in their hands. As I climbed the bureaucratic ladder I saw more and more of this use and always felt uneasy about it. The thin dividing line between use and misuse was difficult to define. I, for one, never made use of this strategy in the Mossad, but I did come across others who resorted to such manipulations. I felt at the time, and feel so today, that in the final analysis, constant resort to this method perverts the system of government if it becomes common practice with frequent risks poisoning the entire machinery of civil service. Key figures, when they realize that they have been used for other purposes, lose their trust in their superiors and naturally take measures and precautions to protect their integrity or, in some cases, they simply walk away and thus inflict damage on the service by denying it the benefit of their continued employ.

This is how I remember some of the principal players in the region. A sixth prime minister, Ariel Sharon, an important figure in the history and progress of the Middle East whom I have not yet spoken of, will be dealt with more extensively in a later chapter. In a certain way, the manner in which they interacted with the powers that be beyond the Middle East serves to illustrate the dependence of the peoples of the entire region on the way forces outside the region have perceived them and acted toward them. The most profound of these external forces has been, without a doubt, the United States. Every day, we see countless examples of U.S. reaction to, and involvement with, key players in the Middle East.

9

CHANGING TIMES—CHANGING PRIORITIES

By the mid-nineties, the world was settling down to its new major configuration. The Communist bloc of countries led by the defunct Soviet Union was gone. Russia was struggling for economic survival and painfully experiencing a regime change that was characterized by symptoms of destabilization. The Balkans were in the throes of a bitter war induced by the disintegration of the republic of Yugoslavia a few years after the death of President Tito, who, alone, was capable of holding together the feuding ethnic groups that constituted his country.

Through my eyes, the eyes of one who had come to Brussels to represent his country as ambassador accredited to the European Union, the situation appeared nothing less than bizarre. On the one hand, the European Union had succeeded in healing the wounds of two successive world wars that had engulfed the continent and had left behind them millions of dead and wounded as well as economic devastation. The fifteen-member Union had become a real economic superpower and had begun to feel its way toward instituting a common currency and a closer-knit political union with the prospects of forging a common foreign policy and defense approach that would gradually evolve into one agreed upon by all member states. Yet the vast economic potential did not appear to translate itself into real political and strategic muscle. First and foremost, because the Europeans preferred to deal with issues outside their immediate orbits and to refrain from sinking their teeth into their own spheres. They were only too eager to deliver a monthly statement on the Israeli-Palestinian dispute and to render judgment on the parties, mainly on Israel. But when it came to a subject like the generation-long dispute in Northern Ireland, for example, they studiously ignored it because it was an issue that involved a member of the Union.

The Middle East was a favorite of the Union and served as a convenient issue for forging a common foreign policy of the fifteen member states. I vividly recall how I was instructed month after month to gather information on preliminary discussions that were held in Brussels at subcommittee level concerning the impending draft resolution that was due to be submitted at the foreign minister meeting that convened every month. Following receipt of the necessary intelligence in Brussels or in the capitals of the member states, we routinely put pressure on leading member states to moderate the drafts, more often than not, to no avail. The Union officials reveled in these exercises. They enjoyed the importance we attached to these monthly bouts of diplomacy and felt as if they were sitting in judgment on the parties in the region, believing that their ultimate pronouncements were of great importance to the future of mankind. Nothing was further from the truth. Looking back at those years it is difficult to understand why so much effort was expended on these monthly bouts of quasi-diplomacy.

Europe was immensely important to Israel. It was its largest trading partner, accounting for more than 50 percent of its annual foreign trade. Europe had its borders very close to the Middle East. It was anxious to make sure that the conflicts of the region, the Arab-Israeli conflict and other conflicts, did not spill over into the European continent. Due to its trade importance to the countries of the Mediterranean basin, Europe strove to pursue its foreign policy interests through the subtle use of trade negotiations. The countries of the entire area sought trade agreements—associate member status—and these agreements assumed ever greater importance as economics played increasing roles in the well-being of every state in the region. The Europeans drove hard bargains in trade talks, but these were also used to exact commitments on issues such as human rights, etc., from potential partners. The European Union attempted to promote a series of agreements with all the countries in the Mediterranean basin and in the immediate vicinity, with the aim of creating a vast trade zone of Europe and the enlarged Middle East by 2010.

To this end an initiative was launched in the mid-nineties named the Barcelona Process, which generated an intricate series of meetings at various levels dealing with issues of economics, culture, and political character. The top layer of this initiative was a periodic foreign minister meeting of the partners to the Barcelona Process, where declared foes like Israel and Syria met around the same table to deliberate on matters of common interest. This was the only international forum, except for the United Nations Assembly, where conflicting states in the region were convened around the same table in a quasi-secluded environment and the union was justly proud of this achievement. The Union did little—almost nothing, in fact—to exploit this unique opportunity to launch private, semiprivate, or secret moves. Similarly, it did not invest any real financial support to activities of the process. It could have used the cultural "basket," as it was called, to convene scholars to discuss a host of academic and cultural topics, and thus it could have created meeting and breeding grounds for dialogue between bitter enemies. Undoubtedly, this required a touch of nonconformist diplomacy, and a modest budget to cover travel costs and accommodations. Rather than this, the Union contented itself with organizing and maintaining these periodic meetings for meetings' sake, in the belief that these exercises were serving to burnish the image of the Union at minimal cost. I recall being invited to preparatory sessions in Brussels together with other Mediterranean heads of missions and sitting across from the Syrian chargé d'affaires in Brussels. I vainly tried to engage him either in a private conversation or in a formal discussion on this or that technical item that was on the agenda. If the European hosts had shown just a little imagination, we might have been able to make something out of the process, but this was not to be.

One of the issues I had to deal with was that of Iran. The involvement of this country in the practice of state terror was well known not only in the Middle East but also in Western European capitals. Iranian agents had been active in the streets of Paris and London murdering enemies of the mullahs' regime in Tehran. We, in Israel, had been on the front line of the Iranian-Shiite offensive and had confronted the Iranian-supplied and -supported Hizbollah terrorist movement for a long period of time. Two major events in the nineties were the bombing of the Israeli embassy in Buenos Aires in 1994 and the subsequent operation carried out against the center of the Jewish community in that city, resulting in the deaths of scores of persons, both in the building and in its immediate vicinity.

It was obvious in those days that the Iranian threat was a global one, that it was directed not only against Israel and not only against the Jewish people in general, but also against international law and order. The E.U. adopted a gingerly approach and tried to engage in a constructive dialogue with the powers that be in Tehran. The European parliament, which I regularly visited in Strasbourg and in Brussels, where it convened alternatively, became the venue of persistent efforts to establish channels of contact and talks. At a given moment the Europeans took the dramatic and courageous step of suspending the dialogue and the member states withdrew their heads of mission from Tehran. I was serving in Brussels at the time and thought that this decision might herald a new era, not only in the confrontation with Iran, but also in the method and strategy that the Union might adopt to deal with concrete threats to the security and well-being of its member states. I was mistaken. Within a very short time, the Iranians had succeeded in puncturing the common front that the union had created and the member states appeared to be competing with each other as to who would be the first back in Tehran. Italy won the dishonorable race and the Iranians concluded then that the Union was little more than a paper tiger. It would take the Union seven years before it could get its act together again, but this time it would be Britain, France, and Germany performing together outside the confines of the union. This time around, in 2004 and 2005, it would be the Iranian nuclear challenge that would spur Europe, or part of it, to confront the Iranians in a diplomatic showdown backed by an implicit threat of action far beyond a withdrawal of ambassadors from Tehran.

Of all the experiences that I encountered during my stay in Brussels, the most vivid was that which involved the murder of a girl of Moroccan origin at the hands of a paedophile, a Belgian. The event was traumatic for Belgian society and was investigated, inter alia, by a parliamentary commission, whose hearings were relayed daily by the local television chains. One of the marginal aspects of this gruesome affair was the airing of a few of the more problematic conditions under which the Moroccan immigrant community lived in Belgium at the time. Thus it transpired that there were no burial facilities for this community in the country and the dead had to be sent back to their native land for interment. The community, as such, enjoyed limited rights and the hundreds of thousands of North Africans who took up residence in Belgium did not have a proportional representation in the organs of government and parliament. The more I learned about the conditions of Muslims residing in Western European countries, the more I realized that, as far as this cardinal issue was concerned, the governments of Europe by and large preferred to ignore the true nature of the problems they were bound to face sooner rather than later. I remember talking about this with a colleague, the then Moroccan ambassador in Brussels, who was in the eye of the storm over the murder of the young girl, and it was clear to us both that within a relatively short time, there would be an eruption somewhere.

From time to time, I met with the security chiefs of the state. This was not part of my brief when I was deputy chief of the Mossad. The Israeli ambassador to Belgium and I were among the few foreign chiefs of mission who enjoyed physical protection of the local security service. Therefore, I was invited to meet the head of the local service from time to time, mainly in order to be reprimanded, albeit in a very friendly but nevertheless firm manner, for evading my protection when I was on my own, primarily on weekends. I took advantage of these sporadic meetings to receive an overview of current problems, and whenever I raised the issue of the local Muslim population I was politely told that there was no such problem at all and that there was no spillover of the Israeli-Arab dispute into the local scene in Belgium. When I explained that this was not the point I had raised, but that I wished to question whether there was any rising tension among the Muslims concerning their inferior status in the country, I was fairly and squarely rebuffed and told in no uncertain terms that the Muslims appreciated the facilities granted them by the host government and that I would do well not to pry into local problems or imaginary ones. Instead, I should do what I could to prevail on my government to ease the plight of the Palestinians who were living under dire circumstances of occupation.

It was during that period that I believe the Muslim problem in Europe assumed not only new parameters, but also an entirely different character than that which had been accepted and understood before. Even before the terrorist attacks of 9/11 or that in Madrid, the writing was definitely on the wall. The problems were complex. On the one hand, Europe was becoming more and more dependent on foreign workers for its menial workforce and a large majority of these millions of manual laborers were Muslims coming from the economically underdeveloped countries of North Africa or from former Yugoslavia and Turkey. These millions of newcomers posed a cultural and ethnic challenge to traditional Western Europe, and in truth, the Europeans not only were ill-equipped to deal with these issues, but also much preferred to ignore them. No serious discussions were held in any forum of the Union on these matters. Even the delicate issue of emigration policy was not tackled at the European level because it was considered too sensitive and controversial. The general theme that I met every time I mentioned the subject was that it was an internal European matter, on the one hand, and that the problem was directly linked to the Arab-Israeli or Palestinian-Israeli dispute, on the other, and that if there was violence or unrest in Europe, this was primarily due to Israeli intransigence on these issues. Europe was "paying the price" for Israel's sins and the moment Israel changed its policy on these subjects and met the Palestinians' justified demands, all would be well. The interconnection between the Muslim challenge in Europe, including but not only exclusively the terrorist component of the "threat," and Israel's policies vis-à-vis the Arab world has served for generations as a convenient excuse for the states of Europe not to focus on the immediate aspects of the confrontation between Arab-Islamic religious trends and Judeo-Christian and secular Europe. Whenever I spoke to my European counterparts in Brussels or Strasbourg on these issues, and whenever I warned of the more violent strands in Islam, I was accused of resorting to Israeli propaganda.

In discussions and debates that I had during my tenure as a diplomat, I often countered the arguments hurled at me by saying that the European positions on the Middle East conflict were primarily driven by self-interest and all the moralizing over Israel's "draconian" policies was a convenient diversion and nothing more. At certain stages of the fierce debates that took place, I told my interlocutors that if one had to take their argumentation to its logical conclusion, then only the disappearance of the State of Israel would succeed in pacifying the insatiable desires of the Arab world. One more step and the "final solution" to

Jewish existence would herald an end to anti-Semitism. There is nothing like bringing an argument to the stage of reductio ad absurdum to startle an audience and to bring it to its senses. And yet I often hesitated to revert to this method of dialogue because its extreme nature laid it open to being labeled as disreputable demagoguery. It was not politically correct to express oneself in such terms. Civility demanded that an Israeli official refrain from appearing to plead for extenuating circumstances based on the terrible traumatic event that befell the Jewish people in World War II, when a third of the entire Jewish community was exterminated by Nazi Germany. Time and time again, I met prominent Germans and other Europeans who took the trouble to tell me that they had been born after 1945, the end of the Second World War, or that they had been little more than infants when the dark pages in the history book of Germany had been written.

It would not be accurate to state, though, that the issue of Muslim presence in Europe was entirely ignored. Under the thin veneer of sophisticated denial, European practitioners realized that the challenge from the Muslim populations in their midst required a policy designed to defuse this social and political time bomb. Much of the pressure came from underprivileged masses in the North African states who sought employment in Europe rather than languish unemployed and impoverished where they had been born and reared. In 1995, the leaders at the E.U. summit meeting in Barcelona decided to create a Barcelona architecture, which was designed to create a system of cooperation between members of the Union and all the countries surrounding the Mediterranean. As previously stated, the architecture of process was ostensibly designed to create a common economic market by 2010 and to accompany this effort at economic cooperation with parallel activities in politics and cultural fields. In effect, this strategy was chosen to divert tensions between the E.U. and the countries along the southeastern shore of the Mediterranean. But the Union was not prepared to invest the funds or the political capital essential to make a real impact on the problem. Similar to its approach to the Arab-Israeli dispute, the sums designated to achieve a substantial result were nowhere near the level required for this purpose. Compared to the billions of European ecus, as they were then, spent in pursuit of the European farming subsidies that were handed out to farmers in key member states on an annual basis, simply to ensure their continued subsistence, the amounts devoted to stem the Muslim tide were pitiful and by and large insignificant. Domestic pressures and needs took precedence over confronting external threats and the "farmers' lobby" was predominant in the list of political priorities of the member states. Under these circumstances the Muslim "wound" was bound to fester on, with its attendant consequences.

As an intelligence officer, I have always been conscious of the limited agenda that any political level can maintain and it has always been essential for the professional level to make its decisions on the agenda that it proposed to its masters. Even the only remaining superpower, the United States, has never possessed unlimited resources and capacities to field an unlimited number of external issues simultaneously. Israel, for example, has to date been unable to promote peace initiatives directed at its neighbors concurrently. Even if it pursued negotiations with more than one state, it has not seen fit to conclude the negotiations at the same time.

In this vein, Europe in the late nineties was primarily concerned with its opening to the east. The accession of ten more member states was a major task at hand and the mandarins in Brussels did not wish to be deflected by having to deal seriously with the Muslim problem looming in the south and southeast. Needless to say, they would strenuously deny this and would reject the allegation as self-serving and unfounded. Yet, in my view, what I have now described was, and to some extent still is, basically accurate. Hence, even if the predominance of the Muslim challenge had been accepted in the capitals of the Union, there would not have been sufficient political will to translate a policy decision into action. It would be correct to state, in no uncertain terms, that the Muslim challenge was clearly identified in Europe toward the end of the twentieth century. Obviously, the precise form it would ultimately assume was not identified, but the basics were there for all to observe. For the reasons I have tried to explain, there was no desire to take up the issue in a meaningful way and to deal with it effectively. Indeed, even today, after the turn of the century and following a number of deadly terrorist attacks, including those perpetrated on European soil, there is still a reluctance to face up to the threat in its entirety and to contemplate solutions that might be unpleasant and controversial. As on many other issues, Europe is trailing behind the United States.

10

THE MASHAL AFFAIR

Relations between nations just as those between individuals have defining moments. The Mashal affair was such an event. Although, on the face of it, the resolution was categorized as a successful one, it was, in the final analysis, a lost opportunity.

It was September 1997. On a Thursday afternoon I was traveling to Antwerp from Brussels, where I had been Israel's ambassador to the European Union for close to two years. The time had come to purchase some furniture for a new apartment that my wife and I were going to move into, on our return home in a few months' time. Antwerp, the commercial center of Belgium, was the right place to go for things that make a home. An unexpected ring on my cell phone interrupted my thoughts of chairs and dining tables. The military secretary to the prime minister was on the line. I was being asked to travel to Israel immediately. Something had happened and my service was required. No explanations could be given because of the sensitivity of the event. I asked that the foreign minister be informed and his approval given. On another occasion I had traveled at the behest of the prime minister to Jordan without the ministry being informed and I had been publicly dismissed in the media and reprimanded. I was determined that this would not happen a second time. I was told that this was impossible. The foreign minister was in New York attending the annual U.N. Assembly session and there was no way of communicating with him in a secure way. I replied that I would not move without the minister being informed. My wishes were honored. The minister was informed and it became my task to find an immediate flight to Israel.

As evening fell, I was back in Brussels and a quick check showed that there was no possible way for me to fly directly to Tel Aviv before the following day. In the meantime, I found out why I was being summoned: A squad of Mossad officers had been on mission in Amman, Jordan, where they had attempted, unsuccessfully, to eliminate a prominent Khammas leader, Khaled Mashal. Six members of the squad were stranded in Jordan. Two were in the hands of the Jordanians and nothing was known about their whereabouts or what had become of them. Four were holed up in the Israeli embassy in Amman, their place of refuge after the mission had been aborted. The head of the Mossad had flown to Jordan to see the king and to put things right. He had seen the king briefly but had not been able to obtain any concession from him on the six men and women. All contact between the Jordanians and Israel had been suspended. Attempts to dispatch senior figures to see the king, like Attorney General Elyakim Rubinstein, who had led the official Israeli delegation in the peace negotiations with Jordan and who was well liked and respected by the king, were rebuffed. He simply did not wish to see any Israeli. He felt betrayed by those whom he had befriended and with whom he had dealt in a spirit of trust and confidence. The Mossad chief, a former military secretary to the late Prime Minister Rabin, had spent a weekend with his family in Aqaba, Jordan, days before the abortive operation that he had commanded on Jordanian soil. To King Hussein, the entire situation was beyond comprehension.

Another incident served to deepen the king's feelings of betrayal. A few days before the incident, he had met with a senior Mossad officer, an officer for whom he had a particular liking. Through this officer, he had transmitted a proposal by Khammas leaders that a thirty-year truce—a *hudna*—be called between Israel and the Palestinians, including the radical Khammas movement. The King had not received any reaction whatsoever to the proposal when the abortive Mossad attempt had shaken his trust that Thursday morning. I was to learn of this later from the king himself. In his eyes, the Mossad operation seemed even more strange in light of the proposal he had passed on to Israel. It later came to light that the message had not been given any priority and the routine treatment it received resulted in the prime minister being informed of its existence only after the operation was over.

There is no way that I can determine whether this offer of the Khammas was serious and if it would have blossomed into a genuine thirty-year or even a thirty-day cease-fire. In the aftermath of the whole affair, conventional wisdom in Israel held that the whole initiative was at best a tactical trial balloon to test the resilience of Israel at a given moment and that there was no merit whatsoever in giving such an offer even the faintest character of legitimacy. At that time, there was widespread consensus that Khammas was a deadly terrorist group that had to be met by force and force alone. This may well have been so; however, we will never know if this method of dealing with them was the only valid one, for there was never a discussion of their offer of a truce at the time it could have been operative.

Throughout the night I was in touch with the powers that be in Israel. I was told that the prime minister had spent the whole night at Mossad headquarters and that he was personally overseeing the steps and moves of the Mossad as they dealt with the incident. The leaders of the intelligence community were there with him together with the IDF chief of staff and others. The crisis was real.

The prime minister wanted me in Israel instantly. I was told to try to hire an aircraft at Brussels Airport. A quick check produced an eighty-thousand-dollar price tag for such a trip and this was without doubt exorbitant by any yardstick. An attempt was made to reroute an Israeli Boeing 747 cargo aircraft to pick me up. Alas, the airport closed around midnight due to environmental restrictions. Constant phone calls reminded me that time was of the essence. The whole story had been placed under heavy censorship, but the fear was that it would burst out at any moment and the result would or could be catastrophic. I could not move before the following day. In all honesty, the more I learned the details of the crisis, the less inclined I was to rush to Tel Aviv without sufficient time for reflection and preparation.

The following day, Friday, I left for Israel and arrived in the early afternoon. I was met at the airport and whisked away to Mossad headquarters.

A strange feeling crept over me. It was like returning to the scene of the crime. I was no longer a member of this illustrious band of warriors, but the fate of their comrades and that of the political future of the principals on either side suddenly seemed to have been placed into my hands.

I was greeted very warmly by my former colleagues and by my predecessor, all of whom assured me that everyone now awaited my solution to the problem. They began by wanting to brief me on the operation. To their surprise I requested not to be briefed. I told my erstwhile colleagues that the less I knew of the operation, the better. If and when I met my Jordanian friends, I wished to be as ignorant as possible about the details of what had transpired. I was no longer a member of the Mossad. Indeed, if I were to have any chance of success, it would only be if my interlocutors were convinced that I had nothing whatsoever to do with what had happened.

All present understood that the crisis could not be solved without some contribution being made to Jordan's well-being. In this spirit, long before my arrival, ideas had been bandied around. They ranged from supplying the Jordanian Armed Forces with a quantity of infrared night sights for tanks to upgrading some of the country's aircraft. I was told all this in passing, as if these ideas had been voiced and then disregarded as incapable of healing such a deep wound. The moment I had arrived the problem became mine and it was clear why I had been so hastily summoned. As one of my now former colleagues put it, "It is your show now and we will be watching you from the balcony."

After listening patiently and sympathetically to what they told me, I said to the many sitting around the table that I had been thinking about the problem and a possible solution all the way to Tel Aviv. All of those present had been focusing on Israel's predicament. I had, instead, been concentrating on the acute embarrassment of King Hussein. He had taken the courageous step of leading his country to sign a peace treaty with Israel in the face of bitter opposition of the majority of his citizens. His land was playing host to hundreds of thousands of Palestinian refugees and their sentiments toward Israel were extremely hostile. Inside Jordan there was a strong and vocal element of extreme Muslim radicals, the Muslim Brotherhood, and they were allied, inter alia, with the Khammas movement operating in the Palestinian territories and mounting operations against Israel. The relationship between the monarchy and the Muslim Brotherhood had been an extremely complex one. There were times when the movement was allowed to run for parliamentary elections and there were others when they were banned from public office. It was a very intricate power play that had been enacted on the Jordanian political stage. The aborted attempt on the life of Khaled Mashal could not have come at a worse time from the king's perspective.

At the same time there was understanding and cooperation between Israel and Jordan at the highest levels and both parties were enjoying the benefits of these unique relations. Now, in the eyes of King Hussein, Israel had betrayed this trust and had placed him in an untenable position. Israeli operatives had attempted to assassinate a Jordanian citizen, a leader of the Khammas–Muslim Brotherhood group on Jordanian territory, in the center of Amman, not that far from the seat of government. The king had a tremendous problem. If we solved his problem, ours would be solved immediately.

Any solution had to take into account all the elements of this complex situation. Any proposal made by us would have to enable the king to defend his decision to release the six detainees publicly if necessary. In this vein I suggested that Israel release the jailed founder-leader of Khammas, Sheikh Ahmed Yassin, and hand him over to Jordan. He would, most probably, subsequently be transferred to the Gaza Strip and welcomed by Arafat and the Palestinians, but it would be no other than King Hussein who had secured the man's release. A deafening silence greeted my suggestion. After the initial shock, my colleagues tore into it mercilessly. There was no way that the Israeli public would understand such a move, since the Khammas had kidnapped an Israeli soldier three years before and demanded the release of Yassin as the price for his release. The prime minister at the time, Yitzhak Rabin, had refused to give in to this ultimatum and had approved a daring rescue operation that had ended in failure. The soldier, Nachshon Waxman, and one of the commanders of the liberating force had paid with their lives. Now I was proposing to secure the release of the six (two of whom were in the hands of the Jordanians) by voluntarily releasing the same figure that Rabin had refused to free. This was morally objectionable and unacceptable. The Mossad, of all in Israel, could not table such a proposal. King Hussein had not even asked for such a gesture. If Yassin were to be released, he should be handed over to the Palestinians. The release of the Palestinian leader to Jordan would be a slap in the face to the Palestinian leader, Yassir Arafat, who was, after all, Israel's principal partner in the tortuous peace process that we were engaged in. After all, it was argued, what had happened was no fault of Arafat's. All this led to an all-out rejection of the proposition.

I responded at some length. What was at stake did not begin and end with the detention and release of six Mossad operatives. The operation had placed the king in an impossible situation. If he simply let the men go he would be unable ever again to look his own security forces in the face; in their eyes he would be seen as no more than a "collaborator" with the Mossad and what it represented. Moreover, I did not think that Jordan could pursue any cooperation of any kind with Israel in the security and defense fields as long as the crisis had not been resolved. If allowed to fester, the situation could well deteriorate to a point where the peace treaty signed between Israel and Jordan might be suspended if not abrogated. In pure political terms this could become a massive blow to the cause of peace in the region and the overall political effect could threaten the continued service of both Prime Minister Netanyahu and King Hussein in their respective roles. The shock effects of such turmoil could affect the entire fabric of peace agreements and negotiations to those ends, which was a basic strategic necessity for Israel.

My audience was not convinced and suggested that I come up with a proposal that was less pretentious and dramatic. I told my former colleagues that I could think of nothing else and the discussion then ceased abruptly and a sense of deep gloom filled the room. Several minutes later, no other suggestion having been made, I was asked to call the prime minister and put the idea to him. "Why me?" I asked. "If you people think it a reasonable idea, you call him!" A short Ping-Pong on this ended with my agreeing to speak to the prime minister. It was late Friday afternoon and he was at home as the Jewish Sabbath was about to commence. I explained the suggestion and its rationale and Netanyahu responded with an immediate rejection. It was unthinkable and he would not even give the proposal any further thought.

I was asked to think of something else. I told my friends that it was up to them to be creative and imaginative. I had tried, in the meantime, to establish contact with my Jordanian colleagues and was told that His Majesty asked that I not become involved in this affair. He valued his relationship with me and did not wish it to be tarnished by this sordid story.

Late that evening I went up to Jerusalem and stayed overnight at my son's apartment. The following morning I drove down to the office where the prime minister caught up with me on the phone. He referred in general terms to our conversation the day before and told me that I was authorized to proceed and try to get a resolution along the lines that I had suggested. Given the delicacy of the matter at hand, I asked the prime minister to be more specific, to mention the name we were discussing, and to be more explicit about the parameters of my authority. He accepted the request and I realized that what had been total anathema only a day before was now legitimate and acceptable.

I asked that my role in the negotiations not be revealed in public. I was no longer serving in the Mossad and therefore the normal rules of secrecy no longer applied to me, but I valued the relationship I had fostered over the years with the Hashemite house and thought that public reference to my role in any shape or form concerning the Mashal affair might taint this asset, which I believed was an asset that had assumed national significance and was no longer just a personal bond of friendship. I did not wish to jeopardize any future role that I might be called upon to play. More specifically, I asked that I not be named as the one who had proposed the release of Yassin. Not that I was in any way ashamed of having raised the unmentionable. Rather, I thought that the anonymity of the proposals of civil servants should be respected and protected so that they might not be inhibited in the future from proposing whatever they thought fit, without fear of public exposure that could restrict them in defending their opinions and challenge their professional integrity. I was assured that my wishes would be respected. The affair had been under press censorship restrictions and nothing had yet been published in the Israeli media. It was therefore possible to lay down the rules in advance of the inevitable publicity and to ensure that my wishes be respected alongside other considerations. Alas, within forty-eight hours the cat was out of the bag and both my role and my authorship of the proposal were revealed in broad daylight. But before all this was to happen, the drama had yet to play itself out.

Saturday was not only the day that marked a turning point in the policy that Israel was to adopt on the crisis. King Hussein had been uneasy ever since Mashal's neck had been smeared with a certain poison application and then quickly administered an antidote by an Israeli physician who had been rushed to the scene on orders of the prime minister. His rapid grasp of the full consequences of the botched operation had led him to make the immediate decision to save the life of the person that was the target of the operation. It was, in my opinion, a masterstroke that averted a real and true catastrophe in Israeli-Jordanian relations. In situations such as these, the prime minister's knack for instant reaction based on a whirlwind mastery of diverse details and complex considerations was second to none. Had Mashal died that morning, I think the task of extricating ourselves from the ensuing entanglement would have been ten times more difficult. Mashal was recovering well, but the king's deepest suspicions had been aroused. What if there was a turn for the worse and Mashal were to die in a Jordanian hospital because the antidote had not worked in the end? How would this reflect upon all of the concerned parties, including the king himself? Would he not be blamed personally for trusting the Israelis after they had betrayed him so terribly?

The king decided that day to turn to the president of the United States and to place the issue at his doorstep. He had summoned to Jordan a trusted American physician and the latter required more information before he could assure the king that all was well. In the meantime, I had relayed the gist of the Yassin proposal to Jordan and was invited to come to Amman the following day, on condition that the king received the necessary assurances the day before. It was late Saturday afternoon and I was to go to Amman on Sunday, if all went well.

We were all gathered in the prime minister's office. Calls were arriving from the United States urging the prime minister to meet the king's demands and to alleviate his deep anxieties. I was on the line to Amman assuring my Jordanian counterparts that we were sincere and truthful in what we were telling them. As evening fell I received word from Jordan that the king was planning to hold a high-profile international press conference that very evening in which he intended to expose the aborted Israeli operation and to announce the suspension of the Israeli-Jordanian peace treaty. He was going to ask that the Israeli embassy personnel leave Amman as soon as possible, and that the four Mossad officers ensconced there be handed over to the Jordanian security services. Were he to be met by a refusal on the part of Israel, crack Jordanian forces were readied to storm the embassy and to apprehend the four operatives. I must admit that during those tense hours I felt that the destiny of so much that had been accomplished in recent years was in the balance, and that I had been catapulted into a truly unique position where I could not afford to fail. I told the prime minister that I did not think that the king was bluffing. Knowing him sufficiently well by now, I believed that I could responsibly advise the prime minister that all this was for real. The air was tense and the number of people around who kept their silence far outnumbered the few who spoke their mind. I have always found that these are the moments in which you truly get to know people. Was there not a silver lining in every tough situation?

The king had his way, and the crisis eased somewhat, but there was still no assurance on his part that the formula I had proposed would indeed get us over the problem. I drove the following day to Amman and insisted on going alone. This was not a Mossad mission and I was not representing the agency that I had served for close to thirty-five years, the last five as deputy chief of the organization.

On arrival, I was received by Crown Prince Hassan and the then chief of the security service, General Batikhi. This was the first time I had met the latter and I did not have the advantage of any previous dealings with him. The prince, a longtime friend, who had played a decisive and historic role in cementing the peace treaty, was very grave and subdued that morning. He related in detail how the operation had been executed by the Mossad. As told by the prince either it was a highly incompetent piece of work or it showed a remarkable disregard for Jordanian capabilities and thus added insult to injury. I knew nothing of all this and had, as recalled, specifically not been briefed on the details of the act. Every juicy detail was put to me and all I could do was nod in sympathy and wait with infinite patience until the story reached its conclusion.

I then put the proposition to the prince and he said it was worthy of consideration. Batikhi took a different line and it was clear to me that he was out to extract as much as he could. He exhibited a wealth of injured pride and was scathing in his rhetoric and widespread accusations of treachery. I made it clear that I was not representing the Mossad but asked, en passant, how the two persons detained by the Jordanian service were faring. Nothing had been heard of them since they were detained and there was much concern in Israel over their well-being. The prince immediately responded that they were in good health, to the open anger of Batikhi, who wished us to remain in the dark on the condition of the two detainees as long as possible. As the discussion went on it became clear to me that there would have to be further negotiations and that the price for solving the crisis would have to be greater and to include more prisoners in Israeli hands.

A pause was called and I was informed that I would be seeing His Majesty in the early afternoon. I rushed to the embassy, reported back to Jerusalem, and met with the four officers trapped there to tell them that I was doing my level best to get them out. I could promise nothing but asked that they be ready at short notice. Back to the palace and within no time I was sitting across from His Majesty, who barely concealed his bitter feelings over what had transpired. I heard at some length how he felt and as he concluded his words, he intimated that he would be accepting the offer of the release of Sheikh Yassin together with others, yet to be specified. In the developing discussion I felt that it had become appropriate to propose that an emergency meeting be convened at the highest level to solidify the understandings being reached. I had obtained authorization to make such a proposal if I thought it had a chance of being accepted. His Majesty accepted this and agreed that the details be worked out with the prime minister himself. To this end, I suggested that the prime minister come over that very night for a meeting, most probably with Prince Hassan and General Batikhi, both of whom were present at the audience. I rushed over again to the embassy and obtained Netanyahu's final agreement to make the trip. As my meeting with the king was nearing its end, and sensing that the hitherto tense atmosphere had eased somewhat, I turned to the king and said that I now felt I could make a personal request of His Majesty. He asked what I had in mind. "That His Majesty perform an act of compassion," I replied. "What exactly are you asking for?" he said. I replied that since I was asking for an act of royal compassion, I did not feel comfortable stating exactly what His Majesty could or should do. "Go and take the four people in the embassy right away," His Majesty told me. Batikhi tried to prevent His Majesty from confirming his decision, but to no avail. The die had been cast. I then turned to His Majesty and requested that the two detained persons be informed in a certain way that we were aware of their condition and that we were working to get them home. The king agreed without hesitation, to the obvious annoyance of Batikhi. I thanked His Majesty for his welcome gestures, took my leave of him, and rushed out to telephone on my cell phone to request that a military helicopter be sent without delay, to take the four persons and myself back to Israel. Within less than thirty minutes we were all aboard and flying back to Israel. It took only twenty minutes to fly directly from Amman to Jerusalem and we touched down at the helipad near the Knesset. I left the helicopter for the prime minister's office to start preparing for the nocturnal meeting of the prime minister in Amman. The others flew on to Tel Aviv and to freedom. Stage one had been successfully completed, but there was much left to do. The ice had been broken and in a letter the prime minister sent me a couple of months later, he acknowledged that without this initial breakthrough the successful outcome would have been in serious doubt.

It became necessary to make sure that all were on board on the Israeli side as to what had been agreed on with the Jordanian leadership before the journey to Amman. As the nature of the deal became known inside the Israeli hierarchy, opposition was voiced by key figures in the intelligence and defense establishments. This was to be expected. There were those who opposed the developing deal on principle, whereas others, as is often the case, lifted their hands against it simply because they had not been brought in at the beginning. Ultimately, the strong backing of the minister of defense, Yitzhak Mordecai, was key to providing the prime minister with vital political support. Ariel Sharon was a subsequent backer of the move and was destined to take over the intricate negotiations with the Jordanians, once the initial stage had been completed.

Toward midnight, a helicopter took off from the helipad in Jerusalem, carrying the prime minister, the minister of defense, and a host of military secretaries, aides, and others. I was there with them in the traditional role I had played in the relationship with the Jordanians when prime ministers Shamir and Rabin were at the helm. As we neared Amman, there was no indication that the Jordanians were there to receive us on the ground. Something had gone wrong in the coordination procedures and for almost half an hour the helicopter flew above the city, virtually aimlessly. I sensed growing danger as the plane went low from time to time, seeking landing options. It was a nerve-wracking experience, during which, more times than one, I suggested to the prime minister to call the mission off, to return to Israel, and to get things back on track. He would hear none of this and instructed the pilots to pursue their search come what may. At the very last minute, a Jordanian helicopter took off, established contact, and guided our aircraft to a landing site. One mistake, and the whole mission could have ended in national tragedy.

The negotiations that ensued that night were led on the Jordanian side by Crown Prince Hassan and General Batikhi. They were driving a hard bargain and it became evident that the release of the two detained men was not going to be imminent. At the end, understandings were reached on the principles of the deal, but much remained for subsequent meetings, at which I was no longer present. These were conducted first by the attorney general, Rubinstein, and afterward by Minister Ariel Sharon and his emissary, Magali Wahaba. I asked to be excused from further involvement in the affair and, once this was granted, flew back immediately to Brussels. Several days later, I was summoned once again to Jerusalem to deal with a mini-crisis in the discussions but made every effort to cut down my further participation to a bare minimum. I honestly desired to distance myself from the entire story. I did not wish to become overinvolved and by association indirectly implicated with my former office, which I had left never to return, or so I believed.

For me, the Mashal affair was a unique experience in dealing with matters of state. I came to learn how brittle the fortunes of political masters and historic figures could become. One moment they were up on high, a minute later their careers hung in the balance. In retrospect, I think that had the problem not been solved in the way I proposed, the course of events in the Middle East might well have taken an entirely different turn. Yassin was released a day after the fateful midnight meeting and found his way to Gaza, after a brief stay in Jordan. King Hussein emerged from the crisis as one who had achieved the impossible and could not be faulted for releasing his prisoners. Public opinion in Israel, by and large, accepted the step as necessary, even if it was not cause for jubilation.

In the past I had been witness to many tense situations involving the political levels of government, but had never felt the intensity of the personal aspect of such predicaments as I did on this occasion. Maybe this was because in this case I was at the epicenter of the potential political and diplomatic earthquake and I felt an acute personal responsibility to bail all the players out safe and sound. Within the space of ninety-six hours I went through a crash program that propelled me through heads of state, politicians, civil servants, and personal aides, the like of which I had never experienced before. There were times when I sensed an acute loneliness. People seemed to melt into the woodwork, when just a moment before they had been all-present and vocal. I could almost hear the wheels turning in their heads and in their hearts: "How will this affect me?" "How will I be perceived in the eyes of my peers, my subordinates, my adversaries and enemies?" I saw friends and colleagues standing aloof, waiting for the other shoe to drop, preparing to distance themselves from my possible failure, and readying themselves to join in the triumph and festivities once success was assured.

This intensive course in political maneuvers was to stand me in good stead up to a point as I was to enter my future incarnations. And yet, I must admit, that notwithstanding my schooling in the sensation of cynicism, egoism, and human deviousness, maybe essential tools in the practice of intelligence, I could never ever reconcile myself to accepting that all human relations must have grains of these ingredients. During those formative days I also met with one or two people who were true and unconditional friends. It was a redeeming feature, a vital antidote in a hostile world of evil passions and unbridled ambitions. If I was to make mistakes from then on, it would be when I wrongly assigned persons to the select category of sincere friends rather than to the more general category of people who inevitably surrounded me in the beclouded corridors of power. And I never succumbed to a persecution complex.

The Mashal affair was to shape my understanding and approach to many of the issues on the agenda of the Middle East and the world at large. When in Brussels I had the opportunity of meeting a rabbi, Menachem Fruman, who was an inhabitant of a settlement in the "disputed territories," but who at the same time held a series of meetings with none other than Sheikh Yassin at his jail. The two discussed religion, theology, and a host of other philosophical subjects. The way I saw it, Fruman had no illusions about Yassin's sentiments concerning Israel. He was a deadly foe. And yet Fruman seemed to believe that dialogue between implacable enemies could produce, if conducted properly, positive results. I continued to maintain contact with Fruman after I returned to Israel and became head of the Mossad, in the belief that one might never know when a given relationship could suddenly become the key to progress or a solution to a particular problem.

Yassin was to become a focal point in the campaign of the Khammas against Israel. From his wheelchair confinement he was viewed as a senior initiator and champion of terrorist acts, some especially gruesome and bloody. He became the target of successive operations designed to eliminate him and was finally killed in 2003. His elimination was viewed as a feather in the cap of the Israeli Security Agency and the Israeli Air Force. I was asked sometimes in years subsequent to the Mashal affair if I did not regret proposing and arranging for his release in the light of the deaths he wrought after he returned to Gaza. I will admit that such thoughts did trouble me from time to time, but I always came back to thinking that there has been, and always will be, only one solitary historical realization. I do not think it can be argued that if Yassin had been kept in an Israeli jail for all the years to come, lives would have definitely been saved. For one, Israeli jails holding Palestinian terrorists had proved to be hotbeds of terrorist planning and inspiration. Israel was never capable of preventing the flow of information, commands, and instruction out of its detention centers, however secure they were in preventing mass escapes. Thus an incarcerated Yassin would not have been prevented from continuing to act as an instigator and as an icon of terror. Similarly, had the crisis between Jordan and Israel not been resolved the way I went about it, the relations between the two countries and their respective political masters could have resulted, as already stated, in the suspension of the peace treaty between the two states, and Jordan might have slid into a new mode whereby its border with Israel would provide terrorists with easy and quick access to the heartland of Israel. No one will ever be able to calculate how many lives were saved by the rapid solution of the grave crisis between Jordan and Israel.

11

PRIORITIES OF A NEW CHIEF

On my return home from Brussels and my abrupt and unexpected appointment as head of the Mossad in April 1998, I found myself once again in the world that I had left less than three years before, but in circumstances that had changed beyond recognition. My time spent in Belgium had, in a strange way, not only provided me with a temporary respite but also furnished me with a detached view of life that was to serve me well in the grueling times that lay ahead.

In 1998, two sets of events propelled the world in the direction of drastic changes in its national and international agendas. The one set was the advent of the Al Qaeda–bin Laden brand of terrorism and the American-led coalition reaction in the form of a cruise missile attack against targets in Afghanistan and Sudan. The other set of events related to the acceleration of the moves to promote proliferation of weapons and capabilities of mass destruction. The world was confronted with the necessity to gather information on these critical subjects and one of the results of this need was that Intelligence, with a capital *I*, suddenly became a key player in the equation of international relations. Why was this fundamentally different from the conditions that had prevailed during the Cold War that followed the end of World War II?

The Cold War as it ran its course over the years had succeeded, so to speak, in fashioning rules of its own and functioning according to them. There was dialogue between the warring nations; there was access, albeit limited, available to all sides beyond the world of intelligence. Embassies in Moscow and Washington, D.C., housed not only hordes of intelligence officers but also diplomats and associated functionaries. Legal travelers from the world of economics, business, and trade journeyed in and out of the powerful countries of the world and the United Nations and semiofficial and nongovernmental groups and conferences provided venues for fraternization and exchanges along a broad front of activity. Access to Beijing was more restricted, but nevertheless it was not solely an intelligence target and there were additional channels of communication.

The circumstances surrounding the principal issues of the late nineties were entirely different. The sole means of access to the principal players were, and to some extent still are, those of intelligence gathering and penetration. The terrorist cells of the various groups practicing international Islamic terror shunned contact with the outside world except by way of their terrorist operations and the publicity they wished to attract to them. Diplomatic, commercial, or academic channels to these groups were never created, and as a result of this, almost absolute reliance was placed on the intelligence net. Similarly, the countries attempting to develop nonconventional weaponry limited access to them to a bare minimum. Of the famous "axis of evil" declared by President George W. Bush after he assumed office, Iraq and North Korea were for all intents and purposes pariah states existing almost entirely in a state of isolation, whereas Iran, which did allow and maintain diversified conduits to the world at large, clearly monitored and controlled them.

Thus, as the free world was propelled into what may someday be seen as the greatest of its tests in living history—its encounter with two deadly menaces to its very existence—the means whereby it was able accurately to gather the vital data it required to assess the dangers were restricted as never before. The difficulties involved in gathering reliable information were colossal. The time span normally applicable to this type of task had to be extended in order to produce results, but the lead time for foiling the evil intent of the enemy was becoming ever shorter.

The expertise and knowledge of political figures in these specialized areas was at the outset quite limited. This was not the conventional field of war and peace that had been studied and researched in depth. Indeed, in the academic world there was no real tradition in investigating these new phenomena, be they cultural, religious, or simply diabolically satanic manifestations of a terrorist scourge, the like of which had not been observed or predicted. The political levels had no one to turn to but the intelligence community, and that community did not enjoy the luxury of being able to tell its masters that it was not ready to tackle the problem and to evaluate the dangers, and that the masters should just go away and come back later.

Thus were the intelligence chiefs in the major countries of the free world catapulted into roles that they had never performed before and for which they were initially ill equipped. Just as they were instructed to gather the vital data without delay, so were they drawn into policy roles or into partnership with policy levels because these policy levels were so thin on their own capacities and capabilities.

Dealing with these amorphous elements rapidly became one of the most tantalizing and frustrating tasks ever undertaken in the realm of intelligence. It was a tormenting experience because it necessitated crash efforts to study languages, habits, and mind-sets of groups and individuals who were, by and large, unidentified and consequently unknown. This is not an apologia for an intelligence failure. It is a simple statement of the accumulative factors that rendered this challenge unique in the annals of the intelligence profession. It was similarly exceptional in regard to the unprecedented menaces facing the political masters of the free world. In their predicament they turned to their intelligence leaders not only for information, but no less for guidance, encouragement, and support.

As a result of these circumstances, I believe it would be accurate to assert that there was never a greater dependence of the political levels on their intelligence chiefs and services than in the fatal areas of international Muslim terrorism and the proliferation of weapons of mass destruction. The burden borne by the intelligence chiefs has been immense. In the final analysis, they have been destined to become equal or near-equal partners of their political masters in making decisions and formulating policies. Subsequently, the intelligence chiefs have been made scapegoats for them if they seemingly went wrong.

The true nature of the threats was extremely difficult to ascertain. The dearth of accurate and confirmed intelligence was a hindrance that was to dog the international community for a decade and more. The purveyors of terror and WMD proliferation were diabolically sophisticated. Their culture and modus operandi did not lend themselves to the traditional methods of intelligence gathering. Thus, just at the time that the intelligence leadership reached unprecedented heights of influence over the political levels of government, the intelligence communities fell short, very short, in their professional achievements in the field.

The delicate interplay between the political and professional levels of intelligence, as already said elsewhere, has been a permanent feature of the Israeli scene ever since it gained its independence in 1948. I was exposed to this reality on many occasions, but did not feel the brunt of this until I assumed the position of head of the service.

One might have thought that there was nothing new for me to learn when I became chief, since I had been deputy chief for five years, a lengthy period without precedent. Normally, the appointment of a deputy heralded his candidacy for the ultimate promotion to the number-one slot. In my case, it was entirely different. When I was offered the number-two position, the relatively new chief, Shabtai Shavit, had made it very clear to me that he did not see me as a possible candidate to replace him when the time came. In view of this, I would serve for two years as deputy and then retire, enabling him to appoint a person to this post who would be groomed by him for the succession. A year later, he partially changed his mind. I was five years older than him and, by tradition, nobody over the age of sixty had ever been appointed head of the Mossad, a difficult job for a person of any age. I was therefore no threat to the chief and as long as I served as deputy, he need not appoint a presumptive successor as deputy, in my stead. Thus I served for five full years as deputy and on many an occasion was acting chief during the frequent absences of the chief. More than once, I handled acute crisis situations, and one might have assumed that when I ultimately was called back to serve as chief, at the age of sixty-four, I simply resumed where I had left off. There was nothing further from the truth.

The ultimate personal and indivisible responsibility of a chief of service has no parallel in other walks of life. It cannot be compared to the accountability of a deputy or any other officeholder. In my first months in office I had a specially onerous mission to perform. Never before had a chief been appointed in such difficult circumstances. My predecessor had resigned after two consecutive intelligence flaps, both of an operational nature. One was the Mashal affair, described earlier on. The second was a failed operation in Switzerland, when a Mossad officer was caught and arrested while trying to attach a wiretap to the telephone line of a person believed to be a terrorist suspect. Both failures hit the media within months of each other and embarrassed Benjamin Netanyahu, who was prime minister at the time.

I had to address myself to three related crises: First, there was a crisis of trust between the political level and the service that I was asked to lead. The prime minister had his reservations concerning the professionalism of the Mossad, making for a very difficult situation. Second, there was a crisis in the public domain between the Mossad and the general public. Much scorn and ridicule was poured on the service and its unknown and unsung officers. And third, a crisis had to be faced within the ranks of the Mossad itself that resulted from the first two stated above—the severe damage caused to the self-confidence and self-esteem of those serving in the ranks. The Mossad's assignments were for the most part fraught with great danger and the dent in the self-confidence of those in the field compounded the dangers in no small measure. It was clear to me that the political level could hardly afford any more mishaps in the immediate future and would expect me to make sure that we performed to perfection. This expectation was never spelled out in so many words, but the body language of my masters left me in no doubt. Yet, on the other side of the equation, I knew full well that if I did not restore the Mossad to full action within weeks, the internal malaise could assume proportions bordering on disaster for the entire organization.

Within months, activities were back on track, and I could truthfully report that we were succeeding in producing quality results that were vital to the continued existence and well-being of the State of Israel. Two events of totally differing natures tested my leadership in the first few months of my tenure, besides the necessity of taking responsibility for decisions involving hazardous operations in a variety of fields and venues. Each illuminated the responsibilities and dilemmas of a chief in modern times.

The one event was the arrest of two Mossad operatives in Cyprus, in a village named Ziggi in the south of the island, in the Greek-dominated

state. The two were brought to trial and sentenced to terms of imprisonment and the whole story was covered at length by the media, which did
not mince words in castigating the Mossad for what was described as
shoddy standards of performance. The division head under whose command the mishap occurred offered his resignation, which I accepted. He
had been considered an outstanding leader and I genuinely regretted having to retire him from the service. Coming so soon after the previous
blows to the prestige of the Mossad that led to my appointment, the
question was raised whether the causes for repetitive failures had been
removed and, by inference, whether I should not hand in my resignation
as well.

I must say that the support I received from Prime Minister Netanyahu
and other ministers, including the then foreign minister, Ariel Sharon,
was reassuring to me and was an important factor in convincing me that
I not only could stay on, but should do so. The degree of my personal
knowledge and involvement in that particular incident was, to me, crucial in making my personal decision. I also thought at the time, and continued to believe so, that if a chief had to resign each time an operation
went wrong, an atmosphere could develop, paralyzing the capacity of
command levels to make hazardous decisions for fear of instant dismissal
due to failure. I formed the belief that command levels must never be cen-
sured for faulty judgment, unless that judgment was blatantly irrational
and reckless. Barring that, only gross negligence could be a motive for
blame.

Once I made the decision that I would stay on, it was clear to me that
the eyes of my subordinates would be directed at me to ascertain whether
I would moderate operations and become demonstratively cautious. This
could have spelled disaster for the organization and I therefore made certain that we would persevere as ever before, myself knowing full well
that I did not enjoy unlimited credit at the top and that my "account,"
though still in the black, had diminished somewhat.

In my initial run in office, I experienced a second test of my powers of
determination and sober evaluation. One bright morning, on February
19, 1999, the Turkish press carried banner headlines announcing that the
leader of the Turkish Kurds, Abdullah Ocalan, had been apprehended in
Nairobi, Kenya, and had been flown under arrest to Turkey to face trial.
The highest government level in Ankara, Turkey, claimed that the arrest

had been made possible through the information provided by the CIA of the United States and the Israeli Mossad. Several days later, Kurds of Turkish origin staged violent demonstrations in European capitals, culminating in an attempt to storm the Israeli consulate general in Berlin. In the ensuing battle, fire was exchanged between the assailants and security guards, who fought off demonstrators which had succeeded in entering the consulate. Three Kurdish demonstrators died that day.

It was clear to me that the fact that the reports in the Turkish press were false was immaterial in the fast-evolving situation. My concern was that if the Kurds in Europe were to remain firm in their belief that the story was indeed true, we would be facing a foe on European soil that would not only seek revenge for what was, albeit falsely, believed to be an act of supreme treachery, but an adversary that could become a permanent feature making our tough tasks that much more lethally dangerous. In these given circumstances it was imperative to send a sharp and clear signal to the Kurds that the Mossad had nothing to do with the capture of their leader. On the face of it, what could be better than an official denial issued by the political level? This, however, would be suspect and in the final analysis would lack credibility. It would be seen as a standard denial, the like of which is issued as a conditioned reflex. I realized that if I raised the matter with my superior, he would decide to publish a denial instantly. I could not argue with him that a statement made on his behalf would be viewed with disbelief.

I chose a method hitherto unused. I sent a personal letter to every serving member of the Mossad clearly stating that the Mossad had nothing to do with the affair and saw to it that the message hit the media. This was, to the best of my knowledge, unprecedented, and I made sure that my original intention was kept unknown. A leading Israeli journalist of impeccable reputation devoted an entire article to criticizing my implicit defense of the prime minister by virtue of my letter to the "troops." He claimed that I was misusing my professional credibility in order to get the prime minister off the hook and that I was guilty of a cheap political ploy. Obviously he missed the whole point of my message and for evident reasons, I preferred to take the rap and not to divulge my true motives. As far as I was concerned, my primary responsibility lay in getting the Kurds to accept that we were out of the loop. It was essential that they not open up a campaign against Mossad officers in Europe, resulting in their return home in body bags. This was my ultimate duty, which transcended all others. This was the kind of decision that I alone could make. In the chain of authority, "the buck" stopped at my doorstep, and my superior was out of the loop and had to remain so. In the final analysis, I achieved my aim. Apparently, the Turkish Kurds did not pursue us and did not jeopardize our men in the field. This, in my understanding, was my ultimate responsibility to my men and women operating in foreign countries, exposed to local threats of both police and security services, and natural prey to the aggressive adversaries in the Arab and Muslim world. Anything I could do to ease their burden and to make their life safer was my number-one priority. This last instance highlighted the unique and personal responsibility that a service chief bore in relation to each and every one of his subordinates. It was, and is, a direct and personal one and it manifested itself in a somewhat extreme form as I dealt with an officer being held by Swiss authorities.

When I assumed the office of chief of the Mossad, following the premature resignation of my predecessor, a Mossad officer was in the custody of the Swiss authorities after he had been caught in the basement of a building trying to fix a wiretap to a telephone line of a suspect connected to Palestinian terror. All the efforts to secure his release, even on bail, had proved futile and the prospect was that the man would languish in jail for an undetermined period of many months until he was brought to trial. The prosecution had not yet decided what charges were to be leveled at him and the future on this matter appeared bleak. Given the shaken morale of those in service, it was clear to me that we must secure the release of the man in jail, even on bail, as quickly as possible. To this end, it became necessary to involve the attorney general in Israel, Elyakim Rubinstein, who was a friend and a colleague of the past. There would have to be a dialogue between him and the state attorney, Edna Arbel, on our side, and the parallel Swiss authorities, on the other. As is often the case, in matters such as this, the involvement of "external" arms of government usually compounded the issue, even if, in this case, they had the best will in the world to be helpful. The negotiations on bail were extensive and protracted. The Jewish feast of Passover was approaching and I was hoping that the procedures and terms for release would enable my man to celebrate the holiday at home. This was not to be. He had to celebrate the freedom of the Jewish people from bondage in Egypt in a Swiss cell, where the Israeli consul was allowed to bring him traditional matzoh, or unleavened bread, on the afternoon prior to the evening of Seder night. The Swiss did not even let him out for a few hours that evening and this was a person who had not yet been indicted, let alone sentenced.

Ultimately, the Swiss agreed to release the man on bail on the following conditions: A bond had to be posted for several million Swiss francs, and the attorney general of Israel had to guarantee, personally, that the released man would return to stand trial when the day came. The attorney general agreed to make the commitment, but insisted that the man himself sign a personal commitment to return as requested and that this personal commitment be signed in jail in the presence of the Israeli consul. This became a serious internal issue in the Mossad. I thought that a commitment on my part to produce the man should be sufficient for the attorney general. It was my responsibility to ensure that the man turn up and not the individual responsibility of that particular officer. My friend the attorney general thought otherwise. He insisted that the man take personal responsibility. This, in my view, ran contrary to the basic codes of conduct in the business. I thought it wrong that in the event of a mishap, the person involved should revert to the status of a private individual in the eyes of the Israeli legal system. Surely, it was just at a moment such as this that the system should "embrace" the individual and assume responsibility for him rather than to apparently separate him from his group and treat him as a lone person. Was I being unnecessarily petty? Was all this just counterproductive? My friend the attorney general claimed that if something went wrong and the man did not return, it would be his professional reputation that would be soiled, and therefore it was only he who could set the conditions. Nobody in government could instruct him to act otherwise. I had no option but to accept this and grit my teeth.

The man was released and he returned home. More than a year later, an indictment was issued by the state prosecutor, Madame Carla Del Ponte, on her last day in office before moving on to the post of chief prosecutor of the U.N. special international court (formed to try persons from the former Yugoslavia, accused of war crimes and crimes against humanity). Some time later, the day of the trial was set, and I prepared to send the bailed officer back to face the Swiss court. A campaign was mounted by ex-Mossad officers to convince me, and the man directly, not to travel to Switzerland. I was told that the dispatch of the person to face trial was unprecedented. I was willfully and consciously placing the man in jeopardy and this ran contrary to the basic ethics of the organization and the "trade of intelligence." It was my duty, so I was told, to keep the man in Israel and to handle the resultant crisis with the Swiss authorities, on the one hand, and the attorney general, on the other, as best as I could. I was accused of preparing to "surrender" a Mossad operative to the "enemy," more or less. More than one of my predecessors was recruited to adopt this position. I was more or less alone on this matter and could not rely on the support of all of my predecessors, which is so vital in such circumstances.

I embarked on an effort of my own, first to convince the person in question to voluntarily agree to travel and face trial. I told him that on the basis of what I knew, there was every chance that he would not have to enter jail again, but that I could not guarantee this. I had several meetings with him and he accepted the rationale of my arguments and agreed to go as per my request. I then spent hours of discussion with the division involved in the unfortunate event and explained to them at length what my considerations were.

Three days before the trial began, I was attending a party at the residence of the American ambassador to Israel when I received a phone call telling me that the military correspondent of the national radio network had just broadcast an item stating that a couple of veteran senior Mossad front-line elite officers had written to the prime minister, detailing what I was about to do. They appealed to him to intervene and announced that in protest they were turning in their badges and would no longer go on reserve duty in their elite unit as they had been accustomed to do until then. The correspondent added that the division involved was in a state of crisis and that its operations had been suspended because the "troops" were refusing to go out into the field. I was accused publicly of being guilty of an act comparable to treason!

I moved rapidly to contain the damage. The report on the strike of the troops was blatantly untrue while the story about the letter to the prime minister was true. I had received it hours before the radio revelation, whereas it had not even reached the office of the prime minister before the public was treated to this juicy piece of scandal. What most con-

cerned me was the effect this publicity might have on the trial and its outcome. After all, if the Swiss powers that be wished to deal a body blow to
the Mossad and to try to cripple its capabilities for some time to come,
what easier move would there be than to sentence the man to a period of
imprisonment and thus to fan the flames of discontent and controversy
inside the Mossad? If ever there was an act of treachery committed inside the Mossad, this was one! The knights of purity and ethics had stuck
their swords deep into the back of their colleague and of the service that
they falsely claimed to serve so valiantly.

I readily admit that I was extremely tense and concerned on the day of
the trial. I was out of Israel on a mission that I could not postpone. The
senior officer that had seen through the whole case on my behalf was in
place and had performed admirably so far. I had implicit trust in him. I
had gone a very long way, personally, in my efforts to ensure that the final outcome would be palatable, to say the least, but I had no way of
guaranteeing the result in advance. When the cell phone rang, I was alone
in a hotel room, somewhere in Europe, and received the welcome news
with a deep sigh of relief. The accused had received a suspended prison
sentence and was a free man.

Immediately on my return to Israel I sent a personal message to every
serving member in the Mossad, detailing the sequence of events and explaining my decision to each and every employee in the organization. I
entitled my message with the words "Without Credibility the Mossad
Will Disintegrate." It was a play on the words of an eminent Jewish
Zionist thinker who had written a famous essay close to a hundred years
before entitled "Without Vision—the People Will Disintegrate." I told
everybody what I had said to the man himself and to his division peers.
We depend on credibility. If we did not keep our word, if we failed to act
on our obligations, nobody would trust us again and we would be on our
own forever and ever. If we failed, no Israeli official outside the Mossad
would accept our word in the future and nobody would come to our aid,
when we needed it. Moreover, if we failed to turn up in Switzerland, we
would never be able to cut deals and understandings in the future with
foreign countries, services, or authorities. Nobody would take our word.
But my decision was based on something greater than expediency. Israel
as a state and its government had made a solemn commitment. The
honor of Israel's legal system as embodied in this case in the personality

of the attorney general was at stake. The Mossad was not an organ of government outside the system. We were part of the machinery of the state and we were duty-bound to act in a manner that would safeguard the integrity and reputation of its institutions. There were times when we were called upon to pay a painful price for this. If we elected not to do so we would not only be causing grievous damage to our country, but we would also at the same time be positioning ourselves outside the fold. This we should never do. This we could never do.

I received strong support from my immediate subordinates for what I had decided and done. A session of the elite unit to which the two reserve "rebels" belonged gave me a very warm reception and their commander told the audience that he had decided to expel them from the unit. One was a close friend and fellow combatant of his. I was convinced at the time, just as I am convinced today, that the step I took established a standard of conduct that was not only a credit to those directly involved, but also a service to the cause as a whole. I have no way of knowing what would have happened if the Swiss court had decided differently. Would this have been the prelude to an internal dispute that would have rent the Mossad in two? I honestly do not know. But this decision, like so many others that I took on the pure operational level, was characteristic of the essence of the art of intelligence. Namely, that any decision is always made in circumstances of uncertainty. There was never, and never will be, a foolproof method of correct decision making in intelligence, and you always have to take risks and be ready to shoulder responsibility for failure just as you are willing to revel in success.

What was and still remains the correlation between the gigantic challenges that intelligence communities face in this age, the priorities that I, as a new chief, had to contend with, and the seemingly petty cases that I related about mishaps and my approach to them? The nature and unique personal hazards confronting the individual officer in pursuit of his missions in far-flung regions around the globe have made it imperative to secure a solid relationship between the chief, as the person ultimately responsible for the safety of his men/women, and the lonely case officer out in the cold. Consequently, I made it my business to meet with individuals and teams leaving on mission, to brief them on their tasks and to look them straight in the face and tell them in advance what my capabilities were, should they get into trouble, and what I personally undertook to do in such an eventuality. This not only created a personal bond, to which I was committed, but also served to solidify a firm ethical code and basis for a service that had no legal framework to support its myriad tasks and activities. If I had failed in this effort of mine, nothing else would have been capable of redeeming my term in office. Failure would result in a definite deterioration of the health, resilience, and quality of the service and would inevitably spell the death of the enterprise as a whole.

The priorities of terror—its local, regional, and international brands—and the threat of WMD production and proliferation, which have been at the forefront of the concerns of the Israeli and international intelligence communities for more than a decade, shaped the character and content of my watch. When I came on board I found many initiatives taken by my immediate predecessors that were both worthy and productive. I had no hesitation in continuing along some of those paths and benefiting from excellent results. In this spirit, I considered it my duty to launch not only short-term projects but also medium- and in rare cases even long-term plans, knowing full well that any successor of mine might cancel any one of them. Such is life in general, yet in the field of intelligence, hidden as it is from the public eye, the flexibility and powers of the chief are infinitely greater than in the overt parts of life.

The well-worn cliché, incessantly repeated in the Mossad almost from time immemorial, has been that the human source is the most precious treasure of the business. This sounded, and will forever sound, fine. It was particularly relevant in the first decades of our existence when people joined the Mossad for a lifetime mission. It fell to me to begin a major change in approach to maintain the high degree of excellence to which we aspired. In modern times it was no longer possible to ignore the rules of the labor market. Young and capable individuals no longer wished to sign up for the duration of their working careers and now preferred to serve their country or people for limited periods of time on a contractual basis. It was therefore imperative to bring about a change in the basic culture of the "business" and to launch a process that would culminate, sometime in the future, with most if not all of them serving short or medium terms. But how should we go about recruiting the best and the brightest? In the past most of the recruits were identified by acquaintances already serving in the ranks. From time to time, there were advertisements in the press seeking candidates on behalf of a "national," anonymous organ of state. I decided that we would start recruitment under the banner of the Mossad, and to this end I hired the services of a leading public-relations firm, one that had promoted and handled the political campaign of more than one prime minister. I also decided to open a Web site to this end. The move aroused strong opposition in the firm and produced heated debates on the ethics of "going public." Some looked upon this step as something bordering on sacrilege! For a few of the veterans these became difficult times, but in the end the results justified this departure from ancient custom.

Needless to say, these aspects of my tenure were by no means the highlights of my four-and-a-half-year term in office. There were the operations and decisions that I had to make on the substantive tasks of the firm, but of them, much needed to remain hidden from sight. The basic requirement and tenet of any intelligence firm is its sworn duty to protect "sources and methods." These must remain sacrosanct not only for ethical reasons, but also because their violation would inevitably result in the cessation of activities. No individual will put his faith and personal fate in the hands of a firm that has proven unwilling or incapable of protecting the identities of its sources and the methods whereby these sources are run.

There was one more aspect of my experience that I wish to dwell upon, since in my judgment, it has significance beyond my particular case. I became chief in unique and unexpected circumstances. I returned "home," so to speak, and the people surrounding me were all known to me, except for one. I had been brought back to steady the boat and a new deputy had been appointed alongside me, a distinguished serving general from the IDF, who was personally revered by the prime minister. The tacit understanding and expectation was that I would be an "interim chief" and that I would groom my deputy as my successor within a two-year-or-so span. When this became clear to me at the outset, I insisted that no time limit be placed on my tenure. I also asked that it be stated publicly, and in no uncertain terms, that I had full authority to run the agency and to make any decision whether short-term or long-term, whatever the case might be. Had these conditions/requests not been met, it would have been impossible for me to accept the offer made to me by the prime minister. In any service, like the Mossad, it would be ruinous to create a situation wherein the "troops" were to believe that their chief was a temporary fixture, here today and gone tomorrow, and that therefore any decision he might make could be overturned within a very short period of time. My new deputy came in about six months after I took over. By then I had decided on a major reorganization of some of the divisions, appointed new division chiefs to some of the major operational units, and all this had been approved by the prime minister. All this was accomplished with a renewal of all the activities of the operational units, including activities implemented in places never visited by operatives of the service. Had I not acted in this way, I would have sent a message within that I was no more than a lame duck at the very outset and this would have spelled the end of my new or old career from the very beginning. Once the direction had been set and most of the management was on board, we could face the new challenges with a degree of confidence and hope. Notwithstanding these steps taken by me, it was inevitable that once my deputy assumed office, there would be those who would begin a countdown to the end of my leadership. Within a very short time, it was only natural that the new man on board would form his opinions on a host of issues and would make his views clear to those seeking his advice. The formula applied by the prime minister in putting in place a two-headed command did not serve a useful purpose and the ensuing tension began to compound a situation that was already laden with complexity owing to the circumstances that had resulted in the resignation of my predecessor. The media became aware of the situation and added fuel to the fire until the prime minister decided that he wished me to stay on to ensure stability and continuity. My deputy resigned, and I stayed on for more than two more years and was thus able to steer the agency in the direction I had chosen with a growing degree of satisfaction over the results obtained.

I have often looked back on those days and have thought that the delicate nature of the Mossad's activities should preclude the political level of government from experimenting with appointments and chains of command. So much of the Mossad's work is always performed under conditions of varying measures of uncertainty. There is precious little that the political master can do to reduce the margins of unpredictability, and on countless occasions not only the chief of the service but also many of his subordinates find themselves locked in the horns of insoluble dilemmas. In the seas of doubt and mystery, in which an intelligence officer is often constrained to function, he or she should sense a rocklike strength and dependability at the top. I well remember meeting with individuals and teams about to depart on dangerous missions in order to review their preparations with them and with a view to encouraging the men and women as they prepared to depart. The final part of any such briefing session was always devoted to surveying what were the weaknesses of a given operation and what might go wrong in the course of its implementation. It was my habit to leave the desk or podium where I was standing or seated and to approach my audience and look them straight in the face. I considered it my sacred duty to impress upon those listening to me that I bore a personal and direct responsibility for their wellbeing and safety and that in the event of their being victims of mishaps, I would personally be involved in efforts to resolve any situation that might arise. I never spoke in vague terms and referred to concrete conditions that might arise and to my personal capacities to act in them. What would I do in cases of detention or arrest? What could I do in situations that put individuals in physical jeopardy? I could not, of course, supply ironclad guarantees of success, but I could impress upon my listeners that I was dead serious and that I indeed had capabilities in such predicaments and that I was not just mouthing empty words.

This was of paramount importance in providing the lone officer or the team with a sense of confidence and security. After all, what "weapon" did the intelligence officer have in his bag when it came to his having to fend for himself? Unlike any soldier in the field, he did not even have a personal gun to give him minimal protection. He had to rely on his brains, on his training, on his ingenuity, and on his confidence that come what may, the chief of the service would spare no effort to extricate him from any situation and that the chief, no other, would be involved in person to do whatever had to be done. Of all my experiences in office, these sessions were the most dramatic and meaningful to me and, long after leaving government service, I had the good fortune to be accosted by people whom I did not recognize and who reminded me of this or that encounter, when I had met with them on such matters, and how these meetings had left an indelible impression upon them. These unique "conclaves" could only be successful if mutual confidence was established, and confidence in the chief was only possible if the troops understood that he was not a transient figure, but one that had a large measure of continuity. It was the duty of those at the political level to ensure such continuity, not permanence, but a sizable degree of stability. The damage to morale and to the efficacy of intelligence work caused by malfeasance of those at the political levels in the performance of their duty is indescribable. This is by no means confined to the Mossad, but is true when it comes to any intelligence service the world over.

12

HUBRIS, ARROGANCE, AND
SELF-CONFIDENCE

The day after I took over as head of the Mossad, I held a meeting with a group of officers led by their division chief to discuss and approve an operation that was to be carried out in a country that was rated particularly hazardous and dangerous from multiple aspects. It involved a series of sessions with a valuable agent who had been in service for quite some time, whose trips abroad from his native country were few and far between. His travels were usually strictly monitored by his security services and his freedom of movement was by nature restricted, and he was therefore unable to go to a venue that might have made it easier for all concerned. It transpired that quite some time had elapsed since Mossad officers had passed through the impending venue; actually, nobody around the table could recall when we had last been there. The operational plan was presented to me in general terms and I responded by posing a series of practical questions, to which there were no answers. The dilemma was compounded by the knowledge that there was no knowing when the agent might travel again. Was it one year, two years later? Neither he nor anybody else could know. It was presented as "now or never"! Less than an hour after the discussion began, talk petered out and a familiar silence came over the room. Everything that could have been said had been said and it was now only a go-ahead signal that was awaited. I had attended countless discussions of this nature in the past and was used to saying my piece. This time it was I who had the last word and it was my decision and my decision alone.

I was conscious of the fact that this was to be my very first decision as chief. Anything I said and my general comportment when saying it would be registered by all those present and would be disseminated in one form or other to a much wider audience in the business. I would be judged by this decision beyond its intrinsic significance and it was immaterial if this was justified or not. I summed up the situation the way I saw it and said that I did not think that the risks had been adequately assessed. I withheld approval and, instead, instructed the division to carry out a dry run without attempting any contact with the agent. On the basis of the operational data collected, a fresh plan should be drawn up in the hope that the agent might turn up again, earlier than expected. This indeed did happen and by sheer luck, he came again three months later and the operation was successfully accomplished.

As everyone left the room that morning, a senior officer who had been in attendance came up to me to say that I had made the right decision. Only a few minutes earlier he had forcefully pressed to approve the mission without reservation. Astounded as I was, I asked him why he had not spoken up and had, instead, "joined the crowd," to which he replied, "It is our task to initiate and press for action; we must press forward. It is your task to weigh the dangers and to apply the brakes if you think fit."

I did not accept this approach or philosophy in the business. From then on, I made it my business to brief every station chief before he went abroad and to tell him, inter alia, that once he was in place, he should consider himself a mini-Mossad chief, and should make it his business to highlight the weaknesses of any proposal no less than its strengths. I made it abundantly clear that only in such a climate would it be possible for me to make bold decisions, in the knowledge that nothing had been hidden from me.

There was another aspect of the situation that I had to take care of immediately after coming aboard. It became known to me that as a result of the flaps that had occurred and that had led to my appointment, the prime minister had ordered an entire division to be suspended until they had worked out a fresh modus operandi, and he himself had laid down the first rules of the new operational approach that he expected to be brought for his approval. In addition to this, he had decided that an entire range of activities should be brought to him for endorsement and this necessitated frequent meetings with the prime minister, where he reviewed operational proposals, expressed his detailed opinions on them, and then gave his consent or withheld it. A few weeks after taking office, I asked to see the prime minister and told him why I thought that he should restore to me all the authority that he had taken from my predecessor. I told the prime minister that I thought he should not enter into the operational field and should not be briefed in such a manner that would be viewed as not only indicative of a lack of confidence in the head of the Mossad, but also as a situation in which the prime minister assumed operational responsibility for the activities of the Mossad. If he continued in this way, he would be the de facto head of the Mossad and would shoulder responsibility for the operational conduct of the business. I definitely accepted that there were types of decisions that would have to be brought to the prime minister's approval, but these should be limited to the bare minimum and in any event, the approval procedure should not embrace entry into the nitty-gritty of this or that project. I must say that Prime Minister Netanyahu accepted my requests and gave me full support and backing. He did not rescind this decision and stood behind me without reservation when I sustained my first flap several months later, when a couple of my men were caught and arrested in Cyprus.

The distinction between the responsibilities of the political and executive levels was one of the issues that both interested me and consumed part of my time and thinking during my tenure as head of the Mossad. It was not an exercise in theory or in political thought. Rather, it was often a very real and immediate subject of concern. I recall that on one occasion we presented a detailed plan of an impending operation and, as was necessary in such matters, listed possible weaknesses in the plan of action. The prime minister, who in a past incarnation had had experience in this very field, went into every detail and tried to instruct us on the technicalities, where to station security personnel, and how to use our equipment. Were these orders of the political level that had to be obeyed or were they what a former minister of defense, Moshe Dayan, had termed "ministerial advice," the minister taking on the role of an adviser? For my part, I would have preferred not to be offered advice at all. If the political level wished to embroil itself in the details, then it should assume total responsibility for the outcome. If, on the other hand, it wished to absolve itself of direct responsibility for the professional conduct of the operation, then it should refrain from offering extraneous advice of any kind. There could be no middle course.

There was one additional aspect to this carefully structured strategy that was designed to cater to the concerns, interests, and sensitivities of the two partners to the equation. I always believed that the political level had the inherent right of deniability when operations failed or went wrong and became public knowledge and, in some cases, the causes of diplomatic crises. It was often imperative that the state—the government of the day—be afforded the possibility of complete public disassociation from acts committed or persons apprehended. After retiring from the Mossad in 1995 and going to Brussels as ambassador to the European Union, I was asked to write an article for a book on intelligence, *Intelligence for Peace*. I titled it "On the Right of Deniability and the Obligation to Loyalty." In it I set forth my philosophy on the right of the state to disassociate itself both from acts and from individuals caught in foreign countries. I fully recognized the necessity to provide political protection for the sovereign state so that it might avoid serious damage to national interests. However, as I claimed, this part of the equation had to be complemented by the state acting in a loyal manner toward the individual who was paying the price for the national interest. Unfortunately, as I stated, the political levels did not always stay true to their obligation.

I cited two instances to prove my point. I will recount only one, which has been given scant attention by the media either in Israel or abroad.

A year before the 1973 Yom Kippur War, when Egypt and Syria surprised Israel by invading it on the holiest of its days, a Mossad operative was caught in Yemen and after interrogation was handed over to the Egyptians, where he was incarcerated during that war. At the end of the war Israel had captured several thousand prisoners, whereas Egypt had managed to capture several hundred Israeli soldiers. Negotiations began for a prisoner exchange and there was obviously much pressure to effect such a transfer as soon as possible. The head of the Mossad at the time, General Zamir, demanded that Baruch Mizrahi, the Mossad officer in Egyptian hands, be part of the deal and the then prime minister,

Golda Meir, acceded to this demand; however, the Egyptians refused, saying that Mizrahi was a "spy" and, as such, did not merit being included in a military prisoner exchange. What I did not relate in my article was that shortly after Mrs. Meir had given Zamir her assurances that she would be steadfast in her position, Zamir departed for a visit to Washington, D.C., where I received him and accompanied him to his various meetings. A day after his arrival, Zamir was informed that the then minister of defense, General Moshe Dayan, had prevailed upon Mrs. Meir to concede and to bow to enormous pressure that had built up in Israel to go ahead with the exchange. The public at large was entirely ignorant of the "Mizrahi issue" and could not understand why the exchange did not proceed. The Mizrahi story was a well-guarded secret and remained so for some time to come.

Upon hearing of the change in policy, Zamir fired off a telegram to Israel, announcing his immediate resignation. He turned to me saying, "I am no longer your superior and you are under no further obligation to me to spend time with me, etc. Cancel all the appointments that you have set up because I am no longer head of the Mossad!" I begged Zamir not to cancel the meetings, which included those with the secretary of defense, James Schlesinger, CIA director Colby, and others. Shortly afterward, a string of telephone calls came in from the prime minister; her deputy, Yigal Allon; and others asking to speak to Zamir. He refused to accept any of the calls and told me I was free to talk to any of those calling but not on his behalf. Ultimately, Zamir extracted an assurance that Mizrahi would be released quietly a few weeks later and, indeed, this did come to pass.

It was my belief that Zamir had rendered a singular service by insisting on the paramount necessity of creating dignified and moral norms that were applicable not only to the civil service, to the service of the intelligence community, but also to the political level and after I left the Mossad in 1995, I welcomed the opportunity to make this public. The Mossad chief at the time thought otherwise. When I submitted the article for approval before publication, he did everything he could to dissuade me from publishing the article. Among the arguments he put forward was one that particularly incensed me. He claimed that my piece would serve to demoralize "the troops," since it would call into question the faith that could be put in the political level. My view was, of course, dia-metrically to the contrary. I thought that publicity would make it that much more difficult for politicians to turn their backs on intelligence of-ficers in distress or in peril. I also strongly believed that officers going into intelligence "battle" had every right to know exactly where their po-litical masters stood.

In the end, I won this round. I published the article in an obscure book and nobody took any notice. Mizrahi died in 2005. One newspaper car-ried an item on his death on an inner page of the paper; there was even cursory mention of Zamir's resignation. The public was otherwise en-gaged and the truth of the matter was that nobody really cared. Mizrahi, like Sylvia Raphael, another Mossad operative who was arrested in the Norwegian village of Lillehamer after a botched Mossad operation re-sulted in the death of an innocent waiter, owing to mistaken identity, re-ceived no national recognition even after death. The task and privilege of rendering the final respects to the dead were left to the intelligence and security services. Governments of the day were only too content to turn their backs on devoted individuals who had served their country with ex-treme valor and distinction. Such are the norms that the political levels in Israel have set and cultivated over the years.

One of the aspects that I had to contend with was the transformation of the Mossad from a "family" into a modern enterprise. When I en-listed in the early sixties the atmosphere that the leadership was bent on preserving was that of an intimate, family one. In those far-off days it was more than just customary to encourage enlistment of family and rel-atives and whenever a crisis arose inside the business, people drew close to each other and acted out of intense devotion not only to the "Cause" but to those who were in jeopardy. When officers retired, they were told that the Mossad would forever be their home and they were invited to maintain the closest of ties with the business. I knew so many of the key figures personally and everybody expected me not only to continue the tradition but to promote it even more, but this was no longer possible, nor was it really desirable. I strictly enforced civil-service rules preclud-ing the recruitment of close relatives to government service under the same roof. Although I continued to assure retirees that the Mossad would always be at their side in case of personal need, I promoted a policy of gradual easing of ties between those still serving and those who were on the other side of the hill. It was by no means easy and it necessitated the investment of much time and effort to make partings of the way as gentle and as considerate as possible. Many expected me to act totally differently. After all, was I not one of "theirs"? But the true interests of the state and the Mossad demanded that I behave otherwise.

THE YEARS 1998 AND 1999 WERE THOSE IN WHICH THE MIDDLE EAST BEgan its course of renewed confrontation, which was destined to erupt in the form of the second Gulf War of 2003. Observed from the vantage point of the Mossad, it was clear that the dual challenges of Iraq and Iran in the sensitive area of weapons of mass destruction were fast taking on ominous indications. The United Nations presence in Iraq was terminated and a new period began. As for Iran, this country had long been singled out for special attention and became a high-level concern both in the WMD field and in the area of international terrorism. There were two distinct aspects to these obvious threats. There was the intrinsic independent threat that these countries posed by virtue of their determined independent pursuit of their aims and ambitions in these fields, and there were the links between the Palestinian terrorist movements, the Palestinian Authority, and both Baghdad and Tehran. Parallel to these concerns, the Israeli governments of Benjamin Netanyahu and Ehud Barak pursued efforts to reach agreements with the Palestinians in the hope that these agreements would not only lower the level and intensity of terror directed against Israel but also facilitate the creation of a common front against the outer threats of WMD and international terror. This was the strategic rationale for reaching agreements with the Palestinians and the Syrians. The estimate, the political estimate, was that once a resolution of the Israeli-Palestinian and the Israeli-Arab conflicts was achieved, the whole of the "inner circle" of Israel and the Arab states, together, would form a common front to confront the "outer circle," Iran, Libya, and the like, which were at one and the same time purveyors of state terror and the proliferation of weapons of mass destruction. This was the time when the strategic threat to Israel assumed international dimensions that forced it to contemplate the limitations on its own independent capacities to cope alone, if necessary, and to fashion a credible response.

Two principal conclusions were drawn in those days: The first was that, even if the aim of reaching a permanent solution of the Israeli-Arab problem was achieved (and the likelihood of this happening appeared to be dim), the inner circle would not have the power to muster sufficient force to confront and defeat the "outer perimeter" on its own. Moreover, even if Syria and the Palestinians were to make their formal peace with Israel, they would not sever their ties with Iran or North Korea. They might well reduce the profile of these strategic assets that they had nurtured over the years, but the current regimes of Bashar al-Assad and of Yassir Arafat would not turn their backs entirely on their erstwhile supporters.

At the turn of the century, North Korea had been singularly successful in penetrating the Middle East. It had sold Scud-C and Scud-D missiles to Syria, the latter with a seven-hundred-kilometer range, and had given the Syrians not only launchers and missiles but also production lines for the two. These were to be the essential delivery systems for the chemical warheads that the Syrians had developed as a balancing deterrent to Israel's known or assumed capabilities in the nuclear field. Parallel to this enterprise, the North Koreans had provided unique aid to Iran in the missile-development field, enabling Tehran gradually to forge medium-range missile systems that could cover most of the Middle East to the east and a comparable distance to both the north and east. Last, but not least, the powers that be in Pyongyang had succeeded in maintaining a long-established foothold in Egypt, through the sale and maintenance of a Scud-B supply to the Egyptians. Notwithstanding the close military ties that had been established between Cairo and Washington after the signature of the Egyptian-Israeli peace treaty of 1979, Cairo did not forego the opportunity to preserve a small but significant independent supply line of Scud-B missiles and it maintained its connections with the North Korean regime to the very end of the twentieth century.

What should the Israeli response be to a North Korean threat which is so all-encompassing and so ominous? I referred to this issue earlier on, when there was a reported attempt to strike a deal between Israel and North Korea, an attempt that was ill-conceived and was doomed to failure because Israel could not and should have never contemplated an independent diplomatic-economic exercise behind the back of the United States.

At the end of the century, the issue was different. The days of the futile and dangerous dreams of brilliant diplomatic creativity were over. What was next? There were those who believed that, come what may, Israel was duty-bound to meet the North Koreans head-on. How exactly this should be done was not entirely clear, given the enormous distance between the two countries and in view of North Korea's well-known track record of violent and bloody reaction to any physical action taken against the interests of Pyongyang. Others, more sober and realistic, held the view that this is where Israel had to acknowledge that there were limits beyond which it was precluded from acting and that there were challenges that had to be left to world powers and, first and foremost, to the United States.

The practical policy followed by Israel in these years reflected the understanding of the political level that the latter approach was the only feasible one—that whereas intelligence gathering should be promoted whenever and wherever possible so that the real nature and extent of the threat could be accurately evaluated, the major task of translating information into direct action, aimed at the "perpetrators," must be entrusted to others.

One of the more complex outcomes of Israel becoming the target of "global" threats at the end of the century was that the theaters of interest of the Israeli intelligence community were to become ever more far-flung. It became vital to know so much more about countries and regions far removed from Israel, to have an in-depth insight into their political and social cultures, and to learn how to operate and function in hitherto uncharted waters. And yet, just as this was being accomplished, the growing awareness of Israel's limitations loomed large on the horizon.

It is extremely difficult for an intelligence officer to receive a true injection of humility. It almost goes against the grain of those who are trained to stretch the boundaries of the "possible" beyond the limits of human logic and reason. One of the basic tenets of the Mossad during its over fifty years of existence has been that in the final analysis there is no mission that is not doable and that it is unacceptable to report to the political level that a clear threat cannot be neutralized in one way or another. Not every mission hitherto had ended in success. There had been failures, some very painful, but up to that time at the end of the century, I cannot recall a situation, in which a negative answer was given, in advance, to an order to thwart a glaring danger. Political levels in Israel certainly did not welcome such responses, especially from traditional "supermen."

There have been, in my view, four issues in the area of proliferation of weapons of mass destruction that occupied the attention of the nations of the Middle East in the last fifteen years. One was the Iraqi challenge that loomed on the horizon as we approached the first Gulf War in January 1991. Since the invasion of Kuwait in 1990, the countdown toward war gathered momentum and the question surrounding Saddam Hussein's plans in the area of nuclear weaponry became ever more acute. I believe that the intelligence community of Israel was able to provide sufficient indications to both its political masters and to the international community to prove that Iraq was on course to obtain operational capabilities in this fateful field. The aftermath of that war produced the evidence that we were dead right. The second issue has been that of Iranian activities and intentions, and on this count, I believe that Israel has scored very highly both in identifying the threat at a very early stage and in taking countless steps to make sure that neither Jerusalem nor any other key capital in the world was caught unawares. If the director of military intelligence could state in an interview on April 29, 2005, that there was little chance that Israel might be caught by surprise on this crucial issue, it can only be so thanks to more than a decade-long concentration of effort invested by the entire intelligence community, led in this instance by the Mossad. The third issue that came to the fore was the Libyan program to forge an independent military-nuclear capacity. None other than Israeli prime minister Ariel Sharon himself chose to reveal this to the Israeli public in a series of media interviews that he gave on the eve of the Jewish new year in September 2002. No person in such a capacity would risk making such unequivocal revelations had he not been in possession of sound intelligence. The fourth regional challenge was the development of an offensive chemical capacity by Syria and its combination with a missile-delivery system. This was clearly identified at an early stage and it became possible to fashion an adequate strategic response.

One of the problems that the intelligence community has faced over the years has been the absolute necessity to protect sources and methods

while, at the very same time, making it possible to keep the public informed about the basic threats to its security. In this regard, there has
been, and will always be, a conflict of interest between the political and
professional levels. Ultimately neither of the two is ever truly satisfied.

13

A NEW ERA: THE INTELLIGENCE OFFICER AS A BROKER BETWEEN NATIONS

Just as the intelligence communities of Israel, the United States, and the rest of the free world were moving to confront the looming issues of international terrorism and the proliferation of weapons of mass destruction, they were also being propelled to become ever more deeply involved in the promotion of solutions and work plans in the region. The first inkling of this came to me as I talked to American colleagues about the policies of the governments under which I served. I found myself representing the thinking and aspirations of my political masters and as such, it was obvious that I was much more than an intelligence officer gathering information for my government. I was simultaneously catapulted into the role of a "source," a high-level source at that, who was providing information to my counterparts on the thinking and intentions of my superior, the prime minister himself. I had to be careful not to divulge what should not be revealed, and I had to be extremely careful not to be quoted in any way that would mislead my interlocutors. I could not afford to be a tool for high-level disinformation because in such a case I would be guilty of deceiving the United States and allies and would immediately lose my credibility and my standing, which if properly preserved could be invaluable in many a delicate situation.

There was no point in my simply parroting the open statements and comments emanating from my country. There would be no added value in that and I would quickly become a redundant and ineffective figure. There was no merit in this. What I did was divide my briefs into three sections. The first was invariably devoted to a professional intelligence brief. The second part was the delivery of messages or themes determined by the prime minister of the day. And the third was a distinct intimate appraisal of key issues as viewed personally by myself. The latter part was always the more difficult and the more hazardous for me. If misquoted, or if quoted out of context, I might cause much damage and be open to accusation that I had gone beyond my authority.

I must say that of all the messages that I passed back and forth, the most significant one I was able to impart to the prime minister was passed to him a short time before the events of 9/11: The president of the United States did not understand the strategy of the prime minister in relation to the Arab-Israeli conflict. He very much wanted to forge a common approach that the two leaders could then follow and support and that gave due weight to the position of the United States in the Arab world. I had the distinct feeling that similar messages had been passed to the prime minister through additional channels, but I did believe that, coming through me, the American side was trying to impress upon its Israeli partner that time was running out and that we could wait around no longer. What was clear to me was that the American side was not, at that particular point in time, working on ideas of its own. Contrary to the period of the Clinton presidency, there was no independent deep thinking on the Israeli-Arab file in Washington in those days. I understood that I was being told that "the field is clear for you to come up with new ideas. We welcome this, but you must table proposals that will serve not only your interests, but also those of the United States in the Middle East as a whole. If you want to be partners of the United States, then you must cater to the interests of your partner no less than for your own. Come up with something credible, and we will go along with you!" That was my understanding of what was being said to me and that was how I relayed it to my political master.

The truth of the matter was that, as I looked around me and sought an individual or a government body that could take up the challenge, I could not find anybody. The IDF had its planning branch, which dealt with strategic-policy issues in the area of defense and security and the senior officers there were men and women of caliber, but they were neither mandated nor equipped with the means to deal with Israel's overall strategy. The national defense council that I subsequently led for one year was not a favored body of the prime minister. In any case it did not have the breadth and depth that could give it a true capacity to suggest comprehensive plans.

In the past I had been a personal emissary of prime ministers, but acting from within the Mossad, as a senior player (but by no means as a lone one). Now I was at the helm of my organization as of 1998 and could mold it in any way that I preferred. Let me be clear on this point: I was responsible to the prime minister, subordinate to him, reported to him, and had to receive his approval for certain types of activity. And yet, to a very large extent, I was quite independent. I saw the prime minister on a largely regular basis, but even this regular schedule tended to vary with the times. When very burdened, the weekly meeting could quickly become a biweekly event of approximately sixty to ninety minutes. I was asked to submit a list of items for reporting or discussion in advance, but the prime minister himself never saw the paper before we met and the military secretary who was the ongoing liaison with the "political level" tried from time to time, in vain, to act as a "mini prime minister" and to ask for elaborations and/or clarifications in advance. When it came to appointments, I had to obtain approval for the appointments of division chiefs and their deputies. In such cases, I appended a one-page description of my choice for this or that position together with a small passport photograph of the candidate. When I met the prime minister, I described the position, presented the candidate's CV, and extolled his virtues. In my four and a half years of service, never once was approval withheld. The prime minister approved the appointments without meeting the candidates and without any prior process of screening or hearing. On one occasion, I came to propose the appointment of a deputy chief. I made my proposal and told the then prime minister that another division chief aspired to the position and wished to be interviewed in person. I suggested that this be done although I clearly indicated my preference. The prime minister acceded to the request, but accepted my recommendation at once and my candidate became deputy chief of the service.

I have detailed this aspect in order to describe the power and prestige that the chief wielded in my day. There was no external interference in appointments within the service and the prime minister, three successive ones, had implicit faith in the decisions taken by the chief. As chief, I enjoyed a freedom of action that was a rarity in public service. My colleagues at the security service had similar powers and authority within their organization.

The subcommittee of the defense and foreign-relations committee of parliament received regular briefs from me and in some respects, their oversight surpassed that of the prime minister. Sessions lasted longer— two to three hours—and they were often guests of the firm and were exposed to facilities and personnel in relatively large numbers. And yet, in truth, it must be said that every prime minister developed a "feel" for the Mossad and held it in high esteem, all except one, Shimon Peres. I recall accompanying my chiefs to meetings with him where he made it abundantly clear that he had very little interest in what was done, and not much respect for those engaged in the profession of intelligence.

And yet, in recent years, at the turn of the century, the added profile of intelligence in promoting and monitoring peace and reconciliation moves was initiated by the United States rather than by the Israelis or Palestinians or Arab states. As the terrorist cycle raged, starting in the latter part of 2001, an initiative was taken to try to bring about a cease-fire or a reduction of hostile acts in the Israeli-Palestinian dispute. The director of the CIA, George Tenet, was mandated by the president to proceed to Israel and to work out a solution to the growing cycle of violence. The product of this mission was the Tenet work plan that purported to be a detailed sequence of steps that each side would have to take on the way to reducing violence. Technically, this was a professional blueprint addressed to the security and military services on both sides. Since the implications of each and every step proposed were political no less than operational, the CIA was in effect plunging into the political imbroglio of the Middle East up front. This was a clear departure from the clandestine role that the agency had played throughout the last fifty years and it was the political level in the United States that had decided to act in this manner. Two or three consequences emerged from this decision, even before the work plan was put to the test. The CIA became an overt player on the scene. Its representative's name in Israel became, overnight, a household name, and his activities in relation to the role of the agency were for the most part public knowledge. The second result of this development was that the CIA assumed the role of an umpire in the dispute. Its representative attended trilateral meetings and these deliberations were often grandstanding events and were treated as such by the direct parties to the dispute. Furthermore, the agency assumed a role of coordinating the training of the Palestinian security forces and ran training courses for them with the participation of Egyptian and Jordanian instructors. Thus the stake, the direct stake of the agency, in securing a success of the whole enterprise was clear for everyone to see. The negotiations to secure acceptance of both parties to the workplan contained all the elements of customary Middle East drama.

Tenet presented a draft of his plan to both sides and invited their comments. I recall that we, Israel, responded with a few amendments, whereas the Palestinians came up with a host of changes they wished to incorporate in the document. Within a few hours, Tenet came back and presented a paper that accommodated a few of our concerns, but by far not all of them. He added that it was a "take it or leave it" proposition. I skimmed through the paper and rushed to the prime minister, after consulting with my colleagues, and urged him to accept the paper "as is." I argued that the majority of the Palestinian strictures had not been accepted by Tenet, and therefore we should rush to say yes, thus precluding any further negotiation. Once we said yes to this take-it-or-leave-it proposal, the entire onus moved to the other side. And this is what happened. Tenet traveled to Ramallah, the headquarters of the Palestinian Authority led by Yassir Arafat, and wrangled with him for close to five hours. Part of the time the two interlocutors were lying on the floor, because George Tenet was suffering from a severe back ailment. At the end, Tenet gave up and departed Ramallah, admitting failure, only to be called back as he was heading for Lod International Airport and to be told that Arafat had knuckled under.

From that moment on, the role and status of the CIA in the dispute underwent a change. Its representatives served as professional watchdogs of the implementation of the Tenet work plan and as such were absorbed into the political arena. After months of failure to bring the Palestinians around to lowering the flames of violence and incitement, the United States designated a marine force general, General Anthony Zinni, as a special representative charged with the mission of getting the parties to implement the Tenet work plan. He, too, failed in the effort and ultimately withdrew after presenting the parties with a somewhat diluted version of the work plan, which Israel, yet again, readily accepted, despite many reservations, whereas the Palestinians dithered about it. A massive suicide attack in Netanya on Passover night in 2002 left Israel no option but to move in force into the West Bank and to confront the terrorists on their own home ground.

The overt involvement of the CIA in the process served no real interest of the United States. The prestige of the Agency and its trusted and highly respected chief in person was placed on the block. The failure highlighted the obvious limitations of one of the most revered arms of the United States government. The professional capabilities of the Agency were similarly compromised, at least in part. After all, if the U.S. government and its Egyptian and Jordanian partners could not put together a credible training program that would produce an effective and powerful professional intelligence and security system, what was there left to be done?

I believed from the outset that going along this path would not only serve no purpose, but that the ongoing liaisons and relations between the intelligence communities of the United States and Israel could be impaired. In the end, this latter danger did not materialize but, on the other hand, as already said, no useful purpose was ultimately served by injecting the Agency into the fray in a role that did not conform to its normal mandate and style.

Coming back to Israel itself, the developments hitherto described absorbed the intelligence community more than ever before into the gray zone that always exists between the operational and policy levels. In the past, we, in the intelligence community, were often assigned roles in the political process of the day by the political master at that particular point in time. As I saw the Agency moving into the arena, and given the almost complete absence of professional initiatives from the policy-making levels, I, and to a lesser extent my two colleagues in the committee of chiefs of services, began suggesting policy options, and gradually we became more and more emboldened in promoting ideas and courses of action.

The unleashing of the IDF offensive, code-named "defensive shield," in March 2002 heralded a new era not only in the doctrine and implementation of low-intensity warfare but also an entirely new approach on the part of the international community to the challenge of dealing with failed regimes. In this respect, I think it would be true to say that the innovative policy proposed on the political level by the Israeli side was a "first," to be emulated in subsequent crises as an integral element in American policies.

As the offensive directed at West Bank centers of Palestinian terror was unleashed, it became obvious from the outset that the operation would be limited in time. The extent to which international public opinion and international political considerations would permit Israel to act with impunity in the territories of the Palestinian Authority could not be clearly determined in advance The IDF chief of staff at the time, General Shaul Mofaz, asked for a couple of months at least of freedom of action, but it was obvious that such a time frame would not be granted. However swift and successful the impending operation might be, it would end without obtaining the long-term objective of the total eradication of terror. If, immediately or shortly after the end of hostilities, terror would raise its its ugly head once again, what long-standing effect would the operation produce? Would it not turn out to be counterproductive in the sense that it would highlight the impotence rather than the strengths of the Israeli defense and security system? Moreover, if the operation came to an end on a given day and nothing was in place, defense-wise or policy-wise, then the vacuum could invite all kinds of initiatives that could well be disastrous from Israel's standpoint. Hence, from every angle it was imperative to take the initiative and to come up with a policy that would be launched on the morrow of the defense operation. This detailed line of thought should not have been the bailiwick of the intelligence officer or the intelligence community, but because of the vacuum in the decision-making process that I have described, we stepped into the breech.

Given the realization that Yassir Arafat had no interest in any real accommodation with Israel, the only possibility lay in promoting a move that would produce an alternative leadership in the Palestinian Authority. In order for such a change to come about, it would be necessary to create a new power center inside the Palestinian parliamentary system. This center would get the Palestinian parliament to create the hitherto nonexistent position of prime minister and this officeholder would be "empowered" to be, in effect, the chief "executive" of the authority. This was the very first time that a proposal to bring about a regime change in the Middle East was tabled for the international community. It took into account the specific conditions prevailing inside the authority, especially the key position occupied by Arafat and the immense popular support that he enjoyed. Therefore, rather than remove him entirely from the scene, the idea was to leave him with his title of president, but to devolve his powers in such a way that he would become a titular head of state, comparable, as the cynics would say, to the queen of England.

A very detailed blueprint was drafted and submitted to the prime minister. First, an empowered chief executive had to be appointed. Second, the Palestinians had to reorganize their security organs and reduce them to three instead of the close to thirteen that each reported separately to the president. The financial system of the Palestinian Authority had to be rethought and grouped under a finance minister subordinated to the prime minister, rather than to the president. If all of these things came about, we knew that there would emerge a credible partner for action and negotiation and that this partner could conceivably go on to rule an independent Palestinian state, functioning side by side with Israel, within provisional borders. As all of this fell into place, negotiations on a permanent status would be postponed to an indefinite date.

These were the main ideas put to the prime minister even as battles were raging in the West Bank. To the best of my knowledge and recollection, this was the very first time that a policy of "regime change" was placed on the international table. It was certainly the first time that such a concept was proposed to the political level in Israel by an intelligence chief and after detailed deliberation by the prime minister and a select group of his personal and political aides, the concept and the detailed blueprint were approved. In a period of no more than ten weeks, the plan was presented in Washington, London, Cairo, Amman, and other key spots both inside the region and beyond. To the surprise of many, inside Israel and without, it was received and adopted with much enthusiasm. As we toured the capitals of the world, General Kaplinsky, the prime minister's military secretary, and I felt that we were making history. We found that once we had taken the initiative and filled the political vacuum before anybody could beat us to it, and once we offered a set of assumptions and proposals that entailed painful but reasonable concessions on both sides, the world was prepared not only to listen, but also to adopt the ideas as if they were its own.

Thus as the White House in Washington prepared to launch its own initiative we were more than anxious to discover how far we had succeeded. On June 24 at 3:47 P.M., the president appeared in the Rose Garden and announced what he termed: "A Call for a New Palestinian Leadership." The title said it all and the rest was a logical sequence of this point of departure. I could not recall another instance when the intelligence community had made such a strong showing in charting strategic trends in the region. Support for the president's plan poured forth both inside the region and outside it. Even countries like Egypt, on the one hand, and Russia, on the other, which continued to pay lip service to the legitimacy of President Arafat, supported the new move on the ground and encouraged the more moderate elements in the Palestinian camp to seize the moment.

The initiative I have just described differed somewhat from others promoted primarily on security issues, but with political consequences. The latter, like the pressure exerted by the Israeli Security Agency to build a security fence along Israel's borders, ultimately had a direct effect on the delineation of Israel's ultimate borders, but the original terms of reference of that proposal were entirely in the domain of security.

In contrast, however, from the very beginning my blueprint for forging a new Palestinian leadership was a direct attempt to effect a regime change in a key player, a key adversary, of Israel, and fundamentally it was much more ambitious and so much more intrusive into the camp of our key adversary. As I look back upon those days, I cannot avoid remembering that no discussion took place on the principle involved in pursuing such a policy. No one asked if it was legitimate for us to openly sponsor steps and policies of this nature. This was not a clandestine effort to pull strings. It was an up-front campaign designed to gain public support and not simply endorsement of a concept, but an actual precise list of measures designed to obtain the desired result.

I was, in truth, confounded by the relative ease that characterized the entire sequence that produced the approval to go ahead and try to secure the objective. I had prefaced my presentation to the prime minister with a series of in-house discussions with my experts who were on the analytical side of the business. Initially it had been difficult for them to understand what I was asking of them. They had never before cast themselves in policy-making roles. On countless occasions I had asked for their assessments on this or that issue; I had involved them in discussion of operational options in the field of intelligence, but never before had I asked them for their ideas on major political action blueprints on key regional issues. It turned out to be a very exciting and rewarding exercise for all those involved and, for myself, I was rewarded by comments and feedbacks that reassured me that I was on the right track. Thus, when I came to the prime minister, I felt extremely confident and, as I vividly recall, was able to make a very strong pitch, which was exceedingly well received. It so happened that at the very same time that I was putting the finishing touches on my proposals, General Giora Eiland, head of the Planning Branch at IDF headquarters, and his staff had reached identical conclusions. Each of us was summoned separately for breakfast at the official residence of the prime minister, Ariel Sharon. Each of us was treated to a sumptuous repast and each of us made his separate presentation in the absence of the other. That morning, the prime minister ate two full breakfasts. I was the second visitor and the host appeared to enjoy his second meal immensely. After that, on the following day, we were summoned together to spend half a day at the prime minister's ranch in the south of the country. There, we met with additional aides and during several hours, under the watchful eye of the prime minister, drafted the final document, a list of talking points, which encapsulated the concept and the plan of action. It was my draft that served as the basis for the final product and I was proud of it. The prime minister asked that the paper be left with him for the weekend, when, I gathered, he was scheduled to consult his "inner circle," composition unknown, and I was to hear from him again at the beginning of the following week.

It took no longer than three days to get approval. The number of persons privy to the plan was minimal at the professional level. I never knew how many people at the political level were involved, nor did I know who they were. What was discussed at that level, what the considerations were for going ahead, beyond what I myself thought of, remained a mystery to me. Within less than a week, a major policy step had been presented, approved, and put into action. In this particular case, due to the way I handled the matter, the whole stratagem had been submitted to a thorough examination of professionals and had been analyzed in great detail. It was my distinct impression that at a later stage this was not so and the consequences were not late in coming.

14

THE POLITICAL MANIPULATION
OF INTELLIGENCE

It was the Passover night in 2002, when a deadly attack of Palestinian suicide bombers on a hotel in Netanya, a well-known tourist seaside resort in the center of Israel, ended with scores of Israeli dead and more than a hundred wounded. This attack was the culmination of a three-month period that had seen a very sharp increase in the incidence of suicide terrorist attacks against Israeli civilian and military personnel, and the military and security services had proved unable to stem the tide. The Palestinian Authority had been encouraging the terrorist elements to pursue their activities with vigor and American attempts to produce a cease-fire of sorts had proved futile. Marine general Anthony Zinni, an American special representative on the spot, had just received word that the Palestinians had rejected his latest proposals designed to lower the flames of attack and counterattack. However, the scope of the Netanya terrorist attack had put a final seal on American attempts to adjudicate the crisis. The die was cast. Israel felt obliged to take matters into its own hands and to enter the entire area of the West Bank in order to subdue the Palestinians, destroy terrorist infrastructures, and uproot the elements that were aiding and abetting terrorism. A government meeting was convened by Prime Minister Sharon on the following evening immediately after the religious holiday ended, and it was set to discuss and to approve the major incursion of the Israel Defense Forces into the Palestinian West Bank. The general outlines of the IDF plans were presented to the government and were quickly approved. The issue, after all, was crystal clear. What had to be decided was whether the Palestinian Authority, as such, should be officially designated an "enemy," and the result would be that Israel would not only enter the territory, but would also act to dissolve the authority which had been set up under the internationally recognized Oslo agreements. There were senior military officers, including the chief of staff, General Mofaz, who argued intensely for this line of action. The international implications and complications of following this path were clear: Israel would not only be moving in to protect itself on an operational level from terrorist attacks but also be legally and formally destroying its nominal negotiating partner on the Palestinian side. Many at the meeting, including myself, thought that such a move would not serve Israel's best interests. Soon after the meeting began, the prime minister proposed that the chairman of the Palestinian Authority, Yassir Arafat, be forcibly sent into exile, since he had become a central figure by inciting his people to violence against Israel and exhorting the Palestinians to converge on Jerusalem as "martyrs." His oft-repeated haranguing catch phrase was that he wanted to see a million *shahids*—martyrs marching on Jerusalem.

The government meeting was attended by all three chiefs of the intelligence community—Avi Dichter, the head of the Israel Security Agency (the ISA, formerly known as the GSS, General Security Service); General Aharon Ze'evi Farkash, the director of military intelligence, the DMI; and myself as head of the Israeli intelligence service, the Mossad. Each of us was asked, in turn, what his opinion was and each of us replied that he did not believe that this course of action would serve Israel's interests. The main reason given was that Arafat as an enforced exile roaming around the world was a greater danger to Israel than an Arafat staying in the territory under our close watch and with our ability to restrict both his movements and freedom of action, if deemed necessary. The three of us were not forewarned that the prime minister was about to tender his proposal to the government; hence, we had no opportunity to discuss the issue among ourselves as we did many other matters that came up over the years. We constituted the Committee of Chiefs of

Services, which I regularly chaired, and we also met periodically as a group with successive prime ministers for discussions of a very privileged nature. Often, the prime minister preceded cabinet meetings with preparatory sessions of the "Security and Defense Establishment," and these meetings enabled the prime minister both to clarify in advance what his immediate policies and lines of action were going to be and to sound us out in advance as to our attitudes and views on this or that matter. On this occasion, nothing of this nature had taken place and we were asked to express our views in open session of the government and each one of us told the full cabinet that we disagreed with the prime minister. The cabinet debate on the prime minister's proposal raged well into the night and time and time again, he pressed his fellow ministers to approve his line of action on Arafat. He spoke of Arafat with much vehemence and said that it would be a terrible mistake to allow him to stay in the heart of the Palestinian territory, in his seat of government in Ramallah, right on the outskirts of Jerusalem. Throughout the debate ministers and others entered and left the cabinet chamber for one-on-one consultations and I was asked by several ministers to explain my opinion to them at great length. I could not recall such a scene in the past.

As dawn broke, the cabinet slowly wound down and a compromise suggestion was tabled and adopted—Yassir Arafat would not be exiled. Rather, he would be confined to his headquarters in Ramallah and would not enjoy any freedom of movement, either inside the territories or in traveling out of the territories to foreign lands. The latter point was later refined to specify that he would be allowed out of his headquarters to travel out of the country, but his return journey could not be guaranteed. In effect he understood that once he left, he would not be permitted to return.

Subsequent to the all-night debate, I often asked myself why it was that the prime minister had resorted to this procedure, which, on the face of it, ran contrary to established custom of the past. It was not for lack of time nor was it because the prime minister wished to wave his special privilege of guiding both the preliminary deliberations and the formulation of the proposals that were to be tabled at cabinet and government levels. Was there not a risk that we, the intelligence chiefs, would hear the prime minister's views and would decide to subscribe to them rather than to object to them? After much thought, I reached the conclusion that the prime minister believed that, indeed, we would oppose his proposal and that this was exactly what he was hoping would happen. Essentially, he did not wish to go through with his idea of banishing Arafat from his seat of government, but he desired that the ultimate outcome of the fierce debate would be for him to "succumb" to the views of his professional intelligence chiefs. Thus he would achieve a dual aim: He would project himself as one who wished to "get rid of the tyrant in Ramallah" yet was dissuaded from pushing through a resolution to that effect because he did not want to go against the professional advice he had been given. History would thus laud him on every count—if the stay of Arafat inside the territories were to prove an unmitigated disaster, then it would be recorded that the prime minister had wished to tackle the threat head-on, but was unable to sway his cabinet, who had preferred to support the advice proffered by the professionals. If, on the other hand, the advice given would prove valid and wise, then it was none other than the prime minister who had bowed to it and had accepted it. Contrary to what might be assumed, I did not consider the above analysis as an act of cynicism. It was precisely demonstrative of the nature of the relationship between the professional and political levels in the minefield of intelligence. It was the mission of the intelligence chief not only to give his very best evaluation of a situation and/or a threat or a challenge. It was inherent in his brief to provide his political master with the option to "play" the advice given to him, to enhance his chances of political survival. That was "the name of the game."

That this was the strategy adopted by the prime minister of the day was borne out by many other instances. During the course of the armed *intifada,* the campaign of violence and terror launched by the Palestinians in 2001, there were many occasions when the prime minister pressed the professional levels to be ever more creative in combating the threat posed by the terrorists, a threat that first and foremost chalked up significant inroads into the morale of the civilian population in Israel. There came a moment when none other than the director of the Israel Security Agency stated publicly in 2003 that the security and defense community had not been able to provide the individual citizen with the an adequate "bag" of personal security and this notwithstanding the spectacular successes of his own service and the military forces in tracking down and eliminating archterrorists and their leaders. Paradoxically, the greater the success of Israel in waging its war against terror and its perpetrators, the greater the growing realization that operational excellence could not provide an ironclad protection for the political level and its policies on the substance of the dispute with the Palestinians.

Once the confrontation between the prime minister and his intelligence chiefs was prominently touted and publicly displayed, it was no longer possible to cast a veil of secrecy over the relationship, especially when differences of opinion arose. The gap between the prime minister and the head of the security agency became even wider when the prime minister launched his unilateral disengagement policy. This policy was designed to effect a withdrawal of Israel from the Gaza Strip as well as the removal of all Israeli settlers, numbering close to eight thousand, from the area. The plan also included a symbolic parallel departure from three settlements in northern Samaria in the West Bank, an area in which the Palestinian Authority would be trying to obtain the greatest possible territorial concessions from Israel. The view of the security agency on this particular decision was that it might not produce the drastic reduction of violence that the prime minister and his trusted political aides were promising the public. This time around, the prime minister took action; he declined the offer of the head of the service to stay in office one more year in order to help oversee the implementation of the disengagement. Similarly, he cooperated with the minister of defense in bringing the term of office of the chief of staff to an end; both left office on the eve of the disengagement.

One argument bolstered these two decisions: It was the privilege of the political level to choose those professional subordinates in whom there was full trust that they would carry out the policies legally approved with utmost faith and diligence. Practically speaking, this meant that not only was the professional level expected to carry out instructions meticulously and faithfully, but it was also expected to subscribe to the evaluations that the chosen steps would, of necessity, produce the desired results. If this was not the case, the professional level was to be removed and was to make way for successors whose evaluations mirrored those of the political level. This is, needless to say, a very precarious path for a professional to negotiate as he or she looks up to the political master.

The inherent conflict of missions that the Israeli intelligence or security chief has experienced has never been more prominent than when he has been requested by his political master to go public and to give his evaluations and estimates to the citizens of the state. Time and time again, the intelligence and security chiefs have been called upon to perform such a duty, not only in the interest of keeping the public informed but to provide professional basis and support for the operational decisions that the political level made. More than once this backfired; thus in May 2005 the director of military intelligence openly stated that the Palestinian Authority president, Mahmoud Abbas, alias Abu Mazen, although delinquent in honoring many of the commitments he had made on taking firm steps to disarm Palestinian armed terrorists, had at the very same time taken serious, other steps in fulfilling parts of his obligations and should therefore be praised and even rewarded politically for his courageous steps. These statements were made at the very same time that the prime minister and his anonymous yet well-known spokesmen poured scorn and ridicule on the Palestinian leadership averring that nothing, yes nothing, had been really done on the other side to assure Israel that terrorism would never again rear its ugly head.

When the needs of politicians and intelligence officers clash, questions about the role of the latter inevitably come to the fore, bringing with them a phalanx of questions about the use and protection of sensitive information: How can intelligence officers preserve their credibility? Who is the intelligence officer's real client and who is the ultimate judge of how intelligence can be put to operational and political use? Who bears the ultimate burden and responsibility of protecting sources and methods? What can or should a professional intelligence chief do if he determines that his political master is acting in a manner that might compromise a source or a method of intelligence gathering? Should he resign or go public and denounce the political level? Should he stay on and claim that it is the ultimate responsibility of the political master, or should he walk away quietly and retire with grace? These are not questions that can be answered lightly in our age of international terrorism.

Before tackling these weighty questions it is more than appropriate to address an additional aspect of this complex and thorny topic. For quite some time successive Israeli prime ministers have used intelligence officers to present information and evaluations to foreign intelligence agencies and partners. This has been, of course, both useful and entirely legitimate; however, there has been a growing trend that does not confine the exercise to the intelligence communities alone. Not only intelligence chiefs are sent, but also officers in lower ranks, to brief both their counterparts and senior officials in the executive branches of government. In several instances, initiatives have been taken to brief the legislative branches as well and even to give select briefings to the media of foreign countries on their own soil. The results of such moves have often been counterproductive, to say the least.

In more than one instance, an American intelligence chief has found himself being briefed in confidence on Monday, the White House briefed on Tuesday morning, Congress briefed on Tuesday afternoon, and *The Washington Post* and *The New York Times* briefed on the following day. Thus the American professional level has been placed in the unenviable position of having to answer to intelligence of a foreign country, intelligence to which it might not subscribe. This has been an understandable cause of much irritation at times and has, simultaneously, allowed senior American officials to discredit Israeli intelligence presentations, labeling them as politically driven and motivated. I was always of the opinion that this was a wrong way of doing business. During my tenure as head of the Mossad, I never briefed the Congress unless this was done at the request of or with the consent of my professional colleagues in the United States. I always thought that the momentary advantage of supposedly circumventing a colleague and going straight to his political master was, at best, short-lived and in the final analysis would be a dead loss. After all was said and done, why would an American president give credence to the Israeli intelligence community over his own trusted intelligence system?

The damaging farce has in recent years been compounded by the openly and proudly announced achievement that, in addition to all existing intelligence channels, a special channel has been set up from the office of the prime minister to the White House to make sure that information was given directly to the president of the United States by the prime minister and was not lost or derailed on its way through normal existing lines of communications. Statements to this effect over the last three years could not have endeared the Israeli leadership to the professional levels in Washington, D.C. Similarly, such elite lines of communication were publicly announced and consecrated between Jerusalem and 10 Downing Street, London. To explain the new connection, informed sources in the prime minister's office in Jerusalem announced to the Israeli public, and by extension to the British public, the following: On a visit to London in July 2003, the prime minister of Israel discovered that precious intelligence passed to the British services had not found its way to the top and, consequently, the British prime minister was not adequately aware of very important items of information. No other explanation was given. Thus the intelligence leaders of both the United States and Britain were found wanting in the eyes of the "wise men" in the office of the prime minister of Israel. In the eyes of the world, the political level in Israel had openly and brazenly tainted Israel's intelligence community by transforming it into a political tool of the current government. Were this just empty bravado, it could be written off as just one more cheap ploy of publicity-greedy, temporizing political hacks. But the real damage wrought by this amateur showmanship can not be overestimated.

In recent years a third element has injected itself into the internal conundrum concerning the interrelationship between different branches of government on the role and function of intelligence. In the Israeli system, the legislative oversight of the intelligence community is performed by a select subcommittee of the Foreign Relations and Defense Committee of the Knesset. The committee is considered the most prestigious and discrete organ of the legislature and its membership is usually made up of the most senior members of the Knesset who are not cabinet members. It is customary that the opposition parties send their top leaders to the committee and thus there are always a number of ex–cabinet members in this six-man group. During my tenure as head of the Mossad and deputy head, a period of close to ten years, Ariel Sharon and Moshe Arens— both former defense ministers—were members of the subcommittee. Both, by the way, were always supportive and helpful to the intelligence community at large. The committee usually held its sessions in private and rarely issued statements of any kind. It was always assumed that anything imparted to the committee was preserved in confidence and this enabled chiefs of services to brief its members freely, which they invariably did. On rare occasions, the committee transformed itself into a parliamentary commission of inquiry. When the aborted operation of the Mossad to kill the Jordanian Khammas leader Khaled Mashal ended in a fiasco, the committee carried out an inquiry that paralleled an investigation by a special commission appointed by Prime Minister Netanyahu. The parliamentary commission's findings were not deemed weighty or credible. Its conclusions were not unanimous and the members differed along political party lines. Ehud Barak, for example, a member of the committee at the time, thought that this was an appropriate opportunity to put the blame for the whole mishap on Prime Minister Netanyahu, thus absolving the then head of the Mossad, my predecessor, General Danny Yatom, a close friend and aide of Barak. The commission, appointed by Netanyahu, produced the opposite conclusion and its credibility in the eyes of the public proved much higher than that of its parliamentary nemesis.

The subcommittee took on a different character when the current chairman, a relatively young and inexperienced Knesset member, Dr. Yuval Steinitz, took office. Within a very short time he became embroiled in controversy with the military establishment on a variety of issues. Matters reached their peak when he decided to set up a commission to explore the shortcomings of the intelligence community during the second Gulf War. The IDF and the director of military intelligence objected to the term "shortcomings," since the title inferred that there had been lacunae in intelligence, before it had been established that this was indeed the case. This problem was overcome and the subcommittee began examining the performance of the intelligence community on the Iraqi war. Among others, I was called to appear before the committee, and I answered questions and made statements as required. During the war, I had been acting as head of the National Security Council and as national security adviser to the prime minister. I had left the Mossad six months before the war began.

Needless to say, I was astounded when the subcommittee published its findings and stated that Israel, and the intelligence community, had been found delinquent when it became clear that they had been totally unaware of Libya's effort to obtain and/or develop a military nuclear capability. This had not been a subject within the mandate of this enquiry commission. The commission had been charged with addressing the subject of Iraq and nothing else. I had been head of the Mossad during the years leading up to the Iraqi war, but not one question on Libya had been directed to me. The commission had published the overt version of its report presented to the public as a sanitized version of the full secret and detailed report before the full report had even been written. Contrary to established custom, I had not been forewarned that this report was about to be published and I had not been afforded the basic privilege of commenting on the document before it became public. I wrote a strong letter of protest to the chairman of the committee and to each of its members and asked that the document be corrected, because what was stated on the Libyan issue was entirely false. None other than the prime minister himself had gone public on the Libyan threat six months before the Iraqi war and he had done so on solid intelligence grounds. I received no response to my letter.

A few months later I happened to come across the committee chairman and he proudly told me that, at his request, the Mossad had launched an investigation into the Libya file and had presented its findings to the committee. These had supported the committee's basic contentions. I was told, of course, that the committee was not at liberty to divulge to me what the Mossad had told them about my stewardship on this subject. I was advised that, if I was interested, I should approach the Mossad and it might decide to show me the findings. I naturally elected not to do so. I could not recall any case in which the Mossad had been asked to carry out an inquiry into the deeds or misdeeds of a former chief, without any recourse whatsoever to him, and had presented the findings to a parliamentary committee. In my view, this was one more step in the politicization of the external scrutiny of the intelligence community.

Events and episodes mentioned here have highlighted the great change that has come about in Israel in recent years concerning the role of intelligence in a free society. Veterans like myself will say that the sacred cow has been slaughtered and now anybody and everybody can partake of the feast at any time.

The last episode involving the legislative branch of government illustrated the manner in which the political agendas of politicians at levels lower, much lower, than that of the political masters of Israel were coloring the already complex relationship between the supreme and professional levels. I made reference to this in an oblique way when I was awarded the Chaim Herzog prize for a singular contribution to the country in the field of clandestine diplomacy and intelligence. The prize, granted by the Hebrew University of Jerusalem and the Chaim Herzog memorial foundation (Herzog was the sixth president of Israel, twice director of military intelligence, a former Israeli ambassador to the United Nations, and a renowned defense and political commentator who played key roles in steadying the fraying nerves of the Israeli public during the conduct of wars), was handed to me at a ceremony in the president of Israel's official residence in Jerusalem on April 13, 2005, in the presence of the president of Israel, Moshe Katsav. In my acceptance comments, I focused on the relationship between the two levels of government and expressed my belief that neither of the two should try to usurp authority by involving itself in the jurisdiction of the other; I recognized the supremacy of the political master, but arged that orderly conduct necessitated that the political level keep its hands away from implementation. Needless to say, I couched myself in respectful terms, as deemed proper for an event such as this. The president, who was the last to speak, departed from his prepared text and turning to me said, "I agree with you, but there is another side to the coin. You must remember that the political level is daily consumed in a struggle for their very survival!" The implication was that in conditions such as those indicated by the president, rules of conduct were thrown to the wind as politicians "struggled" for their survival.

One of the more sensitive items on this overloaded agenda of Israel's intelligence chief has been the passage and use of information by political rivals against each other. Constant monitoring of Israel's enemies has often produced information concerning contacts by members of parliament with an enemy of the state. These occasions have been, admittedly, rare, but they have occurred. One such case involved an Israeli cabinet minister, Ezer Weizman (a future president of Israel), who met with a representative of the Palestinian Liberation Organization at a time when such contact was prohibited by law. The information was in the hands of the political level through the grace of an intelligence gathering. When public use was made of this in order to obtain the removal of Weizman from cabinet meetings, I thought that this was misuse of information. I was not chief at the time, but I often wondered what I should have done had I then been in charge.

There were other instances when cabinet ministers were caught having left classified documentation unprotected. Senior aides to prime ministers were similarly apprehended, but nothing was done to censure them. I cannot recall any instance when a security clearance was cancelled or suspended in reaction to such conduct. And yet I do know of many instances when senior officers in the intelligence services were severely punished, in some cases cashiered and dismissed, for identical offenses. In truth, it must be said that neither I nor any of my colleagues, when we were in service, past or present, ever raised a voice against this double-standard practice. We bowed our heads in obedience and in acceptance, and of this we should not be proud.

The last years of my tenure as head of Mossad and as head of the National Security Council were particularly troublesome when it came to the interface between the political and professional levels. The prime minister, Ariel Sharon, was a very seasoned and experienced practitioner. He had served at length on both sides of the divide and he knew almost every pitfall that there was to know. He, as the supreme commander, had the prerogative and the privilege to use intelligence as he thought fit and he exercised this authority with considerable dexterity. Unfortunately there were those close to him who acted as if they also possessed similar powers and often leaked items and tidbits as they thought fit. No action was taken against them and as time went on, they grew ever more audacious in their practices.

Familiarity breeds contempt and indeed there were those who had never experienced anything near to seeing action in intelligence, but who behaved high-handedly in exploiting their access to information. They also resorted to systematic denigration of intelligence chiefs as they sought fit. I was called "the deceased." My colleague the head of the security agency was dubbed "the watchmaker." The head of military intelligence was disparagingly described as "the man from the Diaspora" (in Israeli traditional slang the Diaspora Jews were considered inferior, weak, and wanting). The chief of staff was unceremoniously dismissed as a "cowhand" and thus the name of the game became that of pouring scorn on functionaries in key sensitive positions and to spread the word among select and handpicked members of the media that these figures had become passé, as those personal hacks laughingly enjoyed stating at every possible opportunity.

As I try to concentrate my thoughts on this critical interface between the political and operational levels I must admit that given the essential elements of a democratic society where the elected representatives of the people reign supreme, that is where the elected representatives embody the ultimate authority in the country. It is the political level and not the professional level that bears the ultimate responsibility for creating the rules of conduct and the prevailing atmosphere wherein the intelligence and security and defense communities operate. However, if events take a turn for the worse, if there is a failure, it is invariably the executive and operational levels that bear the brunt and pay the personal penalty, whatever form that penalty must take. In view of recent history, I believe that those rules of the game must change.

Let us now turn to events in the United States and in the world at large as of September 11, 2001. What, in my view, transpired in the United States during the years between 1988 and 2003, when the United States and its allies invaded Iraq? Did the intelligence community focus on the real issues and did it devote the major part of its resources to gathering information on them and to foiling the aims of those who were promoting international Islamic terror and the proliferation of weapons of mass destruction? I am certainly not in any position to give firm evidence on these matters. I did not have any access to the inner discussions of the American intelligence community during those years. I did have regular, at times frequent, personal contact with the senior levels in the United States, both through visits I made in Washington, D.C., and when visits were made to Israel. If I were to judge by the matters that were raised with me and my colleagues, I would have no doubt in confirming that these topics—preventing international Islamic terrorism and the development of weapons of mass destruction—were at the top of the agenda. They were difficult targets to deal with and once a decision was taken to raise them to highest priority, the lead time required to develop intelligence assets was especially long. There is no doubt in my mind that, however much the intelligence leadership was conscious of the true nature of the threats, it was not in their power to effect a sea change in the basic attitudes of the American public to the matters at hand.

Given the extreme shortage of reliable information on such potentially threatening issues, were the intelligence chiefs duty-bound to present their assessments to the political level regardless of how much hard material they possessed? The reply to this question must be a strong and simple one: yes. The intelligence officer can never tell the political master that he is unable to give an estimate of a threat. Come what may, an officer has to give an estimate, even if it is largely a guess. On issues of life and death the intelligence officer must always err on the side of the threat and not on the side of the optimist. Even if the threat is classified as being of low probability, it must be perceived as real and immediate. This is especially so if the penalty of a mistake would result in the deaths of thousands, major economic catastrophes, and the concomitant problems in public morale and social upheaval experienced by a nation facing such atrocities and problems.

What, then, is the role of the political level in matters such as these? First of all it is the political level that must receive the information, digest it, and set the tone for future discussions and dealings with the subjects at hand. It is not the task or role, generally, of the intelligence officer to make the overall political assessment and to take responsibility for charting alternative operations. The intelligence officer deals first and foremost with the threat, with the adversary. He has to gather the required information on an adversary's capabilities. He must assess his adversary's potential and intentions, both political and operational. It is not his task to evaluate the capability of his own country to cope with the threat. This is entirely outside the purview of the intelligence officer. Indeed, in a democratic society, it is precisely this that characterizes the difference between it and a nondemocratic system. In the latter, the intelligence system is a major arm within the governing system, an essential tool that improves the chance of the political leadership to remain in power. In a democratic system, once the threat has been rightly and credibly identified by the intelligence community, it is the mission of other executive arms of government—not involved with intelligence gathering—to check national defense and operational capabilities in order to determine whether they were adequate to meet the threats. Though these are nonintelligence procedures, the intelligence community must be involved in the discussions on these procedures by offering constant intelligence updates and by estimating the effects of various lines of action on the enemy and on the international scene in general.

It has definitely not been the mission of the intelligence arm to assess the strength of the forces of the United States. This distinction, if made at the time, must have generated a whole series of measures that would provide the president of the United States with the collateral studies and data that would enable him to determine whether the United States was ready to meet the threats that it was facing. This state of readiness was outside the confines of the intelligence community. The state of readiness did not cover the technical aspects of battle readiness of armed forces alone. The state of readiness included the readying of a nation to grapple with oncoming threats in everyday life. It had to deal with delicate issues such as public morale, once violence begins, with legal preparedness, with civilian preparedness, and all that this entailed. None of these issues, as already indicated, had anything to do with the responsibility of the intelligence officers. How can a democratic system of government cope with such tasks and requirements? Does it have the necessary machinery, the organization, and the means to provide for these national necessities? Obviously the answer is invariably "no." If this is the case, then who is to blame? Or is nobody to blame because up until 9/11, no one was even remotely called upon to think in such categories?

It is all too true to say that in times of crisis, the lines between the various arms both within the executive branch and between the executive and legislative branches of government become blurred. This is human nature, pure and simple. An atmosphere of national togetherness, of national cohesion, takes hold of a nation, of a country, and propels it to its ultimate destiny. It is the political master who sets the scene, who forges the vision, who promotes the spirit of the forces which are fated to conduct the struggle—the battle—and to bear the painful and bitter consequences of defeat or the joys and compensations of victory. Intelligence is only one part, one segment of the saga.

As the political level moved in the direction of manipulating intelligence in subtle ways to cater to its needs, so did the intelligence community in Israel become drawn into widening its brief to include creating and promoting political operational options. Whereas in the more distant past it had been deliberately excluded from the promotion of options and had often been intentionally left in the dark when the political level proceeded to engage the enemy politically, during the late nineties and the early years of the new century the intelligence community in Israel became very active in suggesting initiatives and trying to create the conditions that would make some options more realistically obtainable than others. Under the guise of proffering professional estimates and evaluations, the mainstream in the evaluation field painted the Palestinian Authority under the rule of Yassir Arafat as entirely devoid of any desire to accommodate Israel on any real count. The chief evaluation officer in military intelligence, General Amos Gilead, went as far as to claim both in closed cabinet meetings and in public briefs that even after the demise of Arafat, whenever that might happen, no successor would be able to free himself from the extreme legacy that Arafat was bound to leave behind him. What this meant was that the only way that was open to Israel, if it wanted a settlement of sorts with the Palestinians, was one of complete acceptance of three basic demands of the Palestinians: The first demand was total withdrawal of Israel to the 1949 armistice lines, which represented the balance of forces between Israel and the Arab states and Palestinian local units, which had been the warring partners during Israel's War of Independence.

The second demand was the partition of Jerusalem, and the third was the implementation, in some form or other, of the right of return of the Palestinian refugees who had fled from the war zones during the 1948 war. Since these terms were obviously a nonstarter for Israel, the only possible conclusion was that there could not be an accommodation between Israel and the Palestinians in any foreseeable future. Heaps of intelligence items to prove the point were cited and there was never a counterview put forward by the professional level to the political masters. During my tenure, under the premiership of Ehud Barak in 2000, I argued that there was something basically wrong in our telling the political level that the Palestinians would never accept anything less than the fulfillment of their basic demands. This type of approach assumed that Israel had no "red lines," as they were described, meaning that Israel did not have any limitations on its capacity to compromise. This was a false way of observing the scene. My view was that if the Palestinians came to realize that we did have genuine "red lines" then they would, for the first time, be faced with the proposition that if they simply rejected every Israeli offer of compromise or concession as being insufficient, they would run the risk of losing their opportunity for independence and their national movement could well implode.

Often, as I sat through these long cabinet sessions and watched the actors say their pieces, I closed my eyes (some thought that I fell asleep from time to time, but this was not so!), and tried to look beyond the present. This was definitely not my mission. It was not I who should come up with ideas and solutions. Or was it?

In 2001 and the beginning of 2002, I visited Washington, D.C., on several occasions and met my professional counterparts. I also met figures involved in the policy-making level and I sensed that I was being cast in the role of a messenger, similar but not identical to that which I had performed in the nineties, when I was the trusted emissary of both prime ministers Shamir and Rabin and King Hussein. The intelligence channel was being activated in a different way. This was not manipulation in the base sense of the term. It was something entirely different. This time around, the role had been enhanced and it entailed crafting a detailed plan of action to meet the joint strategic interests of the United States and Israel in relation to the Palestinian conflict. We were not only cast in the role of a messenger, but also cast as those that must initiate and generate ideas and concepts that, if approved by the leaders of both the United States and Israel, could serve for years as basic guidelines for the conduct of policies in the region.

15

SHARON'S ACHIEVEMENT

President George W. Bush's statement of June 2002 was without doubt a spectacular achievement of Prime Minister Ariel Sharon. Not only the president of the United States but world leaders around the globe had all adopted the concept of alternative leadership for the Palestinian Authority without requiring the prime minister to travel the globe to gain support for it. It had become an issue in the international interest, not just a parochial—Israeli—one, and therefore the necessity of Israel paying a political or strategic price did not arise. The discussions that surrounded the understanding envisioned an Israeli effort to support the new alternative leadership that was to emerge, as international pressure succeeded in bringing a majority of the Palestinian legislative assembly to adopt the plan. Israel had made commitments in the past concerning its obligations to the Palestinians, obligations designed to bring about the establishment of the Palestinian state, and the president in his statement reiterated these undertakings, but nothing was offered or demanded in return for adoption of the concept of alternative leadership.

Once there arose an alternative leadership what would its first political goal be? There is nothing comparable to a direct quote to clarify this:

And when the Palestinian people have new leaders, new institutions and new security arrangements with their neighbors, the United States of America will support the creation of a Palestinian state whose borders and certain aspects of its sovereignty will be provisional until resolved as part of a final settlement in the Middle East . . .

Toward the end of the statement, the president stated the following:

Ultimately, Israelis and Palestinians must address the core issues that divide them if there is to be a real peace, resolving all claims and ending the conflict between them. This means that the Israeli occupation that began in 1967 will be ended through a settlement negotiated between the parties, based on U.N. resolutions 242 and 338 with Israeli withdrawal to secure and recognized borders.

We must also resolve questions concerning Jerusalem, the plight and future of Palestinian refugees, and a final peace between Israel and Lebanon and Israel and Syria that supports peace and fights terror . . .

He made no mention of additional guidelines concerning the peace process. He gave no timetables on negotiations, no specificity on the transition from the goal of setting up a Palestinian state with "borders and certain aspects of its sovereignty [that] will be provisional . . ." to the ultimate stage of final status negotiations.

This approach was of paramount importance because it conformed to the basic view of the Israeli prime minister that conditions were not ripe for entering into final status negotiations for an interminable period of time. Why? First and foremost, no timetable was possible because the intensity of hatred and distrust between the Israelis and Palestinians was such that the two peoples were too far apart to permit a final resolution of all the many issues. Second, the Palestinians had not yet organized effectively and their long-standing leader, Yassir Arafat, had fanned the flames of violence and hatred for so long as to render him incapable of being a credible interlocutor for negotiations that could move the conflict forward in the direction of any form of reconciliation. His was "a failed leadership," a term that was floated around that time and fast became a common expression, oft-repeated and gradually digested, absorbed by most sides and persons involved directly or indirectly in the dispute. The thrust of the prime minister's argument was that for all practical purposes what was now called for was an interim period that would allow the Palestinians to savor independence, under conditions that were partly provisional. As time went on and the new leadership asserted itself internally, as it established law and order and enforced effective measures to prevent terrorism, conditions would emerge to make a permanent settlement negotiation possible with good chances of success.

Following the president's statement, serious developments in the Palestinian Authority became apparent. Long-standing latent despair with the ways and policies of Yassir Arafat burst into the open. These were fueled by a sustained effort by key figures in the Arab world to force the hand of the Palestinian president and obtain his approval for the creation of the post of an empowered prime minister who would formally serve under him, but who would, in effect, wield the executive powers of government in the territories under the rule of the Palestinian Authority. A prominent figure in this effort was General Omar Soleiman of Egypt, the minister of intelligence in his country, a man who was close to President Mubarak and who was the ultimate chief of all the intelligence and security elements in Egypt. He began what was to become a constant shuttle between Cairo, Ramallah, and Jerusalem, thus projecting Egypt up front as a key player in the Israeli-Palestinian conflict. Space will not permit an extensive description of the many aspects of Soleiman's interventions and contributions in the dispute over the years covered by this book. Suffice to say that, when it comes to surveying the events of the latter part of 2002, it is impossible to do so without reference to the unique role played by General Soleiman.

He was not alone. The Saudis were busy, sending Arafat direct and indirect messages that he must cede power. The Gulf states, particularly Qatar with its colorful and highly impressive foreign minister, Jasem Al Thani, were playing a very effective role in impressing upon Arafat that he must concede. On the international scene, a traditional ally and supporter of the Palestinian cause and its leader, Russia, sent a very persuasive representative to the region, and he, in perfect Arabic, in one-on-one meetings with Arafat, put constant pressure on him to make way, albeit without total renunciation of his powers. Thus it can be said with a large degree of truth that the initiative approved by the prime minister in

March 2002, and subsequently adopted by the president of the United States, had unleashed a torrent of actions and reactions that were propelling events in a positive direction.

It was around that time that the prime minister told me, both directly and through a trusted aide of his, that after four and a half years of my service as head of the Mossad, he was contemplating a leadership change. In truth, I was expecting this for some time. I had assumed the leadership in times of crisis, had put things back on track, and had been privileged to be in command during a critical period in the history of the country at the height of the Palestinian campaign, the *intifada* uprising, against Israel. The Mossad had chalked up several operational successes and its international reputation had been not only restored but enhanced. I had served under three successive prime ministers and I had served at a very late age, in comparison to all my predecessors. No one had been head of the Mossad in his mid- and late sixties and the strain and burden were indeed enormous. However, the prime minister coupled this move of mine with a request that I serve as head of the National Security Council and as national security adviser to the prime minister.

The post was a problematic one. The council had been created in 1999 by Prime Minister Netanyahu in the face of stiff opposition of the defense and intelligence establishments. Successive incumbents had served very short periods and the prime ministers had not given the council that solid support that could endow this new creation with the essential prestige it needed to wield significant power in the establishment. When discussing the council and my specific role, the prime minister made it very clear to me that he wanted me to continue to act as his personal envoy in contacts with leading international figures. He would be sending me on missions around the globe, but this time I would not be doing them under the cloak of Mossad chief, but as the national security adviser at his side. My close family and my very best friends strongly advised me not to take up the offer. They saw all the pitfalls inherent in the situation and told me that, at this stage of my life, I should not inject myself into a position that would force me to engage in incessant turf wars, most of which I was bound to lose. The council that I was to lead had around a score of people working for it and it was ill-equipped to forge a place for itself that could compete with the well-established organs of the defense and intelligence communities.

I accepted the prime minister's invitation largely because it had always been my style to accede to requests or instructions from the political level. To refuse such a request from the prime minister was simply not done. I was also flattered by the notion that I would be able to continue my political and diplomatic work, and this at such a historic time. I also believed that this prime minister was sincerely bent on cutting the Gordian knot that had tied up the conflict of Israel and its surroundings for decade upon decade. Why refuse the opportunity?

There was an added challenge that I found appealing and in some respects tailored to my state of mind at that particular point in time. The National Security Council that had been created by Prime Minister Netanyahu, in 1999, had not gotten off the ground and those who had served as heads of the council had not succeeded in giving this fledgling organ its rightful place in the machinery of government. My concept—my approach—was to be different from those of my predecessors. Since the prime minister was bent on giving me an enhanced role in the implementation and furtherance of his policies by casting me as his personal envoy to decision-making levels both within the region and without, I believed that if I were to succeed in meeting the expectations in that field, my capacity to raise the council alongside me and begin to assure it the prestige that it needed and deserved would be considerable. In short, my success would rub off on the council and propel it to a central position that had hitherto been outside its reach.

I found myself traveling extensively to Washington, Moscow, London, Cairo, and Amman, to mention just a few of the destinations to which the prime minister assigned me.

In September 2002, I was in Moscow alongside the prime minister during a visit that I had previously been sent on to prepare to find out at the very last minute I had been excluded from the key meeting with President Putin. This was strange since the prime minister had designated me to handle the Russian relationship on his behalf. I was told that the Russian side had asked me to be kept out since I was still head of the Mossad and my participation would have embarrassed the Russian president. I was able to check this story out later and found it to be devoid of any truth; however, I was informed that, despite my absence from the meeting, the necessary steps would be taken to create the liaison arrangements for me to continue with my mission. This never happened.

I left Moscow as soon as the official part of the visit was over and traveled west. When I landed and called my office I learned that a sensational story had appeared that very morning in a leading Israeli daily. In effect the story said that I had met the Palestinian leader Abu Mazen who was the natural candidate to fill the post of Palestinian prime minister only a short time before. The story even went as far as to identify the venue of my meeting, a key state in the Persian Gulf. The reporter who had written the story was a reliable journalist, who was in Moscow as a member of the press corps accompanying the prime minister on his visit. It was clear that the leak had occurred in Moscow and I called a member of the prime minister's entourage to complain bitterly about this serious lapse. Within a few minutes I received a call informing me that the leak had not come from anyone in Moscow but from a leading politician in Israel. I was able to check this out and to find that this was not true. At the time I was in the very last days of my service as head of the Mossad, and was already functioning as the national security adviser, in a dual capacity. If the Abu Mazen story of his meeting with me had gained momentum, I and others thought that it could be used as a pretext to launching an assassination attempt on his life.

Shortly after the Moscow visit, the prime minister traveled to Washington. I was, by then, the prime minister's national security adviser and before departure I spoke to the prime minister and said that there was no real point in my accompanying him if I was to be left out of his crucial meetings as was the case in Moscow. The prime minister took note of my comment and I attended all his relevant meetings in the American capital including his intimate meeting with the president. At this juncture I began to realize that something was going wrong in the way I was being allowed to fulfill my duties. From time to time there were reports in the press about some of my more delicate contacts and meetings. There were reports of the prime minister's dissatisfaction with my initiatives, and I was beginning to believe that there was a powerful element in the prime minister's office that was seemingly bent on undermining my efforts and my initiatives. I had two ways open to me: to try to fight it out or to quit. In the months to come it became clear to me that there was no point in staying around, but the clouds were gathering in the east and the Iraqi crisis was about to peak. War appeared to be imminent and I thought that it would be irresponsible on my part to resign on what seemed to be the eve of the war. I mentioned my unhappiness from time to time when I met the prime minister, but these meetings were becoming more and more rare and despite his telling me that he wished to meet with me regularly, those in control of his timetable prevented most of the meetings from taking place. I recall meeting a highly respected former cabinet minister, who was held in very high regard by the prime minister, and he told me that the prime minister had seen him at a social event and had asked why the man had not come in to see him for quite some time. Sharon asked his friend to call the office right away and fix an appointment, which he duly did. For weeks on end, times were fixed for the meeting and subsequently postponed. Eventually the meeting materialized when the regular "gate-keepers" were out of the country.

It was against this background that the drama of the "road map" was to unfold. This was to become, in my assessment, the most grievous error made on our side since the clear success that had culminated in the president's June 24 declaration at the White House about the necessity of allowing a new Palestinian leadership to emerge.

Toward the latter part of the summer of 2002, reports started coming into Jerusalem that persons in Europe in the U.N. and in several U.S. departments were dissatisfied with the president's statement of June, which was deemed to be too tilted in favor of Israel. The outcome of this unease was an idea that it was necessary to supplement the president's statement by drafting a road map that would be a practical "manual," indicating exactly how the president's vision could be translated into a plan of action. By the beginning of October, the principal contours of this document had become known in Jerusalem and the immediate reaction was a very negative one. The prime minister was about to travel to Washington for a meeting with the president and he resolved that everything should be done to avoid the necessity of discussing the draft with the president. Indeed, the draft was not mentioned in any way in the talks between the two leaders. The understanding was that this was a preliminary first draft that had to be worked on and that it would be open for changes and amendments before it was adopted. In any event, this was to be considered as a subsidiary document to the president's main statement of June of that year and hence, if there was any contradiction between the two papers, the principal document would overrule the other.

However clear this understanding was, the prime minister felt that the road map was so damaging to the interests of Israel as to warrant an instruction on his part that little or no comment be sent to Washington. The document and its format were not to be accepted by Israel as a basis for discussion or negotiation. A steering committee was set up under the chairmanship of the prime minister's head of cabinet, and it met irregularly and reviewed minor changes that had been made in the original draft. Major flaws in the document were chewed almost ad nauseam, but nothing practical was done about them. What was basically wrong with the road map?

The name of the document said it all: "A Performance-Based Road Map to a Permanent Two State Solution to the Israeli-Palestinian Conflict." Whereas the president's statement of June had placed the emphasis on the emergence of a new Palestinian leadership that would negotiate an agreement to set up a Palestinian state with provisional attributes, leaving the permanent resolution to a later unspecified time, this new document moved the emphasis to a permanent resolution of the conflict and contained timelines that envisaged a final resolution by 2005. The document outlined three stages and, in its third stage, detailed the substantive guidelines of the negotiation. This is what was stated in no uncertain terms:

> Parties reach final and comprehensive permanent status agreement that ends the Israel-Palestinian conflict in 2005, through a settlement negotiated between the parties based on UNSCR 242, 338 and 1397, that ends occupation that began in 1967, and includes an agreed fair and realistic solution to the refugee issue, and a negotiated resolution on the status of Jerusalem that takes in the political and religious concerns of both sides and protects the religious interests of Jews, Christians and Muslims worldwide, and fulfills the vision of two states, Israel and sovereign, independent, democratic and viable Palestine, living side by side in peace and security.

Of all the elements mentioned in this paragraph, the most serious from Israel's standpoint was that of Jerusalem. Ever since the Six-Day

War when the whole of Jerusalem came under Israel's jurisdiction, successive Israeli prime ministers had vowed that the city would remain united and indivisible under Israel's rule. Israel steadfastly denied that the Palestinians would have a political stake in Jerusalem, which, in Israeli rhetoric repeated time and time again by every Israeli prime minister, would be the undivided capital of Israel for eternity. The wording of the road map equated the political concerns of both sides in Jerusalem. This was a clear deviation from what Israel's policy is and has been, and Israel's acceptance of the road map was, in my view, tantamount to Israel's subscribing to the partition of Jerusalem.

When Prime Minister Ehud Barak went to Camp David in the summer of 2000 and tried to negotiate a permanent settlement with Yassir Arafat under the auspices of President Clinton, he raised the issue of Jerusalem as a negotiating issue and toyed with a variety of blueprints concerning the future of the city. He was roundly condemned for doing so by the opposition in the Israeli parliament led at that time by Ariel Sharon. Shortly after his return from the United States, in late September 2000, Mr. Sharon asked to visit the Temple Mount in Jerusalem and Prime Minister Barak authorized the visit. The purpose of the visit was clearly to assert Israel's undeniable claim to the entirety of Jerusalem, including areas that housed the holy mosques of Jerusalem on the Temple Mount. The visit was followed by riots that signaled the beginning of the Palestinian second *intifada,* the four-year period of intensified conflict causing the loss of thousands of lives on both sides. Hence, the road map on Jerusalem ran diametrically contrary to Israel's declared policy and therefore could not be acceptable without there being a fundamental change in Israel's policy on Jerusalem.

Time dragged on. There was a general election in Israel in January 2003 and Ariel Sharon scored a major victory at the polls. Nevertheless, there was no change on policy regarding the road map. It was still deemed a nonstarter and a real danger to Israeli interests for a variety of reasons. In addition to the elements already mentioned it gave the quartet that launched the road map—the United States, Russia, the European Union, and the United Nations—not only the sponsorship of the whole enterprise but also the ultimate authority to determine whether each side had met its obligations according to the stipulations in the document. Since this was a three-stage plan including numerous detailed tasks and obligations of both sides, the quartet could make allowances for either side as it saw fit. This opened up a whole new aspect of the agreement that each side could well exploit.

That Israel would forfeit its right to determine whether the Palestinians had fulfilled their obligations on issues such as their undertakings concerning terror and would delegate this entirely to the quartet was considered by many to be unthinkable.

My view was that, having achieved a major success in June 2002, Israel should concentrate on getting the moderate Arab states more deeply involved in the political process designed to resolve the conflict. I thought that Egypt, Jordan, and key Gulf states could play a very important role in bringing real pressure to bear on the Palestinians. In the months that followed Israel's massive incursion of the West Bank in March 2002, the Arab states, including Saudi Arabia, had been extremely influential in twisting the arm of Arafat and forcing him to make concessions, the most prominent of which was, without doubt, the creation of the post of prime minister, long before achieving Palestinian independence.

My approach was not approved by the prime minister and he did not allow me to go forward as I had suggested, but neither was anything else done on the issue and a type of paralysis had set in that I could not fathom. Many of my meetings were now being leaked to the press. My initiatives were similarly being paraded and derided publicly and I was being told that the prime minister's closest aides were telling influential journalists in Israel that I was out of the loop for all intents and purposes.

It was clear to me that I had to resign at the earliest possible opportunity. There was no point in staying on; however, the clouds of war were fast looming on the horizon and, as previously stated, I thought it improper to resign on the eve of major hostilities in the Middle East. I thought that it would be unbecoming and irresponsible, especially as the estimate was that Israel might be targeted by Iraq. If missiles carrying nonconventional warheads were to fall upon Israeli territory, I felt that every person serving the State of Israel should be on board.

A week before the outbreak of war, I happened to be in the prime minister's office in Tel Aviv for a routine meeting that had been postponed several times. By then, I had resolved to quit as soon as hostilities were over and was therefore in a mood of resignation and largely at peace with myself. I was therefore surprised to be called in and to be told that I would travel that very evening to Washington together with the prime minister's chief of staff for talks at the White House. Apparently, there were a few misunderstandings concerning Israel's demand for freedom of action, should it come under attack, and the White House wished to be assured that Israel would not act unilaterally against Iraq and thus endanger American troops on the ground. I do not know why I was chosen to be part of the two-man team that was charged with this mission. Was it an American request that I be there? I could not imagine that this was the wish of my partner to the trip.

It transpired that this was for me not only the swan song of my career but also a fascinating half day in the capital of the United States. Upon arrival, we were told that in addition to the original purpose of the trip, another subject would be raised: the road map. This latter matter took center stage during the hours spent in the White House. We were told that, although initially the United States had not wished to link the Israeli-Palestinian conflict with the Iraqi affair and the road map was originally not scheduled for treatment as the United States went to war in Iraq, new circumstances had dictated a rapid change in policy. The British prime minister, Tony Blair, had encountered strong resistance in his Labor party parliamentary faction and there was a group of at least fifty rebels who were threatening to oppose British entry into the war alongside the United States. In order to offset this move, the British had made an almost frantic request that the president officially endorse the road map as soon as possible so that the British prime minister could point to this as an achievement and thus assure himself of the support of the vast majority of his party. Israel was called upon to show understanding for this combination of circumstances, given the stakes of the impending war in Iraq, and the inherent advantage Israel would gain from the removal of Iraq from the list of its active and dangerous foes. In all truth, we had no option but to accept the American request, made on the eve of the war with all its obvious uncertainties.

Originally, the White House appeared to be leaning toward the issue of a press release. It transpired that this was not deemed sufficient to obtain the desired result, so the president made an appearance in the Rose Garden and publicly endorsed the road map and extolled its virtues. Gone was the president's statement of June 2002 as the major defining document of American policy and in came the road map, not as a subsidiary document translating the president's vision into practical steps, but as the major document projecting both the amended vision of the president and the detailed stages of its implementation. Israel kept its silence and in so doing stifled any criticism of the president for acting as he did. Thus did we all slide into the road map as the determining document defining American policy on the Israeli-Palestinian conflict. The link, hitherto latent, between the conflict and America's wider interests in the region therefore received public exposure and recognition. With one lightning movement, brought on by changing circumstances, American policy took a tilt in a direction contrary to the one it had followed hitherto. I saw this happening in front of my eyes and it was a drama that I could not forget.

In Israel, on the eve of the Iraqi war, this major change in American policy passed largely unnoticed. The ordinary citizen was understandably preoccupied with the impending war in Iraq and its possible dangerous fallout on Israel. The cabinet had ordered that gas masks be opened and every citizen was obliged to carry one wherever he went. This was not the time to quibble about documents.

During the very few hours I spent in Washington I was deeply impressed by the concern expressed over the fate of Saudi Arabia as America went to war in Iraq. I recalled that the first Gulf War came to an abrupt end and a cease-fire was hastily ordered when the Saudis let it be known that as members of the American-led coalition they could not stomach the capture of an Arab capital by Western forces. In their estimate, they would be unable to contain the fury that such an event would unleash. This time around the United States was going it alone without the U.N. international sanction that it had during the previous round, more than a decade before, and notwithstanding this impediment, it was clear that the battle plans envisaged the liberation of the entire land of Iraq, including its capital, Baghdad. In such circumstances, I did not believe that Israel could refrain from acceding to United States' demands—requests concerning the road map. I did think that if, in good time, we had entered into a serious negotiation on the map, we would have had had a good chance of mitigating many of its features that were so damaging for us.

Within weeks after the end of the war in Iraq, the United States and the quartet presented the road map to both the Palestinians and the Israelis. This happened shortly after Mahmoud Abbas, alias Abu Mazen, was officially installed as Palestinian prime minister. In mid-May 2003 Prime Minister Ariel Sharon was scheduled to pay a first visit to Washington after the Iraqi war had ended. A terrorist attack on the eve of his departure was cited as the reason for his last-minute decision to stay at home. I sensed that an additional reason for his changed travel plan was his desire not to be confronted with a demand to publicly endorse the road map which he rightly considered as detrimental to Israel's most basic policies and interests. Within the space of less than a week the prime minister's chief of cabinet was summoned to Washington and within less than twenty-four hours the prime minister announced his endorsement of the road map.

At the end of May, the Israeli government convened to discuss and approve the prime minister's acceptance of the road map. During a long and protracted session, the ministers received an abbreviated report of the discussions that had taken place in Washington. They were told that Israel's reservations had been raised, but the American response was withheld from them. They were told that the "body language" of National Security Adviser Condoleezza Rice was understanding and sympathetic. Nothing further was divulged. At one point of the discussion the ministers were told that Israel's reservations had been accepted, but after further probing, this statement was amended. Such acceptance was not there. The United States was quoted as saying that Israel's reservations "would be addressed." This was translated into Hebrew as stating that Israel's reservations had been accepted. Had not one of the ministers questioned the translation, they would have labored under the impression that all was well, and I found it very difficult to accept this "wheeler-dealer" approach to official documents. The government was torn in its attitude to the road map and in order to secure a majority the prime minister agreed that a draft of reservations be appended to the acceptance. Fourteen points that had been a sort of talking-point brief were ceremonially attached to the cabinet's approval and subsequently passed to the United States. Brushing aside Israel's public insistence that these points were an integral part of the agreement, their status was not such as to be part of the acceptance of the road map. The United States did not object to Israel stating its views on any given issue, as long as the road map was formally and unconditionally accepted. No change or correction was permitted in the wording of the road map. We were to take it or leave it and had no alternative but to accept it as it stood.

What troubled me at the time was not only the superficial attitude to the drafting and contents of official documents, but, more, the nature of the background briefs given by the closest aides to the prime minister, his ministers, and others who were told that the road map was of no consequence or danger to Israel. The first stage of the map envisaged a concerted effort on the part of the Palestinians to dismantle terrorist infrastructures. In order for them to do so, they needed to behave like Finns and this, of course, would never come about. Similarly it was claimed that the American side did not really attach any real significance to the road map. Once accepted it could be simply forgotten, with the silent acquiescence of the United States. Knowing a little about the way governments and administrations function, I could not really believe that this was possible, that there could be such a degree of collusion to deceive governments and influence public opinion. Given my background, I knew of silent understandings of the past. I was witness and participant to many an understanding that served the most delicate of interests of both the United States and Israel, but this way of doing business went far beyond what I could genuinely believe. It was obvious to me that I had long not been in the loop, but I was skeptical as to whether those who were in the loop really grasped the rules of the game. This was certainly the time to leave.

Before taking this step, I tried to explain to myself why it was that matters had evolved as they did. Why did the prime minister go full circle and endorse a plan, the road map, which he had defined as so dangerous as to warrant an instruction on his part not to touch it with a barge pole? From whence came the political paralysis that seemed to have caught hold of the entire body politic immediately after the success of June 2002 and the president's statement on the new Palestinian leadership? Why had there been systematic leaks about successive missions that I had performed with the full knowledge and sanction of the prime minister? Could the personal animosity of one government official to another be sufficient to destroy diplomatic assets that were not the property of one single individual, but of a nation as a whole? Why was this allowed to pass without sanction or reprimand? I had no valid answers for this string of queries and since leaving office have yet to discover how all this could come about.

I tendered my resignation twice to the prime minister and twice he asked that I withdraw it, assuring me that I enjoyed his confidence and telling me that he would take steps to meet my concerns. Against my better judgment, I carried on for several more weeks, hoping, if you wish, believing that arrangements would be made to enable me to continue serving the prime minister and the government in a meaningful way. I felt that there was a genuine desire on his part that I stay on. Basically I had confidence in his intention to make historical decisions and in his capacity to carry them out, but I came to realize that, as I saw it, the man was not a free agent and his commitments, very personal commitments to others, tied his hands and prevented him from exercising his prerogatives as he deemed fit. I had no alternative but to go, although resignation was uncharacteristic of me. The third time he accepted my request, but insisted that I stay on for three more months for reasons of his own that I never got to know. I formally left office at the end of August 2003. A short, ineffectual smear campaign orchestrated by some in the prime minister's office petered out after a day or two and that was the end of that.

The year 2003 witnessed the entry of the United States as a front-line player in the Middle East. With a couple of hundred thousand troops in Iraq and in Afghanistan, a military presence in the Balkans, and the prospect of further involvement on the ground should it become necessary to preserve American interests in Saudi Arabia or in the Persian Gulf, it has become essential for every player in the region to treat Washington not only as the only superpower on the global scene, but also as a close neighbor with direct strategic and tactical needs and interests in the Middle East. It has become a power that, if it deems necessary, will impose solutions on states in the region to prevent chaos and danger to world economic or other interests. In the case of the Israeli-Palestinian conflict, the road map will be the instrument whereby an imposed solution might come about. By endorsing it the parties have acquiesced, in principle, to such an outcome. Thus what began as an initiative designed to enable a new Palestinian leadership to emerge and to forge an interim agreement with Israel that would, in time, lower the intensity of the conflict and promote a climate of reconciliation was transformed, overnight, into a formula applied as a solution imposed with the barrel of a shotgun. My feelings at the time were, and are today, that such an approach contains the seeds of future strife rather than a new dawn of peace.

The first Gulf War heralded a decade of negotiations that contained the seeds of possible accommodations. Alas, some of the players were not up to the mark and their failed leadership brought tragedy to their peoples. The second Gulf War was more decisive than the first. The free world, led by the United States, had matured enough to take bold steps to roll back the axis of evil. The initial success wrongly led the victors into believing that they could take lightning steps to turn things around within relatively short time spans. I fear that, on that score, they will be proved wrong. Attitudes and habits of nations and societies do not change overnight. Instant solutions are short-lived and create the parameters for the wars and struggles of tomorrow.

16

TAKING RESPONSIBILITY AND
ASSIGNING BLAME

In our turbulent and dangerous times, one question has trumped all others regarding intelligence services: Who has the ultimate responsibility for making intelligence assessments and who should be judged for them? To answer this very important question, I must, first, think back to 1974. I had just returned to Israel from a four-year tour in Washington, D.C., as Mossad station chief in North America. I was appointed deputy division chief of a new division that had been created in the Mossad in the aftermath of the disastrous Yom Kippur War. It was the assessment division that was created on the specific recommendation of the judicial inquiry commission that had been appointed in the wake of the intelligence and military disaster of the Yom Kippur War. The Agranat Commission as it was called, named after the chief justice who had headed the commission, had recommended that there be "plurality" or "pluralism" in the minefield of assessment, and that three rather than one assessment body be charged with the responsibility of presenting assessments to the political level. It was an exciting and, possibly, rewarding challenge. What more could an ambitious intelligence officer hope for than to be a founding father of an endeavor to set right a major failure that had been responsible, in part, for the loss of more than two thousand dead and several more thousand wounded, let alone the traumatic effect that the war had caused to the morale of the nation.

In addition to the central assessment unit in military intelligence, which was specifically blamed for the disaster, two additional assessment elements were constituted: one in the Mossad and the other in the ministry of foreign affairs. All would supposedly read the same materials and each would reach its independent conclusions. At the outset, the director of military intelligence forbade his officers to receive the assessments of the two new rivals. The rationale given for this was, of course, that the serving officers in military intelligence should be totally free of any outside influence in reaching their conclusions. The truth behind this order was somewhat more complex. Military intelligence, notwithstanding the severe blow it had suffered after that war, was nevertheless the strongest and most prestigious in the field of assessments and it wished to maintain its seniority and to some extent its exclusivity, despite the findings of the commission. Shortly after the war, the government of Prime Minister Golda Meir resigned and Yitzhak Rabin became prime minister. His voice as a junior minister of the outgoing government was the sole voice that rose against the findings of the judicial commission for a variety of reasons. He certainly did not wish to detract from the preeminence of military intelligence and issued a clear guideline stating that military intelligence bore the responsibility for assessing the threats of war against Israel. This ruling immediately established the inferior status of the other two assessment units and that is the state of affairs to this very day. Real life and the ultimate responsibilities of both military and civilian personnel all along the chain of command overcame, and will always overcame, attempts to move authority in various directions when it comes to matters of life and death.

I stayed in my post for just three months. I often told my friends later that it took me six weeks to get into the job and another six to extricate myself from it. Coming from the operational side of the house, I plunged without hesitation into the hurly-burly of assessment production. I was fascinated with the notion that, after Israel had finally repulsed the Syrian onslaught on the Golan Heights which Israel had captured in the Six-Day War six years earlier, Syria might be mature for an approach to reach a peace settlement. I had no hard evidence of this. Despite its painful setback, Syria maintained an excessive degree of hostility against

Israel and the situation along the dividing line between the forces massed on both sides was very precarious. It ultimately took a tough bout of shuttle diplomacy by the U.S. secretary of state, Dr. Henry Kissinger, to reach an accommodation that has permitted both sides to enjoy relative calm for more than thirty years. However, before the shuttle, I put my thoughts to paper and discussed them with my division chief. Frankly, he was horrified by what I had done; I had overstepped the line between assessing the enemies' evil intentions on the ground and giving vent to hypotheses about the prospects of an overall settlement, which, I was told, was way beyond my pay scale.

About a month after we began working, my chief traveled abroad to a very distant country. There was little to no means of communication with him. In his absence, a series of indications were received pointing to a possibility that the Syrians were contemplating a surprise thrust to regain a swathe of lost territory. Was this a serious threat that could result in a major conflagration on our northern front not so long after the Yom Kippur War? I called in the analysts and discussed the information with them in minute detail. Most thought that there was a real threat and under the influence of the intelligence debacle of the previous year certainly did not wish to be caught out by offering an upbeat picture that might prove wrong. A couple of the younger staffers sided with my view that the odds were against an outbreak of hostilities because the penalty of failure was such as to endanger the very survival of the regime. In the end, I myself wrote the division paper, and after analyzing the various aspects and bits of information, gave a definitive assessment that the Syrians would not attack. My division chief returned shortly after and was furious when he learned what I had done. In his judgment, I should have been more sensitive to the views of the majority of analysts and in any event my conclusions should have been couched in much more guarded terms, certainly not dismissing even the faint possibility of a Syrian foray. I was told that, from then on, I would not be authorized to write the definitive division papers in the absence of the chief. I had to go a long way before I could qualify to be a true analyst.

My contention was then, as it is today, that the responsibility of the analyst is similar to that of an officer in the field. There is a hierarchy in analysis just as there is in the operational field. Individuals should be encouraged to speak up and say what's on their mind. In acute cases that contain a variety of assessments, all of the dissenting voices should reach the top; however, this should not—and cannot—detract from the clear responsibility of the assessment chief or deputy chief to give a clear assessment and to be judged for it. "Group think" is not a dirty expression, but it should not lead to a democratic process of assessment evaluation. An assessment of intelligence should not be a subject that is put to a vote as there is no such thing as collective responsibility in intelligence divisions.

As I said, there is a hierarchical structure in intelligence organizations, just as there is a parallel system in the military. Ultimately, the responsibility lies with one single individual who is perched uneasily on the top of a very greasy pole. He is the sole figure responsible for the successes of the agency as he is for its drawbacks and failures. He, or she, alone must stand in judgment and he or she alone must possess the authority—the entire authority—to fashion the organization in a manner that will enable it to cope with its challenges. This is not to say that the intelligence chief can operate outside the confines of the law. He must respect the rule of law and his treatment of his personnel must meet the highest standards in doing so; however, he must have the prerogatives to choose those people with whom he hopes to achieve the desired results. More often than not, in the execution of intelligence operations, individuals are called upon to stretch their efforts far beyond the horizons of normal human imagination. In order to make this possible, ultimately, it is the chief who must retain and exercise the authority to hire and fire. It should be up to him to make all staffing decisions, even at lower levels. That is the reason, in my estimate, that all service chiefs in Israel zealously preserved their authority in the area of human resources. I recall spending long hours meeting with officers at all ranks and not only hearing what they had to say but also taking advantage of these sessions in order to form opinions and assessments of the people working for the business. That is why I spent more than a third of my time outside the country, visiting stations, spending evenings with personnel and their families in so-called "social" events. Intelligence and security in Israel are, and have always been, a very personal affair. Just because the art of intelligence is such a difficult and uncertain occupation, was it not and is it still not natural that, up to a point, officers in command should have a decisive say in deciding who would go into battle with them?

Some of these almost axiomatic rules of conduct have been put to the test in the United States following the events of 9/11 and the Iraqi war. Of the two separate events, I have always felt that the story of 9/11 was most significant when it came to discussing the true significance of some of the basic rules of intelligence. The 9/11 commission appointed by the president of the United States produced a very impressive report and it seemed, on the face of it, to make an extremely persuasive argument. Among other points it raised, it stated that the intelligence community showed a lack of imagination in evaluating the threats to the country. I found this argument especially strange when compared to an almost opposite finding of the Senate commission charged with probing the Iraqi war. In that evaluation, the intelligence community, especially the CIA, was condemned for an overabundance of imagination on the key issue of whether or not Iraq had indeed engaged in attempting to produce nuclear devices that could wreak mass destruction. Was imagination a desirous quality for an intelligence officer or should an intelligence officer be characterized only by his or her complete devotion to the data in his or her possession and by his or her refusal or incapacity to go one inch beyond the black-and-white facts? Since I believe that intelligence is an art rather than a science, an outstanding performer in this field must be blessed with a certain degree of imagination. Only creative minds can think outside the box, so to speak, and only persons with nonconventional approaches can hope to identify hitherto unknown types of threats. But, of course, there has to be a balance between flights of imagination and hard data. Hence, I have always attempted to lead groups of officers who are far from being similar to each other. Indeed, I have tried to include in every pack at least one devil's advocate to stir the waters and to prevent stereotyped thinking.

In the final analysis, authority and responsibility must go together and the chain of command must ensure that he who shoulders the responsibility for the product, for the assessment, or for the procurement of information has direct command of the troops. It is impossible to hold an intelligence chief accountable if he does not have full command of his subordinates. Thus I am convinced that the new intelligence structure that has been put in place in the United States in the wake of 9/11 and the Iraqi war heralds an exceedingly difficult time in the conduct of intelligence in the United States. The creation of the post of director of national intelligence—DNI—immediately calls into question the powers and responsibilities of the director of the CIA. If there is another intelligence failure in the years ahead, who will bear the blame? Is the director of the CIA subordinate to the DNI and, in this case, does the DNI command the Agency? Who appoints the division heads? Who is the ultimate authority for orders in the field? Who micromanages the activities of every intelligence outfit in the nation? If the DNI is empowered to move personnel from service to service, to determine the Essential Elements of Information—or, in other words, the agenda of the community—then he alone is the intelligence chief and all the rest have no real responsibility.

This is an especially important aspect of the conduct of intelligence. In order for an intelligence chief to be credible and reliable, he must have his ear to the ground. He must be up and about, meeting case officers on the scene the world over, familiarizing himself with working conditions and environments, constantly maintaining contact with foreign colleagues, and comparing notes with them. He must develop throughout his tenure gut feelings that are essential to people at all levels and particularly those at the top. And there must be an intimacy that is constantly nurtured between the intelligence leader and his political master. All this is not within arm's reach in the new structure that President Bush has now put in place, under the intense pressure of the legislative branch and the media in the United States. It could well be that there will be an improved flow of information and that coordination at all levels, between agencies, may be advanced; however, this could have been achieved without imposing a heavy layer of officialdom on the top, thus removing the president from that more intimate contact that he must have with the true leaders of the community. Order may be better, but the spirit is gone.

I often recall, with a whiff of nostalgia, the one-on-one meetings that I had with George Tenet, the director of the CIA, throughout my four-and-a-half-year tenure as head of the Mossad. We always had these meetings just before or immediately after the full sessions with our respective staffs and we felt free to discuss anything and everything that was on our minds. A personal relationship was there and it enabled us to serve our masters and our nations in a most effective manner. I knew that certain messages of mine went straight to the top, and he knew that I would communicate to my prime minister directly and give an unadulterated report of what I had heard. We could talk intimately on the situations in the countries neighboring Israel and assess what might happen based on our personal knowledge of the principal players and their strengths, aims, and weaknesses. In the new structure, who will be that vital point of contact in Washington? Will the director of DNI replace the director of the CIA and travel the globe, cementing his personal relations with service chiefs and heads of state? If so, how much time and energy will he have to oversee the vast intelligence community in the United States? If not, who will give the president the indispensable advice based on direct firsthand knowledge of the conditions on the ground? Will the mission be divided up between the two functionaries and, if so, who will bear the ultimate responsibility for the product, the intelligence? This analysis of mine is more than hypothesis and question. When I left the Mossad, George Tenet gave me as a present the book written by his illustrious predecessor, Allen Dulles, titled *The Craft of Intelligence,* published in 1963. In it, I found the following small passage:

> From my own experience in the Agency, under three Presidents, I can say with certainty that the Chief Executive takes a deep and continuing interest in its operations. During eight of my eleven years as Deputy Director and Director of the CIA, I served under President Eisenhower. I had many talks with him about the day-to-day workings of the agency . . .

I believe that little to no attention has been given to one other aspect of the functions of the Agency and in that, as well, there is a similarity with the mission of the Mossad. The CIA has functioned under the provisions of the National Security Act of 1947. Under this law, the CIA is empowered "to perform for the benefit of the existing intelligence agencies such additional services of common concern as the National Security Council determines can be more efficiently accomplished centrally . . . perform such other functions and duties relating to intelligence affecting the national security as the National Security Council may from time to time direct . . ." These seemingly obscure and evasive definitions of the Agency's tasks point to the residual powers and responsibilities that the director of the CIA has had, in relation to national security in the broader sense of the term.

Once one has asked who is responsible for an intelligence agency, one must finally ask the basic questions, "What, then, is 'intelligence'? What can 'intelligence affecting the national security' mean?" I believe that this catch-all term was and still is designed to give the sovereign, the president, the prime minister, et al., the residual power and authority needed to meet future, hitherto unknown, threats to the nation and to direct action to thwart hostile intent through the use of clandestine methods and means. In order for there to be such a capability in place, there has to be an organ, the CIA for instance, that bears responsibility for such a delicate type of mission and that agency must be led by one who not only enjoys the full confidence of the political master, but also has a frequent and close ongoing relationship with him or her. Interposing an interim level of authority scuttles such a possibility from the very outset and renders the implementation of any mission under this provision totally impossible.

I have already alluded to the international aspect of the responsibilities and activities of an intelligence chief. In the current age, given the threats to international stability posed by the twin menace of international Muslim terror and the proliferation of weapons of mass destruction, interservice cooperation between nations is essential. Without such close cooperation, there is no chance that the threats might be contained and ultimately removed. This necessitates, first and foremost, mutual recognition and respect at the top of the pyramid. Relationships have to be created and cultivated and a firm basis of personal trust must be maintained. Who will be the counterpart in the United States for intelligence chiefs the world over, given the new structure? George Tenet, during his particularly long and mostly successful tenure, projected human qualities and professional capacity that earned the United States invaluable assets in the pursuit of its most difficult mission. The manner in which the body politic in the legislative branch set upon him and literally threatened to hound him out left an indelible impression on intelligence communities the world over and caused untold damage to future cooperation. Who will there be around to pick up the pieces? Will it be the new directors of the CIA, shorn of their prestige and power, or the DNI who will virtually be physically unable to shoulder all of the responsibilities thrust upon him?

The United States of America and its intelligence services span the globe. Similarly the leading European services—Britain's famed MI6, Germany's secret intelligence service, the Italian and Russian services— all have international interests and contacts. I was privileged to have meaningful contacts with them all and there was never a moment when I had to make contact through a representative. There was never a moment, when I was making direct contact, that I was turned away. With some colleagues, I continue to enjoy personal contact, even now, when both they and I are no longer in office. At times, these became very intimate links that served political masters as I have related before. I fear that the manner in which the U.S. government conducted its probes into both 9/11 and the Iraqi war will have a negative effect on the international network as a whole for quite some time to come.

In spelling this out, I will not hide my deep respect and affection for George Tenet who, for all intents and purposes, led a unique coalition of intelligence and security services in the international battles that spread all over the world at the turn of the century. He chaired no international conferences or gatherings, nor did he create a massive communications network to enable him to lead as he did. He led by the sheer force of his personality and the immense power that he was able to generate in the name of his country. George Tenet was capable of extracting nuggets of cooperation that others would never have been able to extract. It will, as they say, be a very difficult act for anybody to follow and even more so in the light of the restructuring that the American system will be undergoing in the years to come.

Tenet's relationship with me was certainly not the only one that he cultivated and nurtured during his stewardship. When I was preparing to leave the Mossad, we met in Washington and he honored me both by giving me the book written by Allen Dulles (it was a used copy and as such I valued it that much more) and by conferring upon me the Director's Award created by General Washington, to be issued ". . . whenever any singularly meritorious action is performed . . . not only instances of unusual gallantry, but also of extraordinary fidelity and essential service in any way . . ." I know of no other Israeli who received this award before.

The citation read, ". . . in recognition of his unswerving commitment and dedication to the relationship between Israel and the United States of America . . ."

I would have liked to detail the reasons for a director of central intelligence (in his capacity as leader of the intelligence community of the United States) giving this rare citation to a foreign-service chief, but I am bound by the rules laid down by none other than George Washington himself, who wrote:

> The necessity of procuring good intelligence is apparent and need not be further urged. . . . All that remains for me to add is that you keep the whole matter as secret as possible. For on secrecy success depends in most enterprises of the kind and for want of it they are generally defeated however well planned and promising a favorable issue.

The citation mentions the fact that George Washington was the first intelligence chief of the nation and personally directed agents to collect specific information and instructed them in the clandestine arts. I do not assume that in these times the president could function likewise, but surely this example of days gone by reflects the intimate involvement of the political master in the conduct of that vast field of endeavor named "intelligence."

Throughout this book I have referred from time to time to instances where imagination has been the better or the worse counsel for the intelligence community. Yes, there always has to be someone to blame and if you do not know whom to blame, then why not put it upon someone or some country that you would dearly hope is to blame? Hours after 9/11, before any real intelligence had been gathered on this unprecedented act of terror, the word was out in the Arab world: This was a provocative act committed by none other than Israel and the instrument for this horrendous deed was, naturally, the Mossad. So deep has the prejudice been over scores of years that within no time the lie was out and was relayed through television and other media both near and far. Evidence was quickly spread to the effect that the Mossad had been careful to warn Americans of the Jewish faith to stay away from the Twin Towers in New York. As time went on and the lie appeared so obviously and so wickedly false, a fresh version was disseminated claiming that the Mossad had prior knowledge of the impending attacks but chose to withhold it from its American colleagues. I was Mossad chief at the time and I can attest to this being an outright and vicious lie. No such claim has ever been made by any responsible American official and the fact that, even to this day, the rumor lingers on is a testament to the great dangers inherent in warped and sick imagination.

My criticisms concerning the reports of the two commissions that investigated the two failures might indicate that I am opposed to change and enamored with the status quo. Nothing is further from the truth. I myself instituted great structural changes in the Mossad when I came in, but these were wedded to the immediate challenges that we faced. They had no relation to political considerations of the political level and were approved after I had made an adequate case for them. The new structure put in place in the United States, in effect, insulates the president from the practical conduct of—and therefore from the true responsibility for the supervision of—the intelligence community. Whether this is politically expedient I do not know, since I do not pretend to be sufficiently versed in that aspect of American life. What I do know, and know full well, is that professionally this is a grave mistake.

There is one major change that should have been made and recommended by the 9/11 commission, and that is the creation of a fully fledged security service in the United States. The principal failure that allowed such a terrible event to occur was the absence of a security service whose prime and only mission should be the prevention of terrorist or other subversive activities inside the United States. Law enforcement, which has been the prime task of the FBI since its inception, does not go hand in hand with security. Quite the contrary. Whereas the FBI agent is trained from the very outset to believe that the end product of his activities is the massing of sufficient admissible evidence in court to secure an indictment and a guilty verdict, the security agent is first and foremost trained to prevent an act from being committed, to reveal the environment and support systems that make an act possible or probable, and to gather sufficient evidence—sufficient intelligence—to enable the political level to obtain a clear picture of the menaces and what they entail for the individual. Nowhere in the world, except in the United States, are the two functions combined. When, on one occasion, I shared a platform with a member of the 9/11 commission I aired this idea, only to be told that I was advocating a totalitarian-style system that was contrary to the principles and ideals of the American way of life. I beg to differ: A security service—a domestic service functioning under the rule of law, but with know-how and an organizational culture tailored to its mission— would have been launching intelligence operations within the United States shortly after being made aware of the fact that an attack of sorts directed against the territory of the country could not be ruled out. Indeed, long before the Al Qaeda attacked the U.S.S. *Cole* near Aden, the security service would have analyzed the twin attacks on two American embassies in Africa in 1998, and would not have confined itself to sifting the rubble in the hope of finding clues that would lead to the apprehension of those who actually committed the crime. As long as there is no security service in the United States, there shall remain a yawning gap in the defenses of that great nation. There can be no substitute for a security service, entirely independent and separate from the FBI. That could well be one of the reasons for the success of any future attack on American territory.

The heart of the new American structure almost ensures that if something goes wrong in the future, it will be almost impossible to identify any particular individual who was responsible for what went wrong. This might be good or it may be very bad, but this is not the worst outcome of the new setup. The real fault in this fresh system is that, a priori, no one is really in charge. The men who command the troops are no longer directly accountable to the political master, whereas the titular head of the community lacks the substantive command of the organs that are subordinate to him. This is a recipe for disaster. As of now nobody is truly responsible and therefore nobody will ever be to blame. This feeling of a lack of responsibility will permeate the ranks and impress upon the troops in the field that there is no real authority at the top. The results of such a cultural milieu lacking control by any real figure of authority emerging within the U.S. intelligence community, are too horrendous and too frightening to contemplate.

17

FROM MY NEW VANTAGE POINT

Writing more than two years after leaving government service, I now have had both the privilege and the opportunity to follow events from the outside and to compare what I knew then to what I know now. At this time of writing, seven years have passed since Al Qaeda launched its attack against the United States and destroyed two American embassies simultaneously. As I've said before, I see these events as the declaration of World War III, but it took another three years and the events of 9/11 to galvanize both political and public opinion and to propel the president of the United States to lead the world in battle against this elusive and deadly enemy.

In rapid succession, the invasion of Afghanistan has been followed by the liberation of Iraq from the despotic regime of Saddam Hussein. Although the troops have been on the ground for some time now in both theaters of operation, victory on these two battlefronts appears further away than ever. In realistic terms, the war may last a generation or more before it comes to an end.

Terrorist attacks in Madrid and in London have produced contradictory results and reactions. In the case of Madrid, the public was able to respond instantly, since the heavy toll of victims in the attack on a central railway station traumatized the voters on the eve of a general election. The government of one of the most successful and competent Spanish prime ministers in modern times, Prime Minister Asnar, was ousted and replaced by that of Prime Minister Zapatero. And the new cabinet under Zapatero hastily moved to withdraw the Spanish contingent that had been serving in Iraq alongside the armed forces of the United States. The attack had been politically motivated and had obviously been designed to effect both the removal of the Spanish forces and the weakening of U.S.-Spanish ties that had been a mainstay of support for President Bush in his effort to gain the European underwriting of his policy in Iraq. Initially, Al Qaeda achieved all of its objectives as the result of one isolated operation. The repair of U.S.-Spanish relations, undertaken by both sides, has consumed time and effort. Two years after the bombing, they have not been restored entirely to the point they were at before the elections.

In sharp contrast to the Spanish experience, the series of terrorist attacks mounted against multiple targets in London's underground transportation system on July 7, 2005, had an opposite effect on both the body politic and, in consequence, the practical steps taken by the law enforcement authorities. Initially the main body of political power in the country, both the governing party and the principal opposition, lined up behind Prime Minister Blair to promote a very tough legal and practical response to the threat. However, when fresh legislation was urgently being pushed through to give the men on the ground the means to sustain a prolonged combat effort designed to weed out potential threats, both from outside the country and from within, as speedily as possible, a split in Parliament scuttled a principal provision that would have permitted a detention period of ninety days without charges being formally brought. Blair staked his reputation on getting the measure passed and was defeated in Parliament. It remains to be seen how this setback will be viewed by the "enemy" and how they will try to take advantage of this climate of hesitation and indecision.

Indeed, of the many aspects that have characterized the terrorist activities of the past couple of years, those that relate to the London bombings are the more ominous and necessitate the closest attention. The perpetrators were, basically, not activist foreigners who had come from outside the system. They were, rather, young people from a second-generation

immigrant class, who had apparently been bent on integrating themselves into the British way of life, supposedly striving to adopt British
values and the English way of life. In carrying out their acts of violence
and in adopting the course of suicide, they aligned themselves both politically and culturally with the suicide bombers of Palestinian terror and
the Al Qaeda attackers in New York, Washington, and Madrid. They
were not "outsiders" coming in to perpetrate a crime on foreign soil.
Rather, they were indigenous second-generation citizens who had not renounced their citizenship but were acting within it.

The British phenomenon of Muslim terror is, therefore, separate and
distinct from all the rest. In searching for a parallel, I believe the status of
the Arab minority in Israel bears some similarity to that of the growing
communities of Muslims in Europe, in general, and in Britain, in particular. There are, of course, major differences, but I have been struck by
the resemblance especially when observed from the vantage point of national security and from the tasks that intelligence and security services
must face in handling this extremely delicate issue.

I alluded in a previous chapter to the manner in which the European
Union approached the problem in the final years of the twentieth century, a manner characterized by a desire to ignore the more serious aspects of the developing challenge that the Muslim communities were
posing as their numbers swelled from year to year. Denial and psychological suppression were the order of the day. Whereas the Madrid attack could still be defined as an operation perpetrated from the outside,
the London suicide operations of "Seven-Seven" came from the inside
and, virtually overnight, the public at large was faced with the searing
dilemma of how to deal with a large minority of its citizens out of whose
midst emerged suicide bombers motivated by a religion that was the basic common denominator of the whole minority.

Every citizen in Britain is, of course, entitled to enjoy the full gamut of
rights that the system bestows upon him or her as a citizen of that country and as a human being. Parallel to this basic rule of law and society, it
is reprehensible to taint an entire community and to visit on it the crimes
and attitudes of a small and numerically insignificant number of people
who grew up in their midst. These are the principles involved, but are
they able, in all truth and sincerity, to be practiced to the letter? Didn't
the small group of perpetrators enjoy the general support and sympathy

of a much larger circle of people who shared the same faith and who might feel that, although the means employed might be blameworthy, the Cause—with a capital C—that they set out to serve was most worthy? Professionally, this means that the communities as such must take on the status of targets that need to be covered adequately so that the capacity to obtain intelligence that might foil future attacks would be considerably enhanced. Such an approach, while professionally essential, presents the political levels in governments throughout Europe, including that of Britain, with a daunting dilemma. A decision taken to target the Muslim communities as such, even if taken under the veil of secrecy, cannot remain hidden from the public eye for very long. Recruiting sources and launching a variety of operations will very soon be felt and become known both inside the community and outside it and could arouse intense debate and bitter reprimand.

The problem has been compounded by the fact that the growing presence of Muslim communities on the European continent is fast becoming an issue that must be faced by the continent as an issue of paramount concern. The exact number of Muslim immigrants presently living in Central and Western Europe is unknown. The official figures do not represent the final tally, because there are a large number of persons who entered illegally and their numbers are by no means insignificant. Given the high birthrate among Muslims, their number—in my estimate—will very shortly surpass 10 percent of the entire population across the board.

A minor illustration of the problem of the burgeoning Muslim population and its influence on the operation of a state was provided when one of the suspects in the second, aborted attempt to carry out an attack against the London underground transportation system fled to Italy, where extradition proceedings were still incomplete more than a month after the event. The current laws governing extradition have been refined in recent times to facilitate the effective combating of crime, with emphasis on organized crime and extreme cases involving violence or extensive financial transactions of a serious criminal nature. They were not designed to cater to the needs of facing up to terrorism and the imperative necessity to act speedily. As the suspect appealed to the highest legal instance in Italy against the decision of a lower court, he had no problem in claiming that given the hostile atmosphere in Britain he would not be granted a fair trial there and that he should therefore not be sent there against his own will. The final decision to approve extradition made months after the act could not provide the British authorities with the timely information they needed to develop intelligence leads and to obtain what might be vital early warning information.

The British dilemmas are basically those that confront a large number of countries, which have not, hitherto, suffered in any way from the terrorist threat. The question of how to convince the public in those societies that they must take stern measures to face up to something that they have not experienced is a grave problem. Much has been said and written about the necessity of international cooperation to confront the common threat, but the crux of the matter does not lie only in the direction of promoting cooperation between countries, yet no less in the individual approaches that each separate state takes to the problems confronting them. There is no universal legislation on these matters and what is plain and simple in London may be entirely unacceptable in Berlin. What the powers that be in Britain might be prepared to countenance in the United Kingdom, when it comes to dealing with communities originating from Pakistan, might well be nonstarters for a German government facing the Turk and Kurdish communities numbering several million in united Germany.

I sincerely doubt that a common approach, an identical set of laws and regulations, can be fashioned in the years to come unless, as well might happen, the incidence of further acts of mass terror will propel the peoples of Western civilization into almost instant reaction from which they still recoil. I do not pretend that these choices are easy. These choices are very hard and they also bear on additional political issues that are commanding the attention of the international community.

The issue of possible acceptance of Turkey into the European Union is one such problem with a semi-hidden factor of immense importance. The debate on the subject has already split opinion in major members of the Union. Can the Union absorb an eighty-million-strong Muslim country into what has been a predominantly Christian or non-sectarian society? The United States has strongly advocated the entry of Turkey into the Union, as has Britain. Germany and France are divided on the subject, but, as intimated, there is also a partly hidden terrorist aspect to the matter at hand. Turkey is not only the land of the Turks. In addition to the Kurdish minority, the eastern boundaries of the country border on Syria, Iraq, and Iran. In addition, there are powerful minority groups in the heart of the country. In Istanbul alone, there are over two million inhabitants of Iranian origin and they obviously feel a sense of affinity to their mother country, and some, most probably, would extend that sense of affinity to its extremist regime. Would Turkish membership in the Union improve the prospects of handling terrorism bred and nurtured in the east or would it provide the terrorists with Trojan-horse facilities that would add considerably to the jeopardy facing the free world? These are serious questions and there are no simple clear-cut replies to any of them. Indeed serious public debate of these problems is, by and large, circumscribed because the questions themselves are viewed as being not politically correct and therefore best left alone. Thus we see that the issue of international terrorism is beginning to loom as a distinct factor in a growing number of political areas, both domestic and international, and controversy surrounding them is in itself a factor weakening the national resolve in many states and societies.

In my view, the situation which I've only barely sketched out in this chapter will ultimately intensify the determination of states and societies to take action to protect themselves with diminishing regard for considerations of national sovereignty of independent states. In the face of distinct threats and ominous early warning, states may resort more and more to what I might call "self-help" methods, reaching out to deal with the enemy by themselves without necessarily waiting for the country that is harboring potential or proven terrorists. The Afghan war of 2002 is one such example on a grand scale, but, in the future, there may be more than one instance in which a state will take active preventive measures on its own.

The upshot of this will be that the very fundamentals of conventional international law will be swept away by the dictates of basic national survival. Governments and their senior executive officials will take action, the like of which has rarely ever been dreamed of in the past. Preemption will not await U.N. Security Council resolutions or relatively long-term creations of international coalitions. I predict that there will be a concentration of measures, sometimes complementary and at other times independent, tailored to deal with a rapidly evolving situation. Legislation will create an entirely fresh set of ground rules to deal with challenges. Executive authority will be empowered to take action as seldom before. International law or custom will either bend to the change or be circumvented as necessity demands.

If the combination of all these measures achieves the ultimate aim of defeating terrorism and a safer world emerges, then all the reservations implied in a conservative, more minimal approach will evaporate. The doubters will join in to rejoice in the salvation of humanity. If, however, the desired result is not obtained, then the future will be stark indeed and the powers that be aided by the best minds will have to come up with better solutions. For the present, sadly, I know of none.

18

DIPLOMACY—THE ART OF THE POSSIBLE; INTELLIGENCE—THE CRAFT OF THE IMPOSSIBLE

The impact of international Islamic terror on both the domestic and international scenes of the last seven to eight years cannot be underestimated. As I clearly indicated in the previous chapter, these terrorist achievements have not been the random results of those who carried them out; but rather, in many instances, they were the fulfillment of clearly defined political, economic, and social objectives. From time to time, documents and manifestos of terrorist groups, such as Al Qaeda, have been deliberately exposed, allowing the aims and goals of the group to be consumed by the public at large. For instance, one such goal, revealed in mid-October 2005 on Arab television, put forth the current priorities of the movement. It stated, among other things, that Israel, rather than being near the top of the list, had moved quite far down and would have to await its turn at a much later stage of the master agenda. The destruction of the United States and its way of life, as well as the annihilation of the moderate "infidel" Arab regimes, take precedence over the complete restoration of Palestine, including that part that is now the State of Israel, to its rightful owners—the Palestinians.

From pronouncements such as these, we can see that Al Qaeda has set its sights on the entire world with the goal of effecting an Islamic international revolution that will encompass the entire planet. It is as simple and diabolical as that. It is not a hidden blueprint. It is stated up front for everyone to read and to absorb. It is one more proof that the true masterstrokes of history are not only found through research in secret archives and intelligence files. Rather they appear in the broad daylight of public documents, speeches, and pronouncements all distributed through the interlocking components of the international media. I have always believed that one should accept as credible and genuine that which a political leader tells his audience or what a terrorist helmsman divulges to the media. These pronouncements should be taken at face value unless proven otherwise. One ignores them at one's own peril.

Careful analysis produces a very clear and systematic picture of the enemy that we are facing. The Islamic terrorist movement is an enemy that has strategic planetary goals and clearly defined strategies designed to reach those goals. The weaponry to be used for this purpose is also exceptionally well defined. They will use anything that is available at any given moment from the roadside bomb to the civilian aircraft, seized and directed at the World Trade Center in New York City. If the enemy succeeds in getting their hands on a nonconventional device—nuclear, biological, or chemical—they will have no reservation about employing that device at any moment considered appropriate and against any target, civilian or military, across the globe. The strategy of the Islamic terrorist movement is a long- and short-term strategy combined. On the one hand, time is of the essence. More frequent attacks launched sooner, rather than later, are better. And yet, on the other hand; there is really no rush or hurry to race against time because victory, ultimate and complete victory, is assured, they believe, by Allah's divine decree.

What are the strategies that the free world can employ in an effort to thwart the aims of its deadly adversaries and can these be subjects of genuine public debate? In the previous chapter, a long list of actions on both the domestic and external fronts has been suggested. But these, in and of themselves, do not add up to either a long-term or short-term strategy to defeat the terrorists, and there can be no doubt that a strategy is essential in order to defeat such a committed adversary. What is a "strategy," a term often used, but rarely adequately defined? In the words of *Webster's New International Dictionary,* a strategy is "the science and art of employing the political, economic, psychological, and military forces of a nation or group of nations to afford the maximum support to adopted policies in peace or war." And there is a second, complementary definition: "the science and art of military command exercised to meet the enemy in combat under advantageous conditions." Strategy entails planning based on science and art. It has to be preceded by the determination of policy and followed by the accurate definition of an aim or the goal that makes this policy a reality. Since the activities envisioned are of such a varied nature, as detailed in the definitions quoted herein, the policy or political directive cannot be defined solely in terms of preventing the enemy from achieving its goals. Even if the defensive element is one of the vital ones in securing the desired result, the complete defeat of the enemy—not simply the prevention of its success—must be number one on the list of aims and policies. Given the character and methods employed by the Islamic terrorists, only their total destruction will produce the ultimate solution.

The difficulties involved in reaching clear definitions in this World War III have often been highlighted in this book. Their repetition is unnecessary. One result of these unique peculiarities is that the free world has found great difficulty in discussing strategy, let alone finalizing the discussions with clear-cut strategies to be translated into action. Invariably, in similar situations, the powers that be have reverted to a policy of listing things one cannot do rather than things one can do. This strategy is, among others, the "refuge" of the human-rights activist, who is often so eloquent in reciting the list of steps and actions that are prohibited and, in many cases, reprehensible. The same person is also the one who inevitably flounders when called upon to draw up a plan of positive permissible and effective action to achieve the ultimate goal of survival of free society, which is dearest to his heart.

Having defined the policy, we cannot escape the necessity of defining how we intend to go about implementing it. How urgent is it to define the policy and the strategy? Given the basic fact that we are in the throes of a world war, one would assume that there is nothing more urgent on earth than to draw up the necessary plans to bring it to its successful end. The well-worn phrase "time is of the essence" has never been more applicable than in this case. The pressing aspect of time is all that more crucial. The members of the terrorist groups have clearly signed up for the long haul and are able to maintain the momentum almost indefinitely because of many things, including their dedication to a cause and their size being small enough to make them compact and elusive. Those defending their nations against the Islamic threat form groups that are, on the other hand, numerous, large, and easy targets. They are often internally divided on fundamental issues pertaining to the war and their capacity to see things through to the bitter end is forever in question. Public support, public opinion, political resolve, and periodic elections that often result in dramatic changes on the political scene all combine to intensify the fateful nature of time's march against success.

It is these factors that heighten the feeling of insecurity of the political masters in a free Western society. They are constantly waging a struggle for political survival and they are usually incapable of thinking beyond the term of office that they are currently experiencing. Even when expounding on lofty visions for the future in generational terms, for all practical purposes, the "game plan"—so to speak—is confined to a relatively short period of time. In the case of those seeking the office of the president of the United States, one of the most powerful positions on the international scene, it doesn't extend beyond four or eight years. One would expect that under these extremely adverse circumstances and given the portentous nature of the matter at hand, the powers that be would be devoting day and night to discussing and perfecting the policies and strategies to be put into instant motion in order to clinch victory in our lifetime.

Rather than to propose my own set of ideas, I would have much preferred to present the results of leaders and administrations and to add my own personal notes to this or that item. I am sad to say that this is not possible because I know of no effort made to draw up anything near what appears, on the face of it, so elementarily essential. I know of no public utterance of any leader who has not contented himself with exhorting his people to "stay the course" but who has accompanied this generalized clarion call with a plan of action. Much has been said and written about the Iraqi conundrum and there have been statements about the need to uproot terror and to fight it worldwide, but little or nothing has been said on a concerted strategy, either national or international, to secure an absolute victory.

There is no doubt in my mind that this almost inexplicable absence of discussion and planning is not geared to any shortage of brain power in the free world. On the contrary, there is an overwhelming surplus of this commodity in the West as compared to that which the terrorists can muster. I think the main reason for the absence of extensive offensive planning is to be found in the reluctance of the public at large to come to terms with the reality of terrorism and the subsequent reticence of those on the political level to go much further than they have gone already for fear that they might lose their constituencies. No matter how horrifying the acts of terror committed or how high the level of fear instilled in the public at large, there seems, as of yet, to be no real reaction in the public at large. The average individual prefers to avoid confronting the true and inevitable conclusions of what he must clearly see. Herein lies the well-known dilemma of the statesman-politician trying to choose the lesser of two evils: Should you roll along with public opinion and restrict yourself to those antiterrorism measures that can be marketed to the public, risking only a gradual reduction in public willingness to stay the course, or should you go for the jugular and launch an all-out terrorism offensive, pulling no punches and risking the erosion of the political base and a conclusion wherein one loses everything?

These being the overall variables influencing the march of contemporary history, based on recent experience I suggest that there is a very short time span beginning immediately after a terrorist operation and lasting no more than two to three months when the public is attuned to the adoption of extreme measures to counter the threat. This time span is of very short duration, but nevertheless it can be used to push through the approval of at least a few of the vital steps required to cope with the threat. The British parliament debated the harsh measures proposed by the prime minister four months after the last major terrorist act of 7/7, and they rejected his policy. The French parliament debated strong draconian measures one week after riots in the *cités,* and they approved all the government's policies. Forces both domestic and military should be kept in a state of awareness in anticipation that they will be sent into action at short notice. Targets, both local and foreign, should be prepared in advance and they need not be related directly to any specific terror attack. Just as the terrorists have decided that the entire planet is a legitimate theater of operations, so should the free world respond in kind and consider the entire globe as its theater of operations. Any nation under attack can decide to act where it believes that danger lurks and any nation can take advantage of attack on one of its allies in World War III to retaliate when a terrorist act is committed.

Forward planning must look at those vulnerable spots around the globe that are both festering grounds and safe havens for terrorists. The concept of safe haven assured under the guise of the individual sovereignty of nations should no longer be respected and if a host country provides such safe haven, its territorial integrity and its general diplomatic rights should be considered suspended until the duration of the war has run its course.

In order to achieve maximum results in minimal time, a joint master plan should be drawn up by those countries who feel that they either are targets of terror or have already been victims thereof. A specific time frame should be agreed upon and openly announced by those interested nations, the idea being that the plans and the strategies of all countries should be focused on the issue of time. The strategy should not be open-ended and pressures, both domestic and international, should be raised to the highest level possible in order to improve the chances of success. If a two- or three-year period is publicly announced as one during which no effort will be spared and operations of diverse natures will be put into action, the world will be galvanized into what I could call "an executive mode," meaning that all will pull together to their utmost knowing that the operational plan has a clear target date. At the end of the stated time frame, achievements and failures can be duly assessed and practical conclusions drawn. By so doing the rules of the game will not be set exclusively by the terrorists, as they are now, but will be determined no less by those who have hitherto adopted a relatively defensive posture. The purpose of this strategy, though extreme, would be to up the ante and to accelerate the rate of physical confrontation before the terrorists have the opportunity to upgrade the sophistication of the weaponry they have at their disposal. If this line of action is not adopted, we all risk having to ask ourselves, in the future that may be grim, why it was that the powers that be sat on their hands and did not adopt some or all of the measures suggested here. This time around, it will not be the professional intelligence levels that will take the rap, but the political masters themselves. They will not be able to claim that they were not forewarned.

The war will not be won simply by entering an offensive mode. It should be recognized that the Islamic fundamentalist terrorist threat will not evaporate into thin air under the onslaught of the combined efforts of the Western world. Primarily, the battle is an internal struggle within Islam. The world at large cannot pretend to move in and effect a result. So, what is left for us to do? Should we just sit on the sidelines and await the outcome of the battle royal? Here is where I believe that much more creativity and originality must be sought and ultimately put to good use. It is true that terrorism cannot be seen as anything other than what it is and should not be rewarded, come what may. It is also true that we must not succumb to the wish of some to differentiate between shades and causes in terror and to legitimize those strands of terror that pretend to be acceptable as tools in wars of so-called national liberation. Having said this, though, war is both a science and an art and, within the terrorist movement, there are subtle and important differences. One must not, for instance, be blinded to the fact that the Al Qaeda brand of terror is a category in itself and those who harbor or abet or permit its operatives to function are a group apart from all the rest. Why is this? Al Qaeda and its satellites all over the world are not only devoid of any territorial dimension, but their goals are, similarly, unattached to territory. They do not wish to conquer country A or country B. They do not wish to secure this or that tract of land. Their aims and aspirations are universal. This is not the case with movements like Khammas or in possible future circumstances even the Hizbollah. Granted they are deadly enemies, particularly of Israel, but not of Israel alone, and there are sharp differences between the Hizbollah and Khammas. The former has launched deadly attacks against Israel outside the Middle East and has caused the deaths and injuries of scores of innocent citizens in places like Buenos Aires in 1993 and 1994. Khammas has pointedly refrained from action outside the Palestinian territories and its aims are clearly territorial, namely the complete destruction of the State of Israel.

Let's look at a further example of differences between these groups. Although the aims of Al Qaeda and Khammas appear to be identical, as far as Israel is concerned, there is, nevertheless, a difference between the two. Khammas is not solely a terrorist group. It has political and social interests. It has participated in the election process in the Palestinian Authority, and several of the local municipal councils are controlled by Khammas majorities and have Khammas mayors. In their own way, they aspire to be part of the system and not, as Al Qaeda aspires, to destroy it. Khammas leaders have constituencies, property, educational programs, and social systems that they wish to preserve. A movement that has so much to lose must realize that it has a price to pay and that price could be all or most of its assets. When Israel carried out its unilateral disengagement from Gaza in the late summer of 2005, Khammas co-operated in a cease-fire of all Palestinian movements and was an important factor in allowing the orderly and dignified withdrawal of the Israel Defense Forces to take place. Khammas correctly assumed that, had it acted otherwise, Israel would have unleashed fury that would have put their major assets in serious jeopardy.

The behavior of Khammas was all the more remarkable and wise since it had waged a relentless terrorist campaign against Israel during four years of *intifada,* the violent resurrection that had wrought a sea change in Israeli policy. After all, was it not Prime Minister Sharon, the man who had steadfastly resisted any pressure to remove even one Jewish settlement from the disputed territories, who suddenly decided to evacuate the entire Gaza Strip and to forcibly destroy more than a score of settlements? What greater temptation was there than to launch action against retreating Israeli forces and thus not only enjoy the sweet taste of victory, but also celebrate it for all to observe? Khammas was and at the time of writing is still a sworn enemy of Israel. And yet Khammas leaders have met with Israelis and have dialogued with them. Israeli journalists have interviewed them and Khammas maintains a large web of complex contacts with countless countries, groups, and organizations the world over. It maintains a whole system of Web sites and diffuses its information and propaganda in many languages. Khammas is trying to act simultaneously as a political-social movement and as a terrorist front. This dual role is, at present, being rejected by the United States, the European Union, and Israel at one and the same time. At the time of writing, it is not politically correct for a responsible Israeli or American or European to contemplate bringing Khammas into the fold and legitimizing its participation in the Palestinian political process.

And yet, when Khammas is being told loud and clear that its dual approach of politics/terror is reprehensible and unacceptable and that it must choose between the two, there is an inherent belief that Khammas has a choice and that therefore circumstances could arise in which Khammas might be invited into the tent. No such choice will ever face Al Qaeda. By their very nature they could never be partners. When might Khammas be brought into the fold? It could well be that we will experience more violence before the situation matures to a point when this can happen. In assessing the advantages and disadvantages of including

Khammas, the free world led by the United States with Britain, the European Union, and last but not least Israel, will have to consider the impact and contribution that such a development could have on the global war against Al Qaeda and its associates and weigh the possible benefits of their participation against a crime of political "incorrectness."

The Hizbollah is a similar movement, entertaining territorial designs and basically estranged from Al Qaeda. However, it has one more characteristic that distinguishes it from Khammas and Al Qaeda: It is a Shiite movement allied with Iran, a specific foreign country. The Hizbollah has, as stated, operated a long distance from the Middle East. Its international terrorist arm, though, is a threat that the free world cannot tolerate. In these respects, the Hizbollah will have to renounce much more than Khammas if it wishes its dreams of respectability to come true. The decisions of neither Khammas nor the Hizbollah are foregone conclusions and I think it would be wrong to second-guess them. There can be no doubt that if conditions were created to enable two such groups to join the United States, the European Union, and Israel to engage Al Qaeda within the Muslim world, they could play a singular role in confronting the threat from within. These views might seem, at present, entirely in the realm of fantasy, but the events of the last few years have stretched the limits of imagination as never before.

I do not think these are ideal options and the two examples just mentioned are by no means any near-perfect potential partners. Yet there is never an ideal situation and no partners are ever perfect matches. What will determine the feasibility of the aforesaid is the existence of concrete common interests and goals, as well as the relative reliability of strange partners brought together under the pressures from joint enemies.

Khammas and possibly the Hizbollah are only two examples of the type of partner that the free world may be constrained to seek if it wishes to win the war against terror, international Muslim fundamentalist terror. In order to reach the desired goal, the free world will have to seek similar alliances in other regions. There will be hard bargains to drive, but in the final analysis, was it not a hard bargain to enlist the Taliban and bin Laden in a supreme effort to oust the Soviets from Afghanistan and to hand them a resounding defeat that contributed to the demise of the Soviet empire? Is the game of nations not one where each side chooses between tough alternatives, only to find itself exchanging sides when the ally of yesterday is the sworn enemy of today? We will be obliged to sup with the devil, but we must beware at all times that he does not poison our chalice.

In these games of nations, the leaders and their people pay the heaviest price. On each occasion and at each crossroad, evaluations change. Each party assesses its position and makes its decision. I believe that the United States and Britain will have to make fateful decisions concerning their Middle East policies in the next few years. They are directly involved in conflict and they cannot simply gather their troops and head for home. They must adopt a firm exit strategy, and I am convinced that any successful exit strategy will entail not only a real positive contribution of Israel to the Cause—with a capital C—but also Western sensitivity to Israeli interests and visions. Yet, in addition to all this, there will have to be due attention to co-opting additional partners to the cause and I have indicated a few possible candidates for such a role. The partner will have to pay an acceptance fee in the form of acknowledgment of Israel, but it will also exact a price and every one of the Western partners will have to give its dues. Rarely in recent history has such a tough pack of bargains and bargaining been on the table and rarely have the stakes been so high. The beginning of our journey in this book took us to Baghdad and to the key player—Saddam Hussein—confronting the Shiite revolutionary hurricane emanating from Iran. Hussein was then the savior of the moderate Arab world and the vital interests of the United States in the region. Fifteen years later, he is in the dock facing trial and his country in the throes of a fierce battle over its future. Fifteen years ago, Washington was celebrating its victory over the Soviet Union and the ultimate demise of the Soviet empire with the Taliban and bin Laden as miniheroes of a fifty-year-old Cold War won at last. And now—*quo vadis?* Where do we go?

In war and peace, diplomacy and negotiations are both a science and an art. The world of today will need the powers of science and the faculty of art as never before, but, above all, we shall be in great need of the craft of intelligence, which is more art than science. Much of what lies ahead can only be achieved in a clandestine manner and much of the terrain will have to be studied and absorbed by true experts in the science and art of information. In order to triumph, we shall have to reach to the stars and beyond. While diplomacy is the art of the possible, intelligence is the craft of the impossible. And life is fast becoming more impossible than ever in human history.